CSET Physical Education

129
130
131

Teacher Certification Exam

By: Sharon A. Wynne, M.S.

XAMonline, Inc.
Boston

Copyright © 2018 XAMonline, Inc.
All rights reserved. No part of the material protected by this copyright notice may be reproduced or utilized in any form or by any means, electronic or mechanical, including photocopying, recording or by any information storage and retrievable system, without written permission from the copyright holder.

To obtain permission(s) to use the material from this work for any purpose including workshops or seminars, please submit a written request to:

XAMonline, Inc.
21 Orient Avenue
Melrose, MA 02176
Toll Free 1-800-301-4647
Email: info@xamonline.com
Web www.xamonline.com

Library of Congress Cataloging-in-Publication Data
Wynne, Sharon A.

    CSET Physical Education (129, 130, 131): Teacher Certification / Sharon A. Wynne.
    ISBN 978-1-60787-648-9

1. Physical Education   2. Study Guides.   3. CSET
4. Teachers' Certification & Licensure.   5. Careers

Disclaimer:
The opinions expressed in this publication are the sole works of XAMonline and were created independently from the National Education Association, Educational Testing Service, or any State Department of Education, National Evaluation Systems or other testing affiliates.

Between the time of publication and printing, state specific standards as well as testing formats and website information may change that is not included in part or in whole within this product. XAMonline developed the sample test questions and the questions reflect similar content as on real tests; however, they are not former tests. XAMonline assembles content that aligns with state standards but makes no claims nor guarantees teacher candidates a passing score. Numerical scores are determined by testing companies such as NES or ETS and then are compared with individual state standards. A passing score varies from state to state.

Printed in the United States of America
CSET: Physical Education (129, 130, 131)
ISBN: 978-1-60787-648-9

TEACHER CERTIFICATION STUDY GUIDE

California State Credential in Physical Education (Single Subject Credential)

A Single Subject Teaching Credential authorizes the holder to teach Physical Education in departmentalized classes (usually grades 7-12), but he/she may also teach any subject in this field at any grade level (i.e. Preschool, K-12, adult classes).

Requirements:

1. Complete a Baccalaureate or higher degree, except in professional education, from a regionally-accredited college or university.

2. Pass the California Basic Educational Skills Test (CBEST).

3. Verify subject matter competence by either:

    A. Achieving a passing score on all three subtests of the California Subject Examinations for Teachers (CSET).
    OR
    B. Completing a commission-approved subject-matter program and obtaining verification of completion from the authorized person in the department of the program.

4. Complete a single subject teacher preparation program including successful student teaching, and obtain a formal recommendation for the credential by the California college or university where the program was completed.

About the CSET Examination in Physical Education

The Physical Education CSET is a test lasting five hours. All Single Subject subtests are administered during the afternoon session (1:30pm-7:00pm) on the test administration day except for CSET: Physical Education Subtest I, which is administered during the morning (7:30am-1:00pm) and/or afternoon sessions. The CSET is a criterion-referenced exam, meaning it is used to measure an examinee's knowledge and skills in relation to an established standard rather than in relation to the performance of other examinees.

To pass, the candidate must pass each subtest, which is scored separately and evaluated against established standards. Passing status is determined by the total subtest performance. The total subtest score is based on the number of raw points earned on each section, and the weighing of each section. Raw scores are converted to a scale of 100-300, with the scale score of 220 representing a minimum passing score.

PHYSICAL EDUCATION

TEACHER CERTIFICATION STUDY GUIDE

Applicants must achieve a passing score at a single CSET exam. If you do not pass one or more of the subtests, you may register for and retake the subtests an unlimited number of times.

Subtest	CSET: Physical Education Domains	Number of Multiple-Choice Questions	Number of Constructed-Response Questions
I (129)	Growth, Motor Development, and Motor Learning	20	1 Focused
	The Science of Human Movement	20	1 Focused
II (130)	The Sociology and Psychology of Human Movement	10	1 Focused
	Movement Concepts and Forms	24	1 Focused
	Assessment and Evaluation Principles	6	None
III (131)	Professional Foundations	16	None
	Integration of Concepts	24	1 Extended

Physical Education Subtest 1 (Physical Education 129): Growth, Motor Development, and Motor Learning; The Science of Human Movement:

Comprised of forty multiple choice questions (20 for Growth, Motor Development, and Motor learning, 20 for The Science of Human Movement) whicht are scored electronically and based on the number of questions answered correctly. There is no penalty for guessing. Also contains two focused constructed-response questions dealing with the relevant topics.

Purpose:
1. To demonstrate an understanding of human growth and development processes, as well as how these processes interact with and influence motor learning.

TEACHER CERTIFICATION STUDY GUIDE

2. By analyzing motion according to scientific principles and applying this knowledge with consideration for individual differences, the candidate demonstrates an understanding of the scientific bases of human movement.

Physical Education Subtest II (Physical Education 130): The Sociology and Psychology of Human Movement; Movement Concepts and Forms; Assessment and Evaluation Principles:

Comprised of 10 multiple choice questions and one focused essay dealing with The Sociology and Psychology of Human Movement, 24 multiple choice questions and one focused essay dealing with Movement Concepts and Forms, and 6 multiple choice questions dealing with Assessment and Evaluation Principles.

Purpose:
1. To demonstrate an understanding of the sociology and psychology of human movement and how physical activity provides a context for experiences that can promote personal and social developmental concepts and skills.
2. To demonstrate a broad understanding of movement concepts and forms and to develop a program that will address a variety of ability levels and create challenging, appropriate tasks in a variety of movement forms.
3. To demonstrate an understanding of assessment principles and procedures in order to be able to evaluate the effectiveness of physical education strategies and activities.

Physical Education Subtest III (Physical Education 131): Professional Foundations; Integration of Concepts:

Comprised of 16 multiple choice questions dealing with Professional Foundations and 24 multiple choice questions as well as one extended constructed-response question dealing with Integration of Concepts.

Purpose:
1. To demonstrate an understanding of the philosophical, historical, and legal/ethical foundations of physical education and to plan and implement programs that align with the approved Physical Education Framework.
2. To demonstrate an understanding of the integration of themes and concepts in physical education and the interrelationships between physical education and other subject areas.

TEACHER CERTIFICATION STUDY GUIDE

TABLE OF CONTENTS

Pg.

PART I: CONTENT DOMAINS FOR SUBJECT MATTER UNDERSTANDING AND SKILL IN PHYSICAL EDUCATION

DOMAIN 1. PROFESSIONAL FOUNDATIONS 1

Candidates demonstrate an understanding of the philosophical, historical, and legal/ethical foundations of physical education. To plan and implement programs that are aligned with the approved Physical Education Framework or other approved state documents and the <u>Challenge Standards for Student Success: Physical Education</u> (1998), candidates must have a broad and deep understanding of issues that affect the field, of the professional responsibilities of physical educators, and of the past and present philosophies of physical education and their impact on contemporary programs.

COMPETENCY 1.0 PHILOSOPHIES OF PHYSICAL EDUCATION 1

Skill 1.1 Demonstrate knowledge of past and present philosophies of physical education and their impact on the goals, scope, and components of physical education programs 1

Skill 1.2 Demonstrate an understanding of the organization, purposes, and goals of contemporary physical education programs 2

COMPETENCY 2.0 HISTORICAL DEVELOPMENT 3

Skill 2.1 Demonstrate knowledge of the historical development of physical education, including contributions of noteworthy physical educators of various backgrounds, races, ethnicities, genders, and national origins 3

COMPETENCY 3.0 CURRENT RESEARCH, TRENDS, AND ISSUES 8

Skill 3.1 Analyze current research, trends, and issues that affect physical education (e.g., inclusion, lifelong fitness, the sharp increase in obesity-related diseases among U.S. youth) and their impact on physical education programs and goals 8

Skill 3.2 Demonstrate an understanding of legal and ethical issues in physical education, such as those related to supervision, liability, confidentiality, equity, disability, and diversity 11

TEACHER CERTIFICATION STUDY GUIDE

COMPETENCY 4.0 INTERRELATIONSHIPS OF THE SUBDISCIPLINES OF KINESIOLOGY 18

Skill 4.1 Demonstrate an understanding of the interrelationships of the subdisciplines of kinesiology 18

COMPETENCY 5.0 PROFESSIONAL RESPONSIBILITIES, ORGANIZATIONS, AND RESOURCES 19

Skill 5.1 Demonstrate knowledge of professional responsibilities, organizations, and resources that support physical education (e.g., AAHPERD, American College of Sports Medicine, National Council for the Exceptional Individual) 19

Skill 5.2 Demonstrate knowledge of current state and national standards for physical education 20

COMPETENCY 6.0 RELATIONSHIP BETWEEN HUMAN MOVEMENT ACTIVITIES AND VALUES 21

Skill 6.1 Demonstrate an understanding of human movement activities as instruments for maintaining traditional values and/or for examining and changing traditional values 21

Skill 6.2 Analyze the role of physical education in promoting equity for diverse groups 22

DOMAIN 2. GROWTH, MOTOR DEVELOPMENT, AND MOTOR LEARNING 23

Candidates must demonstrate an understanding of human growth and development processes, as well as how these processes interact with and influence motor learning, in order to teach the movement knowledge and skills contained in the <u>Challenge Standards for Student Success: Physical Education</u> (1998). Foundational knowledge of physical growth, motor development, and motor learning helps ensure that candidates are prepared to provide students, including students with disabilities, with an appropriate, safe, and effective physical education program.

COMPETENCY 1.0 INDIVIDUAL DIFFERENCES 23

Skill 1.1 Demonstrate knowledge of individual motor and physical fitness variables such as agility, balance, flexibility, coordination, strength, and speed 23

Skill 1.2　Analyze individual physical changes and their impact on mechanical and physiological aspects of motor performance 24

COMPETENCY 2.0 PERCEPTUAL-MOTOR DEVELOPMENT 25

Skill 2.1　Know components of perceptual-motor development such as visual, auditory, tactile, and kinesthetic discrimination and how they relate to skill acquisition and performance 25

COMPETENCY 3.0 PHYSICAL AND DEVELOPMENTAL CHANGES 26

Skill 3.1　Demonstrate an understanding of physical changes that occur with growth, development, and age, and analyze their impact on mechanical and physiological aspects of motor performance 26

COMPETENCY 4.0 MOTOR LEARNING 29

Skill 4.1　Relate classical and current theories and models of motor learning to fundamental concepts underlying skill acquisition such as transfer, feedback, retention, practice, readiness, and observational learning . 29

Skill 4.2　Apply knowledge of motor task analysis as it relates to motor development, enabling students to select or design motor tasks that are appropriate to the process of learning movement skills 31

Skill 4.3　Analyze conditions that affect growth, motor development, and motor learning such as diseases, disabilities, and social, emotional, and environmental factors 32

Skill 4.4　Demonstrate an understanding of developmental differences in motor learning and factors that affect motor skills acquisition for individuals with disabilities 34

TEACHER CERTIFICATION STUDY GUIDE

DOMAIN 3. THE SCIENCE OF HUMAN MOVEMENT 38

Candidates demonstrate an understanding of the scientific bases of human movement. To guide students in meeting the goals identified in the Challenge Standards for Student Success: Physical Education (1998), candidates must be able to analyze motion according to scientific principles and apply that knowledge with consideration for individual differences, including disabilities. A broad and deep understanding of the sciences involved in human movement, including anatomy, physiology, kinesiology/biomechanics, exercise physiology, and health-related fitness, enables candidates to understand and explain motion; recognize changes in body systems resulting from practice, development, and response to exercise; and provide instruction in safe and efficient body mechanics.

COMPETENCY 1.0 BODY SYSTEMS 38

Skill 1.1   Demonstrate knowledge of the skeletal system, the general organization of the nervous system, the actions of muscles and major muscle groups, and the interaction of these systems with one another and with the external environment in producing motion 38

COMPETENCY 2.0 BASIC KINEMATIC AND KINETIC PRINCIPLES OF MOTION 49

Skill 2.1   Apply knowledge of basic kinematic and kinetic principles of motion including, but not limited to, summation of forces of equilibrium, vectors, and force-velocity relationships 49

COMPETENCY 3.0 BIOMECHANICAL PRINCIPLES 51

Skill 3.1   Apply knowledge of biomechanical principles (e.g., Newton's laws of motion, center of gravity) to a broad range of movement activities 51

Skill 3.2   Apply knowledge of biomechanical principles in relation to individual differences and to body mechanics for safe and efficient movement/motion 55

COMPETENCY 4.0 MOVEMENT ANALYSIS 59

Skill 4.1   Apply knowledge of movement analysis to movement patterns, including technologies for movement analysis 59

Skill 4.2   Effects of Exercise: Demonstrate knowledge of acute and chronic effects of exercise on body systems (e.g., pulmonary, cardiorespiratory, muscular, skeletal, neural, endocrine) and on energy systems utilized during exercise 61

COMPETENCY 5.0 COMPONENTS OF WELLNESS 65

Skill 5.1 Demonstrate an understanding of components of wellness, such as nutrition, stress management, cardiorespiratory risk reduction, and physical fitness (i.e., cardiorespiratory endurance, flexibility, muscular strength and endurance, and body composition) 65

Skill 5.2 Analyze the effects of various factors on physical fitness 71

COMPETENCY 6.0 PHYSICAL FITNESS TESTING AND PRESCRIPTION 74

Skill 6.1 Demonstrate knowledge of physical fitness testing, exercise prescription, and fitness programs for all individuals, including those with disabilities, as well as the components of health-related fitness and technologies for fitness testing and training 74

COMPETENCY 7.0 FACTORS AFFECTING PHYSICAL PERFORMANCE 78

Skill 7.1 Analyze the effects of factors such as gender, age, disability, environment, and substance abuse on physical performance 78

COMPETENCY 8.0 SAFETY, INJURY PREVENTION, AND FIRST AID 79

Skill 8.1 Demonstrate an understanding of safety-related topics such as the prevention and care of injuries, cardiopulmonary resuscitation, and first aid 79

COMPETENCY 9.0 PHYSIOLOGICAL PRINCIPLES OF FITNESS 85

Skill 9.1 Apply knowledge of physiological principles (e.g., overload, specificity, FIT, reversibility) to the components of physical fitness 85

DOMAIN 4. THE SOCIOLOGY AND PSYCHOLOGY OF HUMAN MOVEMENT 90

Candidates demonstrate an understanding of the sociology and psychology of human movement. Physical activity provides a context for a broad range of experiences that instructors can use to promote the personal and social developmental concepts and skills contained in the Challenge Standards for Student Success: Physical Education (1998). A broad and deep understanding of the sociological and psychological aspects of movement activities helps ensure that candidates are prepared to promote students' motivation for physical activity, regardless of students' abilities, and their development of positive, responsible personal and social behaviors that encourage lifelong physical activity.

COMPETENCY 1.0 PERSONAL DEVELOPMENT 90

Skill 1.1   Analyze the relationship of movement to the development of individual identity, including the development of self-awareness, self-concept, self-discipline, self-expression, and body image 90

Skill 1.2   Theories Related to Motivation: Demonstrate an understanding of contemporary theories such as attribution, social learning, competence, learned helplessness, self-efficacy, and other social/psychological theories as they relate to motivation in physical activities 96

COMPETENCY 2.0 SOCIAL DEVELOPMENT 98

Skill 2.1   Analyze the relationship of movement to social interaction and the development of group member identity through physical education activities 98

Skill 2.2   Identify strategies and activities for promoting appropriate skills and behaviors for cooperation, competition, problem solving, trust building, and risk taking 99

COMPETENCY 3.0 ROLE OF MOVEMENT ACTIVITIES IN SOCIETY 101

Skill 3.1   Demonstrate knowledge of the role of movement activities in society and the relationship of movement activities to social norms, ethics, values, and institutions 101

Skill 3.2   Demonstrate knowledge of the role of movement activities in the development of social interaction skills, a sense of group identity, and a sense of productive participation with others 102

Skill 3.3 Demonstrate knowledge of the role of movement activities in promoting positive social behaviors and traits (e.g., loyalty; compassion; fairness; understanding and appreciation of similarities, differences, and abilities) 103

COMPETENCY 4.0 FACTORS INFLUENCING ACTIVITY CHOICES 105

Skill 4.1 Analyze factors that influence an individual's activity choices (e.g., gender, age, ethnicity, culture, disability) 105

DOMAIN 5. MOVEMENT CONCEPTS AND FORMS 106

Candidates demonstrate an understanding of the movement concepts and forms contained in the <u>Challenge Standards for Student Success: Physical Education</u> (1998). These include but are not limited to aquatics; dance; fitness activities; fundamental and creative movement skills; individual, dual, and team sports; nontraditional activities and games; outdoor education activities; and gymnastics. To develop a balanced program that will address a variety of ability levels and create challenging, appropriate tasks in a variety of movement forms, candidates must have a broad and deep understanding of movement and fitness activities as well as an ability to integrate and apply movement concepts to a broad range of physical education activities and environments.

COMPETENCY 1.0 FUNDAMENTAL AND CREATIVE MOVEMENT SKILLS 106

Skill 1.1 Demonstrate knowledge of fundamental movement skills such as basic locomotor and nonlocomotor skills, movement patterns, manipulative skills, and basic rhythmic movement, as well as knowledge of elements and qualities of movement (e.g., space, time, force, flow, level) 106

Skill 1.2 Demonstrate knowledge of creative movement such as exploration, improvisation, and problem solving 110

COMPETENCY 2.0 DANCE CONCEPTS AND FORMS 111

Skill 2.1 Demonstrate knowledge of skills used in rhythmic activities, creative dance, and structured dance forms (e.g., modern, ballet, jazz, tap, social, folk, country, ethnic, classical) 111

Skill 2.2 Demonstrate an understanding of the use of dance to express perceptions, feelings, images, and thoughts 115

Skill 2.3 Demonstrate an understanding of dance concepts, forms, and basic vocabulary 115

TEACHER CERTIFICATION STUDY GUIDE

COMPETENCY 3.0 GYMNASTIC MOVEMENTS 116

Skill 3.1 Demonstrate knowledge of gymnastic forms such as rhythmic gymnastics and educational gymnastics 116

Skill 3.2 Demonstrate knowledge of gymnastic movements such as stunts, tumbling, apparatus work, and floor exercise 118

COMPETENCY 4.0 AQUATIC SKILLS 119

Skill 4.1 Demonstrate knowledge of aquatic skills such as water safety, swimming strokes, diving, and water fitness activities and games 119

COMPETENCY 5.0 INDIVIDUAL, DUAL, AND TEAM SPORTS AND GAMES 121

Skill 5.1 Demonstrate knowledge of techniques, skills, critical elements, scientific principles, and equipment for individual, dual, and team sports and games 121

Skill 5.2 Apply knowledge of developmental progressions for sports activities 154

Skill 5.3 Demonstrate an understanding of principles of game strategies 156

Skill 5.4 Demonstrate knowledge of safety, etiquette, fair play, and fair competition 160

Skill 5.5 Apply knowledge of how to promote critical-thinking, decision-making, problem-solving, collaboration, communication, leadership, conflict-resolution, and teamwork skills through participation in sports and games 161

Skill 5.6 Demonstrate knowledge of the application of motor learning principles (e.g., transfer, game-like conditions) in instruction for sports and games 163

COMPETENCY 6.0 OUTDOOR EDUCATION 165

Skill 6.1 Demonstrate knowledge of techniques, skills, and safety issues for outdoor education activities 165

Skill 6.2 Identify long-term psychological, physiological, and lifestyle benefits of participation in outdoor education activities 169

TEACHER CERTIFICATION STUDY GUIDE

COMPETENCY 7.0 NONTRADITIONAL AND COOPERATIVE ACTIVITIES 171

Skill 7.1 Identify examples of nontraditional, global, and cooperative games and activities (e.g., Pickle ball, bocce ball, team juggling) 171

Skill 7.2 Apply knowledge of how to promote critical thinking, decision making, problem solving, collaboration, cooperation, leadership, and communication through participation in nontraditional and cooperative activities 172

COMPETENCY 8.0 COMBATIVE ACTIVITIES 173

Skill 8.1 Demonstrate knowledge of one or more basic combative activities (e.g., fencing, wrestling, self-defense) and related safety issues 173

COMPETENCY 9.0 FITNESS ACTIVITIES 175

Skill 9.1 Demonstrate an understanding of fitness activities such as aerobic conditioning, resistance and weight training, and stretching that increase cardiovascular efficiency, muscular strength and endurance, and flexibility 175

DOMAIN 6. ASSESSMENT AND EVALUATION PRINCIPLES 197

Candidates must demonstrate an understanding of assessment principles and procedures in order to be able to evaluate the effectiveness of physical education strategies and activities in promoting student achievement of the goals presented in the Challenge Standards for Student Success: Physical Education (1998). A rigorous knowledge of assessment helps ensure that candidates can determine whether individuals, including those with diverse backgrounds, varying abilities, and special needs, have progressed and achieved specified goals in physical education. Candidates must be able to select, adapt, and develop appropriate assessment instruments and strategies based on sound research principles related to physical, motor, and fitness attributes and needs of individuals and classes.

COMPETENCY 1.0 EVALUATION METHODS IN PHYSICAL EDUCATION 197

Skill 1.1 Demonstrate knowledge of evaluation methods used for the various domains of learning in physical education (e.g., physical, psychomotor, cognitive, social, affective) 197

TEACHER CERTIFICATION STUDY GUIDE

COMPETENCY 2.0 TECHNIQUES OF TEST CONSTRUCTION, EVALUATION, AND ADMINISTRATION 202

Skill 2.1 Demonstrate knowledge of basic strategies of test construction, evaluation, and administration for traditional, holistic, and authentic assessments such as developing and using criteria to assess attainment of goals and objectives 202

Skill 2.2 Test Characteristics: Apply knowledge of test characteristics such as validity, reliability, and objectivity 203

Skill 2.3 Assessment Techniques and Tools: Apply knowledge of assessment strategies and instruments, including technology, that are appropriate for individuals with diverse backgrounds, special needs, and disabilities 204

Skill 2.4 Types of Evaluation: Demonstrate an understanding of types of evaluation such as norm-referenced, criterion referenced, content-referenced, and authentic assessment 205

Skill 2.5 Types of Evaluation: Demonstrate knowledge of formative and summative evaluation strategies 205

COMPETENCY 3.0 BASIC STATISTICAL APPLICATIONS 207

Skill 3.1 Demonstrate knowledge of basic statistical applications, including central tendency and variability, standard scores, norms, and correlations 207

COMPETENCY 4.0 INTERPRETATION AND COMMUNICATION OF ASSESSMENT DATA 208

Skill 4.1 Apply skills for interpreting assessment data and for communicating test results, performance profiles, and assessment data to various audiences (e.g., students, parents, school board members) 208

DOMAIN 7. INTEGRATION OF CONCEPTS 209

Candidates must demonstrate an understanding of the integration of themes and concepts in physical education and the interrelationships between physical education and other subject areas in order to create effective learning environments and experiences that provide students with opportunities to achieve the goals contained in the Challenge Standards for Student Success: Physical Education (1998).

TEACHER CERTIFICATION STUDY GUIDE

COMPETENCY 1.0 INTERPRETATION AND APPLICATION OF THE SUBDISCIPLINES OF KINESIOLOGY 209

Skill 1.1 Interpret and apply knowledge of the subdisciplines of kinesiology to facilitate student skill acquisition and performance 209

COMPETENCY 2.0 SELECTING, ADAPTING, AND MODIFYING ACTIVITIES 211

Skill 2.1 Use developmental information to appropriately select, adapt, and modify sports and games based on goals, skill levels, individual needs, and disabilities 211

COMPETENCY 3.0 DEVELOPMENTAL PROGRESSIONS 214

Skill 3.1 Demonstrate knowledge of appropriate developmental progressions within and between individual movement skills 214

COMPETENCY 4.0 LEARNING CONCEPTS AND PRINCIPLES 216

Skill 4.1 Use concepts and principles of learning to analyze observed individual differences 216

COMPETENCY 5.0 CONNECTIONS BETWEEN PHYSICAL EDUCATION AND OTHER DISCIPLINES 218

Skill 5.1 Demonstrate knowledge of connections between physical education and other subject areas such as life and physical sciences, social science, health, mathematics, language arts, and visual and performing arts 218

ANNOTATED LIST OF RESOURCES 220

SAMPLE TEST 222

ANSWER KEY 249

RATIONALES WITH SAMPLE QUESTIONS 250

SAMPLE WRITTEN ASSIGNMENT & RESPONSE 291

PART II: SUBJECT MATTER SKILLS AND ABILITIES APPLICABLE TO THE CONTENT DOMAINS IN PHYSICAL EDUCATION

Candidates apply knowledge of the theoretical and scientific bases of human movement to design, select, and modify physical activities that reflect students' developmental characteristics and individual differences. They draw upon knowledge of the subdisciplines of kinesiology to ensure that students are able to participate safely and effectively in physical education activities designed to develop and enhance their movement skills and movement knowledge. Candidates understand significant factors and influences in developing, analyzing, and assessing basic motor skills. They know how to structure developmentally appropriate activities to promote maximum participation, inclusion, and active engagement in a wide range of movement forms, including traditional and nontraditional games, sports, dance, and fitness activities. They select and create cooperative and competitive activities that promote trust building, problem solving, collaboration, leadership, and strategic planning. They design fitness programs and recommend exercises and activities that are based on sound physiological and fitness training principles. Candidates understand the short-term and long-term benefits of a healthy, active lifestyle and know how to demonstrate and communicate these benefits to students. Candidates apply knowledge of the sociological, psychological, philosophical, historical, and cultural dimensions of physical education to select and develop activities and approaches that promote students' development of positive personal and social behaviors, including social interaction and communication skills. They are aware of the role of movement activities in helping participants develop a sense of individual identity and group member identity. Candidates use knowledge of historical and cultural influences on games, sports, dance, and other physical activities to enhance student awareness and appreciation of cultural and artistic diversity, the role of movement in society, and the use of physical activity for enjoyment and self-expression. They recognize the importance of inclusion, fair play, and etiquette, as well as respect and consideration for self and others. Candidates understand that many factors influence an individual's activity choices and carefully evaluate the appropriateness of activities in terms of participants' age and developmental levels, motor proficiency, gender, cultural background, and physical strengths and limitations. Candidates apply knowledge of student development and learning to select activities and approaches that help students experience the benefits of individual challenges and successes, and they use principles of learning and motivation to spark students' interest in physical activity and their desire to engage in lifelong physical activity. Candidates use their knowledge of assessment principles and procedures to collect, analyze, interpret, and summarize assessment data. They know physical fitness testing principles, technologies, and techniques and are prepared to administer the state-mandated physical fitness assessment. Candidates are able to interpret and communicate test results, performance profiles, and other types of assessment information in a meaningful and sensitive way.

Candidates understand connections among the subdisciplines of kinesiology, as well as connections between physical education and other subject areas and use this understanding to provide learning activities that promote student skill acquisition and performance. Candidates select, adapt, and modify activities based on program goals, individual differences, and individual needs so that all students have an opportunity to develop their understanding and application of movement skills and concepts and to use this knowledge in exploring other academic and life skills areas.

TEACHER CERTIFICATION STUDY GUIDE

Great Study and Testing Tips!

What you study in order to prepare for the subject assessments is the focus of this study guide, but equally important is *how* you study.

You can increase your chances of truly mastering the information by taking some simple but effective steps.

Study Tips:

1. Some foods aid the learning process. Foods such as milk, nuts, seeds, rice, and oats help your study efforts by releasing natural memory enhancers called CCKs (*cholecystokinin*) composed of *tryptophan*, *choline*, and *phenylalanine*. All of these chemicals enhance the neurotransmitters associated with memory. Before studying, try a light, protein-rich meal of eggs, turkey, and fish. All of these foods release the memory enhancing chemicals. The better the connections, the more you comprehend.

Likewise, before you take a test, stick to a light snack of relaxing and energy boosting foods. A glass of milk, a piece of fruit, or some peanuts release various memory-boosting chemicals and help you to relax and focus on the subject at hand.

2. Learn to take great notes. A by-product of our modern culture is that we have grown accustomed to getting our information in short doses (e.g. TV news sound bites or USA Today style newspaper articles).

Consequently, we've subconsciously trained ourselves to assimilate information better in neat little packages. If your notes are scrawled all over the paper, it fragments the flow of the information. Strive for clarity. Newspapers use a standard format to achieve clarity. You can make your notes much clearer by using proper formatting. A very effective format is the *"Cornell Method."*

Take a sheet of loose-leaf lined notebook paper and draw a line all the way down the paper about 1-2" from the left-hand edge.

Draw another line across the width of the paper about 1-2" up from the bottom. Repeat this process on the reverse side of the page.

Look at the highly effective result. You have ample room for notes, a left hand margin for special emphasis items or inserting supplementary data from the textbook, a large area at the bottom for a brief summary, and a little rectangular space for just about anything you want.

PHYSICAL EDUCATION

3. **Get the concept then the details.** Too often, we focus on the details and don't gather an understanding of the concept. However, if you simply memorize only dates, places, or names, you may well miss the whole point of the subject.

A key way to understand things is to put them in your own words. If you are working from a textbook, automatically summarize each paragraph in your mind. If you are outlining text, don't simply copy the author's words.

Rephrase them in your own words. You remember your own thoughts and words much better than someone else's, and subconsciously tend to associate the important details to the core concepts.

4. **Ask Why?** Pull apart written material paragraph by paragraph and don't forget the captions under the illustrations.

Example: If the heading is "Stream Erosion", flip it around to read "Why do streams erode?" Then answer the questions.

If you train your mind to think in a series of questions and answers, not only will you learn more, but it also helps to lessen the test anxiety because you are used to answering questions.

5. **Read for reinforcement and future needs.** Even if you only have 10 minutes, put your notes or a book in your hand. Your mind is similar to a computer; you have to input data in order to have it processed. *By reading, you are creating the neural connections for future retrieval.* The more times you read something, the more you reinforce the learning of ideas.

Even if you don't fully understand something on the first pass, *your mind stores much of the material for later recall.*

6. **Relax to learn, so go into exile.** Our bodies respond to an inner clock called biorhythms. Burning the midnight oil works well for some people, but not everyone.

If possible, set aside a particular place to study that is free of distractions. Shut off the television, cell phone, and pager and exile your friends and family during your study period.

If silence really bothers you, try background music. Studies show that light classical music played at a low volume aids in concentration.

Music that evokes pleasant emotions without lyrics are highly suggested. Try just about anything by Mozart. It relaxes you.

7. Use arrows not highlighters. At best, it's difficult to read a page full of yellow, pink, blue, and green streaks.

Try staring at a neon sign for a while and you'll soon see my point. The horde of colors obscures the message.

A quick note, a brief dash of color, an underline, and an arrow pointing to a particular passage is much clearer than a horde of highlighted words.

8. Budget your study time. Although you shouldn't ignore any of the material, *allocate your available study time in the same ratio that topics may appear on the test.*

TEACHER CERTIFICATION STUDY GUIDE

Testing Tips:

1. Get smart, play dumb. Don't read anything into the question. Don't assume that the test writer is looking for something else than what is asked. Stick to the question as written and don't read extra things into it.

2. Read the question and all the choices *twice* before answering. You may miss something by not carefully reading and re-reading both the question and the answers.

If you really don't have a clue as to the right answer, leave it blank the first time through. Go on to the other questions, as they may provide a clue as to how to answer the skipped questions.

If later on, you still can't answer the skipped ones . . . ***Guess.***
The only penalty for guessing is that you *might* get it wrong. One thing is certain; if you don't put anything down, you will get it wrong!

3. Turn the question into a statement. Look at the wording of the questions. The syntax of the question usually provides a clue. Does it seem more familiar as a statement rather than as a question? Does it sound strange?

By turning a question into a statement, you may be able to spot if an answer sounds right, and it may also trigger memories of material you've read.

4. Look for hidden clues. It's actually very difficult to compose multiple-choice questions without giving away part of the answer in the options presented.

In most multiple-choice questions, you can often readily eliminate one or two of the potential answers. This leaves you with only two real possibilities, and automatically your odds go to fifty-fifty with very little work.

5. Trust your instincts. For every fact that you have read, you subconsciously retain something of that knowledge. On questions that you aren't really certain about, go with your basic instincts. **Your first impression on how to answer a question is usually correct.**

6. Mark your answers directly on the test booklet. Don't bother trying to fill in the optical scan sheet on the first pass through the test.

Just be very careful not to miss-mark your answers when you eventually transcribe them to the scan sheet.

7. Watch the clock! You have a set amount of time to answer the questions. Don't get bogged down trying to answer a single question at the expense of 10 questions you can more readily answer.

TEACHER CERTIFICATION STUDY GUIDE

DOMAIN 1. PROFESSIONAL FOUNDATIONS

COMPETENCY 1.0 PHILOSOPHIES OF PHYSICAL EDUCATION

Skill 1.1 Demonstrate knowledge of past and present philosophies of physical education and their impact on the goals, scope, and components of physical education programs.

The various philosophies of education greatly influence the goals and values of physical education. Important educational philosophies related to physical education are Idealism, Realism, Pragmatism, Naturalism, Existentialism, Humanism, and Eclecticism.

Idealism – The **mind**, developed through the acquisition of knowledge, is of highest importance. Values exist independently of individuals. Fitness and strength activities contribute to the development of one's personality. Horace Mann, Wadsworth, Kant, Plato, and Descartes were Idealists.

Realism – The physical world is **real.** A realist believes in the laws of nature, the scientific method, and mind and body harmony. Religion and philosophy co-exist. Physical fitness results in greater productivity, physical drills are important to the learning process, athletic programs lead to desired social behavior, and play and recreation help life adjustment. Aristotle was a realist.

Pragmatism – **Experience** is key to life. Dynamic experience shapes individuals' truth. Education is child-centered. Varied activities present experiences that are more meaningful. Activities are socializing. Problem solving accomplishes learning. John Dewy and Charles Pierce were pragmatists.

Naturalism – This philosophy is materialistic. Things that actually exist are found only within the physical realm of nature. Nature is valuable. The individual is more important than society. Self-activities accomplish learning and activities are more than physical in nature. Naturalists promote play and discourage high levels of competition. Physical education takes a holistic approach.

Existentialism – The chief concern is **individualism.** Existentialists do not want the individual to conform to society. They promote freedom of choice and a variety of interests. Individuals need to have their own system of values. Playing develops creativity and the discovery of the "inner self." Sartre, Soren, and Kierkegaard were Existentialists.

Humanism and **Eclecticism** – The modern philosophies of physical education that most schools follow today. The basis of the Humanistic philosophy is the development of individual talents and total fulfillment that encourages total involvement and participation in one's environment. Humanists encourage self-actualization and self-fulfillment.

Curriculums based on the Humanistic approach are more student-centered. The Eclectic approach combines beliefs from different philosophies and does not resemble any single philosophy. When blended skillfully, the Eclectic approach affords a sound philosophy for an individual.

Skill 1.2 **Demonstrate an understanding of the organization, purpose, and goals of contemporary physical education programs.**

The main goals and purpose of physical education is to introduce students to fitness, activity, and nutrition concepts and allow students to be physically active during the school day. Proper structure and organization allows the realization of these goals. The following is a list of physical education goals derived from different philosophies of education:

Physical/Organic Development Goal (Realism philosophy) – activities build physical power by strengthening the body's systems, resulting in the ability to sustain adaptive effort, shorten recovery time, and develop resistance to fatigue. The core values are individual health, greater activity, and better performance by an adequately developed and properly functioning body.

Motor/Neuromuscular Development Goal (Realism philosophy) – develops body awareness producing movement that is proficient, graceful, and aesthetic and uses as little energy as possible. Students develop as many skills as possible so their interests are wide and varied to allow more enjoyment and better adjustment to group situations. Varied motor development skills affect health by influencing how leisure time is spent. Values include reducing energy expenditure, building confidence, bringing recognition, enhancing physical and mental health, making participation safer, and contributing to aesthetic sense.

Cognitive Development Goal (Idealism philosophy) – deals with acquiring knowledge and ability to think and interpret knowledge. Scientific principles explain time, space, and flow of movement. Learning physical activities requires thinking and coordination of movement and mastering and adapting to one's environment. Individuals also should acquire knowledge of rules, techniques, and strategies of activities. Cognitive values include healthy attitudes and habits such as body awareness, personal hygiene, disease prevention, exercise, proper nutrition, and knowledge of health service providers.

Social/Emotional/Affective Development Goal (Existentialism philosophy) – deals with helping individuals make adjustments – personal, group, and societal – by positively influencing human behavior. Performance defines success, and success develops self-confidence. Wholesome attitudes throughout the various growth stages promote the development of an appropriate Self-Concept, which is very important. Values include meeting basic social needs (sense of belonging, recognition, self-respect, and love) that produce a socially, well-adjusted individual.

TEACHER CERTIFICATION STUDY GUIDE

COMPETENCY 2.0   HISTORICAL DEVELOPMENT

Skill 2.1   Demonstrate knowledge of the historical development of physical education, including contributions of noteworthy physical educators of various backgrounds, races, ethnicities, genders, and national origins.

KNOWLEDGE OF THE HISTORY OF PHYSICAL EDUCATION AS A PROFESSION

Leading men and women in physical education

Physical education (P.E.) is a course of study in the curriculum of most educational systems designed to utilize both mental and physical capacities. The goal of this course of study is to instill in students the knowledge, skills, and enthusiasm required to maintain a healthy lifestyle into adulthood. Physical education is not necessarily dependent on an individual's physical capabilities. Physical education is a class that provides students with an understanding of rules, concepts, strategies, and teamwork that will benefit students throughout their lives.

The term physical education derives from the Latin word "physica," meaning *physics*, and "education," meaning the training of the bodily organs and powers to promote health and strength. We can trace the history of physical education back to the Greeks who held the first Olympic Games in 776 BC, which equated honor and fame with physical strength and skill. In 1420, an Italian physician named Vittorini da Feltre recognized the importance of the simultaneous development of mind and body and initiated physical education classes for children in Italy. Physical education classes did not begin in the United States until Charles Beck initiated them in 1825.

Jean-Jacques Rousseau was an Enlightenment philosopher of the 18th century who made great contributions to the field of educational theory. Rousseau argued that humankind was subject to a system of justice derived from nature rather than society. He called this set of rules "natural law," and was a strong advocate of equal education for children of all social classes and physical abilities. Rousseau promoted the training of the body as well as the mind in schools and other educational systems because of the close and interconnected relationship of mental and physical processes, believing that if the body exercised, so did the mind.

Horace Mann was another figure involved in the promotion of education of the entire body in United States school systems. Mann served in both the Massachusetts House of Representatives and Senate in the 1830s, but generated the most educational reform as secretary of the Board of Education of Massachusetts in 1837. Mann's primary goal for education was to create a more equal playing field for the masses, believing that an education would provide the means to better one's lot in life. Mann argued that acquiring knowledge was the same as acquiring power, and placed equal importance on the teaching of academic subjects such as spelling and arithmetic, and the teaching of non-academia such as music and physical education that promoted healthy living habits.

Contributions of early societies to the profession

Games often had a practical, educational aim like playing house. In addition, games such as gladiatorial games had political aims. Economic games included fishing and hunting. Families played board games. There were ceremonial reasons for games found in dances. Finally, ball games provided an opportunity for socialization.

Early society - The common activities performed in early societies included war-like games, chariot racing, boating and fishing, equestrian, hunting, music and dancing, boxing and wrestling, bow and arrow activities, dice, and knucklebones.

Egyptian - The common activities performed in Egypt were acrobatics, gymnastics, tug of war, hoop and kick games, ball and stick games, juggling, knife-throwing games of chance, board games, and guessing games (e.g how many fingers are concealed).

Bronze Age - The activities performed during the Bronze Age (3000 to 1000 BC) were bullfights, dancing, boxing, hunting, archery, running, and board games.

Greek Age - The Greeks are best known for the Olympic Games, but their other contributions were the pentathlon, which included the jump, the discus, and the javelin. The Pankration was a combination of boxing and wrestling. The Greeks also played on seesaws, enjoyed swinging, hand guessing games, blind man's bluff, dice games (losers had to carry their partner's pick-a-back), and hoop and board games. There also were funeral games in The Iliad.

Romans - The Romans kept slaves and were advocates of "blood sports." Their philosophy was to die well. There were unemployment games. Roman baths were popular, as were ball games, stuffed feathers, pila trigonalis, follis, and balloon or bladder ball. The Capitoline games were held in 86 AD. These union guild athletes were paid for their activities, which included artificial fly-fishing. The games that were popular during this period were top spinning, odds and evens, riding a long stick, knucklebones, and hide and seek.

Chinese - The Chinese contributed the following: jujitsu, fighting cocks, dog racing, and football. In Korea, Japan, and China, children played with toys and lanterns. Common activities included building snowmen, playing with dolls, making/playing with shadows, flying kites, and fighting kites. Children enjoyed ropewalker toys, windmills, turnip lanterns, ring puzzles, and playing horse. Noblemen engaged in hopping, jumping, leapfrog, jump rope, seesaw, and drawing.

Major events in the history of physical education and the historical relationship of physical education to health and fitness

Egypt - Sport dancing among the nobility, physical skills among the masses, and physical training for wars.

Cretans - learned to swim.

Spartan and Greeks - emphasized severe physical training and NOT competitive sport.

Athenians - believed in the harmonious development of the body, mind and spirit.

Romans – The Romans established the **worth of physical education**. During the dark ages, children learned fitness and horsemanship. The squires learned how to become knights by boxing and fencing. Swimming was also popular. During the Renaissance, people developed the body for health reasons. The Romans **combined the physical and mental** aspects of exercise in their daily routines.

1349-1428 - Physical education was necessary for a person's total education and also a means of recreation.

In **1546,** Martin Luther saw PE as a substitute for vice and evil.

Sweden - Ling in 1839 strove to make PE a **science.**

Colonial period - religions denounced play. Pleasures were either banned or frowned upon.

The **National Period** began in 1823. Games and sports were available as after school activities. There was an introduction of **gymnastics and calisthenics.**

Civil War (1860) - Gymnastics and non-military use of PE.. Physical Education became **organized**. PE became part of the school curriculum and held a respectable status among other subjects. **YMCA's** were founded. Gulick was the Director of PE at NYC and Dudley Allen Sargent was teaching physical education at Harvard.

Great Depression of the 1930s - Physical fitness movement. Bowling was the number one activity. Dance, gymnastics and sports were popular. The Heisman Trophy was awarded in 1935. After WWII, outdoor pools were common for the average American.

Major trends since WWII influencing physical education

WWII - Selective Service examinations revealed the poor physical fitness condition of the country's youth. Thus, **physical education classes focused on physical conditioning.**

1942 - President Roosevelt established the **Division of Physical Fitness** run by John B. Kelly (who alerted Roosevelt about the poor fitness levels of youths). This division was dissolved and **placed under the Federal Security Agency** [FSA] with numerous organizations **promoting fitness**. Under the FSA, Frank Lloyd was Chief of the Physical Fitness Division, William Hughs was Chief Consultant, and Dorothy LaSalle was head of the work for women and children. **After WWII ended, the eagerness for fitness waned.**

1953 - **Kraus-Webber tests** - Of the 4,264 USA participants, 57% failed a general muscular fitness test. Only 8.7% of Europeans failed. Again, John Kelly alerted the President (Eisenhower) of the **need for a fitness movement.** Eisenhower ordered a **special conference** that was held in **June 1956.**

1956 - AAHPERD Fitness Conference established the President's Council on Youth Fitness and a President's Citizens Advisory Committee on the Fitness of American Youth.

Modern dance gave way to contemporary. Gymnastics had new equipment, including a higher balance beam, trampolines, and uneven parallel bars. The Swedish gymnastics boom was over, and ropes and ladders, wands, dumbbells, and Indian clubs were no longer fashionable. Core sports for boys were football, baseball, basketball, and track and field. Core sports for women were basketball and volleyball.

John Fitzgerald Kennedy changed the name of the President's Citizens Advisory Committee of Fitness of American Youth to the **President's Council on Physical Fitness.**

Lyndon Baines Johnson changed the name to **President's Council on Physical Fitness and Sports.**

1972 - **passage of Title IX** of the Educational Amendments Act to ensure girls and women receive the same rights as boys and men for educational programs - including physical education and athletics

1970 to Present Trends - Preventative medicine, wellness, physical fitness, and education that is more scholarly, more specialized, and more applicable to all segments of population such as the elderly, handicapped persons, and those out of organizations (Non-School sports): AAU - mid 20th century controlled amateur sports; Little League; North American Baseball Association.

International Amateur Sports: Olympic Governing Committee.

Intercollegiate: National Collegiate Athletic Association (NCAA scholarship in 1954); National Association of Intercollegiate Athletics (NAIA); National Junior College Athletic Association (NJCAA).

Interscholastic Sports: National Federation of State High School Athletic Associations.

Organizations for Girls' and Women's Sports: Athletic and Recreation Federation of College Women (ARFCW); the Women's Board of the U.S. Olympic Committee; National Section of Women's Athletics (NSWA - promoted intercollegiate sports such as US Field Hockey and Women's International Bowling and established special committees). The Women's Division of NAAF merged its interests in the NSWA of AAHPERD changing its name to National Section for Girls and Women's Sports (NSGWS). **Mel Lockes, chairperson of NSGWS in 1956, was against intercollegiate athletics for women.** In 1957, NSGWS changed its name to Division of Girls and Women's Sports (DGWS), still a division of AAHPERD. A lack of funds hurt DGWS.

COMPETENCY 3.0   CURRENT RESEARCH, TRENDS, AND ISSUES

Skill 3.1   **Analyze current research, trends, and issues that affect physical education (e.g. inclusion, lifelong fitness, the sharp increase in obesity-related diseases among U.S. youth) and their impact on physical education programs and goals.**

In most educational systems, physical education (PE), also called physical training (PT) or gym, is a course in the curriculum that utilizes the learning medium of large-muscle activities in a play or movement-exploration setting. It is almost always mandatory for students in elementary schools, and often for students in middle schools and high schools. Although some people refer to Physical Education as "P.E.," the preferred titles include Lifetime Fitness, Kinesiology, and Physical Activity.

The primary aim of physical education is to equip students with the knowledge, skills, capacities, values, and enthusiasm to maintain a healthy lifestyle into adulthood, regardless of their physical abilities. Activities included in the program promote physical fitness, develop motor skills, instill knowledge and understanding of rules, concepts, and strategies, and teach students to work as part of a team or as individuals in a wide variety of play-like and competitive activities.

During the past 20 years, obesity among adults has risen significantly in the United States. The latest data shows that 30 percent of U.S. adults 20 years of age and older and over 60 million people are obese. This increase applies to children as well as adults. The percentage of young people who are overweight has more than tripled since 1980. Among children and teens aged 6-19 years, 16 percent (over 9 million young people) are overweight. These increasing rates raise concerns because of their implications for the health of America.

Being overweight or obese increases the risk of many diseases and health conditions, including hypertension, dyslipidemia (for example, high total cholesterol or high levels of triglycerides), type 2 diabetes, coronary heart disease, stroke, gallbladder disease, osteoarthritis, sleep apnea, respiratory problems, and some cancers (endometrial, breast, and colon). Although one of the national health objectives for the year 2010 is to reduce the prevalence of obesity among adults to less than 15%, current data indicates that the situation is worsening rather than improving.

Currently there are programs designed to help states prevent obesity and other chronic diseases by addressing two closely related factors - poor nutrition and inadequate physical activity. The programs support states by helping to develop and implement science-based nutrition and physical activity interventions. The program's major goals are balancing caloric intake and expenditure, increasing physical activity, improving nutrition through increased consumption of fruits and vegetables, reducing television time, and increasing breastfeeding.

Currently 21 states receive funds of $400,000 to $450,000 for capacity building. Seven states receive funds of $750,000 to $1.3 million for basic implementation, bringing the total number of funded states to 28.

Current research, trends, and issues greatly affect the goals of physical education and the programs for achieving them. Issues and trends that exert a strong influence today include:

- **Inclusion** – In the past, a "mainstreaming" approach was used with children experiencing difficulties in class (school staff would occasionally periodically remove students from the class in order to provide special remedial attention). Today, the trend is to replace the mainstreaming approach with "inclusion" (where the child experiencing difficulty remains in the class, and receives remedial attention in the same setting as the rest of the children). This creates a new challenge for physical educators, because they must modify their lessons to accommodate children who may have modality problems (poor vision or hearing), or cognitive difficulties that may render visual or auditory instructions difficult to process. Sequencing of tasks and events may also pose a challenge to some children.

- **Lifelong fitness** – The trend in national standards for physical education is increasingly towards the development of an attitude among students that will promote the integration of movement activities into their routines over an entire lifespan. This requires a greater emphasis on the benefits of physical activities to health and well-being, and a greater knowledge among students of the underlying mechanisms of human movement, so they will be able to make informed choices about the movement activities that best compliment their changing set of skills, interests, and needs.

- **Increase in obesity-related diseases among U.S. youth** – We can attribute the recent sharp growth of obesity-related diseases among U.S. youth to a decrease in quality and quantity of physical activities among youth (a move "from playground to PlayStation"), and a decrease in quality of diet (more fast food, which incorporates high levels of sugar, salt and fats). Countering this trend requires the creative application of human movement activities to stimulate interest and participation among children. Also important is the integration of more theoretical and practical knowledge of nutrition in physical education activities.

Trends towards Kinesiology in physical education

Educators encourage aspiring teachers to draw upon knowledge of the sub-disciplines of kinesiology, including human anatomy, physiology, neuroscience, biochemistry, biomechanics, exercise psychology and sociology of sport, to ensure that students are able to safely and effectively participate in physical education activities that aim to develop and improve their movement skills and knowledge.

Candidate teachers should be able to understand significant factors and influences in developing, analyzing, and assessing basic motor skills; know how to structure developmentally appropriate activities to promote maximum participation, inclusion, and active engagement in a wide range of movement forms, which include traditional and nontraditional games, sports, dance, and fitness activities; select and create cooperative and competitive activities that promote trust building, problem solving, collaboration, leadership, and strategic planning; design fitness programs and recommend exercises and activities based on sound physiological and fitness training principles; understand the short-term and long-term benefits of a healthy, active lifestyle; and know how to demonstrate and communicate these benefits to students.

Trend towards student-centered activities

A prime goal of physical education is to promote student development of positive personal and social behaviors, including social interaction and communication skills. To do this, candidate teachers should apply sociological, psychological, philosophical, historical, and cultural dimensions of physical education to select and develop appropriate activities and innovative approaches. Would-be-teachers should be aware of the role of movement activities in helping students develop a sense of individual identity and group member identity.

This physical education strategy prepares the would-be-teachers to use knowledge of historical and cultural influences on games, sports, dance, and other physical activities to enhance student awareness and appreciation of cultural and artistic diversity, the role of movement in society, and the use of physical activity for enjoyment and self-expression. The teacher should emphasize the importance of inclusion, fair play, etiquette, and respect and consideration for self and others. There are many factors that influence an individual's activity choices and careful evaluation of the appropriateness of activities in terms of participants' age and developmental levels, motor proficiency, gender, cultural background, and physical strengths and limitations is a priority. Knowledge of student development and learning curve is critical to select activities and approaches that help students experience the benefits of individual challenges and successes. To accomplish this, the principles of learning and motivation are necessary to spark students' interest in physical activity and to help motivate them to engage in lifelong physical activity.

Knowledge of assessment principles and procedures to collect, analyze, interpret, and summarize findings are important if physical educators are to succeed in motivating students. This means that teachers should know the rudiments of physical fitness testing principles, technologies, and techniques and they should be prepared to administer the state-mandated physical fitness assessment programs. This means that they must be able to interpret and communicate the test results, performance profiles, and other types of assessment information in a meaningful and sensitive way.

Skill 3.2 **Demonstrate an understanding of legal and ethical issues in physical education, such as those related to supervision, liability, confidentiality, equity, disability, and diversity.**

PROFESSIONAL AND ETHICAL STANDARDS AND CODES AND LEGAL REQUIREMENTS AND RESPONSIBILITIES

There are many issues related to the legal responsibilities of the professional physical educator. Failing to foresee potential hazardous conditions and to take practical steps to avoid these situations can result in litigation. In general, teachers must follow the standard of care expected of any physical education practitioner with a similar level of education and training. Liability refers to a legal responsibility. Often in litigious situations, the term liability refers to negligence, or breach of duty. Negligence refers to actions that do not meet the minimum standard of care. In successful litigation, the defense proves the existence of the following: duty, breach of duty, injury, and proximate cause. When determining liability, courts will determine whether the injury was foreseeable.

To avoid legal action, professional physical educators must meet their legal responsibilities in several areas: equipment and facilities, instruction, supervision, and general safety. Regular inspection of the instructional area identifies potential hazards. When physical educators find hazards, they should submit written notification to the principal immediately. Students should also receive proper instruction of equipment use prior to the first use. In an instructional setting, the physical educator protects students from unreasonable harm. Students receive appropriate training before and during activity. Supervision of all activities in a school setting is mandatory. An unsupervised student in the school at any time or on the school grounds during the school day is unacceptable. The approach to overall safety should be proactive.

Physical educators participate in safety in-service programs each year. The teacher or another school medical professional reviews student medical records prior to allowing participation in physical education. Physical education practitioners teach the safety rules for each activity at the beginning of each unit. When a student sustains an injury in physical education class, the school nurse or other medical professional evaluates the student. The physical educator completes and files an accident report the same day that the accident occurred.

An Emergency Action Plan (EAP) should be in place for the physical education department at each school. The EAP identifies the following: emergency care procedures and the individual responsible for rendering care, the individual responsible for parental notification, the individual responsible for activating the emergency medical system (EMS), the policy for transportation of injured students, and a copy of a blank student accident report. To reduce the financial consequences of litigation, each teacher should purchase and maintain personal professional liability insurance. Teachers should not rely on school district legal liability insurance for personal financial protection.

In addition to legal responsibilities, the physical educator also has ethical responsibilities. Teachers are responsible for helping each student to realize his or her abilities. Physical educators are accountable for the welfare of each student entrusted to their care. Teachers should maintain a professional relationship with their students. Teachers should maintain confidentiality. Physical educators should follow national, state, and district or school curricular standards. Teachers should establish and maintain a classroom routine that promotes student achievement. Finally, the physical education teacher is responsible for promoting healthful living within the school community.

EMERGENCY ACTION PLANS

The first step in establishing a safe physical education environment is creating an Emergency Action Plan (EAP). The formation of a well-planned EAP can make a significant difference in the outcome of an injury situation.

Components of an Emergency Action Plan
To ensure the safety of students during physical activity, an EAP should be easily comprehensible yet detailed enough to facilitate prompt, thorough action.

Communication
Instructors should communicate rules and expectations clearly to students. This information should include pre-participation guidelines, emergency procedures, and proper game etiquette. Instructors should collect emergency information sheets from students at the start of each school year. First-aid kits, facility maps, and incident report forms should also be readily available. Open communication between students and teachers is essential. Creating a positive environment within the classroom allows students to feel comfortable enough to approach an adult/teacher if she feels she has sustained a potential injury.

Teacher Education
At the start of each school year, every student should undergo a pre-participation physical examination. This allows a teacher to recognize the "high-risk" students before activity commences. The teacher should also take note of any student that requires any form of medication or special care. When a teacher is aware of his/her students' conditions, the learning environment is a lot safer.

Facilities and Equipment

It is the responsibility of the teacher and school district to provide a safe environment, playing area, and equipment for students. Instructors and maintenance staff should regularly inspect school facilities to confirm that the equipment and location is adequate and safe for student use.

First Aid Equipment

It is essential to have a properly stocked first aid kit in an easily reachable location. Instructors may need to include asthma inhalers and special care items to meet the specific needs of certain students. Instructors should clearly mark these special care items to avoid a potentially harmful mix-up.

Implementing the Emergency Plan

The main thing to keep in mind when implementing an EAP is to remain calm. Maintaining a sufficient level of control and activating appropriate medical assistance will facilitate the process and will leave less room for error.

STATE LEGISLATION

State governments (Department of Education) are primarily responsible for education. Departments of education establish policies for course curriculum, number of class days and class time, and amount of credits required for graduation.

STANDARDS FOR PHYSICAL EDUCATION

The imperatives of the health and fitness concerns have resulted in the enactment of standards for physical education. In January 2005, the California Department of Education adopted the Physical Education Content Standards. These standards represent the essential skills and knowledge that all students need to maintain a physically active and healthy lifestyle.

Standard 1: Students must be able to demonstrate motor skills and movement patterns needed to perform a variety of physical activities.
Standard 2: Students must be able to demonstrate knowledge of movement concepts, principles, and strategies as they apply to learning and performance of physical activities.
Standard 3: Students must be able to assess and maintain a level of physical fitness to improve health and performance.
Standard 4: Students must be able to demonstrate knowledge of physical fitness concepts, principles, and strategies to improve health and performance.
Standard 5: Students must be able to demonstrate and utilize knowledge of psychological and sociological concepts, principles, and strategies as applied to learning and performance of physical activity.

ADAPTED PHYSICAL EDUCATION NATIONAL STANDARDS

Physical education standards adapted for disabled students include:

STANDARD 1 HUMAN DEVELOPMENT: Sets the foundation of proposed goals and activities for individuals with disabilities. Grounded in a basic understanding of human development and its applications to those with various needs.

STANDARD 2 MOTOR BEHAVIOR: Sets the standard on teaching individuals with disabilities, which requires knowledge of typical physical and motor development as well as understanding the influence of developmental delays on these processes.

STANDARD 3 EXERCISE SCIENCE: The focus of this standard is on the principles that address the physiological and biomechanical applications encountered when working with diverse populations.

STANDARD 4 MEASUREMENT AND EVALUATION: Sets the standards on the measurements in gauging motor performance that is, to a large extent, based on a good grasp of motor development and the acquisition of motor skills covered in other standards.

STANDARD 5 HISTORY AND PHILOSOPHY: This standard sets the basic knowledge base of educators on legal and philosophical factors involved in current day practices in adapted physical education (APE). This standard also covers a review of history and philosophy related to special and general education.

STANDARD 6 UNIQUE ATTRIBUTES OF LEARNERS: This standard refers to information based on the disability areas found in the Individuals with Disabilities Education Act (IDEA).

STANDARD 7 CURRICULUM THEORY AND DEVELOPMENT: Sets the standards on knowledge of certain curriculum theory and development concepts, such as selecting goals based on relevant and appropriate assessment.

STANDARD 8 ASSESSMENT: This seeks to establish the parameters and conduct of assessment, which goes beyond data gathering to include measurements for the purpose of making decisions about special services and program components for individuals with disabilities.

STANDARD 9 INSTRUCTIONAL DESIGN AND PLANNING: Administration must develop standards on instructional design and planning before an APE teacher can provide services to meet legal mandates, educational goals, and, most importantly, the unique needs of individuals with disabilities.

STANDARD 10 TEACHING: This standard integrates many of the principles addressed earlier in covering areas such as human development, motor behavior, and exercise science. This will ensure that schools meet other standards to provide quality physical education to individuals with disabilities effectively.

STANDARD 11 CONSULTATION AND STAFF DEVELOPMENT: This standard sets the key competencies that an adapted physical educator should know in relation to consultation and staff development.

STANDARD 12 STUDENT AND PROGRAM EVALUATION: Sets the standards on how to conduct program evaluation, integrating the entire range of educational services.

STANDARD 13 CONTINUING EDUCATION: This standard sets the parameters on ways teachers of APE can remain current in their field.

STANDARD 14 ETHICS: This standard ensures that teachers of APE not only understand the importance of sound ethical practices, but also adhere to and advance such practices.

STANDARD 15 COMMUNICATION: This standard includes setting the quality of information on how to communicate with families and other professionals effectively. The standard encourages a team approach to enhance service delivery to individuals with disabilities.

IMPACT OF EDUCATION REFORMS AND FEDERAL LEGISLATION

Enrollment went up and there was renewed administrative, parental, and student support. Additional impacts include: coeducational classes, separate teams for boys and girls and men and women (otherwise the school must create a coeducational team), equal opportunities for both sexes (for facilities, equipment and supplies, practice and games, medical and training services, academic tutoring and coaching, travel and per diem allowances, and dining and housing facilities), and equitable expenditure of funds for both sexes.

The Department of Health and Human Services recommended legislative changes - including those for education. **Title IX** prohibits sex discrimination in educational programs and **PL 94-142** requires schools to provide educational services for handicapped students. In 1990, Congress passed the **Individuals with Disabilities Education Act** (IDEA) that amended earlier laws. IDEA specifies physical education as a required educational service. In addition, IDEA defines physical education as the development of physical fitness, motor skills, and skills in-group and individual games and dance, aquatics, and lifetime sports.

Title IX takes precedence over all conflicting state and local laws and conference regulations. Federal aid (even aid not related to physical education or athletics) must comply with Title IX. Finally, Title IX prohibits discrimination in personnel standards and scholarships selection.

Finally, Congress enacted the Physical Education for Progress (PEP) Act in 2000. The PEP program provides funds that the Department of Education uses to award grants to help initiate, expand, and develop physical education programs for Kindergarten through 12th grade students.

LIABILITY CONCERNS IN PHYSICAL EDUCATION

Historically, common-law rules stated that individuals could not sue government agencies without consent of the agencies. However, federal and state courts have begun to allow individuals to sue both federal and state governments. Thus, public schools and school districts are now subject to liability lawsuits.

Compulsory elements of the school curriculum, such as physical education, prompt courts to decide based on what is in the best interests of the public.

Although school districts still have immunity in many states, teachers do not have such immunity. Whether employed by private person or a municipal corporation every employee owes a duty not to injure another by a negligent act of commission.

The following is a list of common legal terms and conditions applicable to physical education.

1. Tort – a legal wrong resulting in a direct or indirect injury; includes omissions and acts intended or unintended to cause harm.

2. Negligence – failing to fulfill a legal duty according to common reasoning; includes instruction and facility maintenance; instructors must consider sex, size, and skill of participants when planning activities and grouping students.

3. In Loco Parentis – acting in the place of the parent in relation to a child.

4. Sports Product Liability – liability of the manufacturer to the person using the manufacturer's product who sustains injury/damage from using the product.

5. Violence and legal liability (intentional injury in sports contests) – harmful, illegal contact of one person by another (referred to as battery).

6. Physical education classes held off campus and legal liability – primary concern is providing due care, which is the responsibility of management and staff members of sponsoring organization; failing to observe "due care" can result in findings of negligence.

7. Attractive Nuisance – an object that results in physical injury that the responsible party should have foreseen.

ACTIONS THAT CAN AVOID LAWSUITS

1. Knowing the health status of each person in the program.

2. Considering the ability and skill level of participants when planning new activities.

3. Grouping students to equalize competitive levels.

4. Using safe equipment and facilities.

5. Properly organizing and supervising classes.

6. Never leaving a class.

7. Knowing first aid (Do not diagnose or prescribe).

8. Keeping accident records.

9. Giving instruction prior to dangerous activities.

10. Being sure that injured students get medical attention and examination.

11. Getting exculpatory agreements (parental consent forms).

12. Having a planned, written disposition for students who suffer injuries or become ill.

13. Providing a detailed accident report if one occurs.

COMPETENCY 4.0 INTERRELATIONSHIPS OF THE SUBDISCIPLINES OF KINESIOLOGY

SKILL 4.1 Demonstrate an understanding of the interrelationships of the subdisciplines of kinesiology.

MOVEMENT SCIENCE AND KINESIOLOGY

The systematic study of human movement applied to the field of physical injury. It is concerned with the understanding of how and why we move and the factors that limit and enhance our capacity to move. This particular field also relates to studies about exercising for health or the regaining of function of an injured body.

Human Movement is based on a solid liberal arts and science education designed to foster development of human values and effective interpersonal skills. A scientific foundation is necessary for the study of the ability to function both didactically and clinically.

The aim of the study of human movement is to further the understanding of the mechanisms and processes underlying skilled movements and the means by which they are influenced by physiological, biomechanical, psychological and social factors.

Finally, kinesiology encompasses human anatomy, physiology, neuroscience, biochemistry, biomechanics, exercise psychology, and sociology of sport. Kinesiologists also study the relationship between the quality of movement and overall human health. Kinesiology is an important part of physical therapy, occupational therapy, chiropractics, osteopathy, exercise physiology, kinesiotherapy, massage therapy, ergonomics, physical education, and athletic coaching. The purpose of these applications may be therapeutic, preventive, or high-performance. The application of kinesiology can also incorporate knowledge from other academic disciplines such as psychology, sociology, cultural studies, ecology, evolutionary biology, and anthropology. The study of kinesiology is often part of the physical education curriculum and illustrates the truly interdisciplinary nature of physical education.

COMPETENCY 5.0 PROFESSIONAL RESPONSIBILITIES, ORGANIZATIONS, AND RESOURCES

SKILL 5.1 Demonstrate knowledge of professional responsibilities, organizations, and resources that support physical education (e.g. AAHPERD, American College of Sports Medicine).

PHYSICAL EDUCATION PROFESSIONAL ORGANIZATIONS AND ACTIVITIES THAT PROMOTE PROFESSIONAL DEVELOPMENT

1. Amateur Athletic Union (AAU) – protects amateur sports from becoming corrupted. Conducts pre-Olympic trials.

2. American Alliance for Health, Physical Education, Recreation, and Dance (AAHPERD) – works with legislatures concerning education and research, works with president's council on physical fitness and sport, and influences public opinion. Various associations make up the alliance.

3. American College of Sports Medicine – promotes scientific studies of sports and conducts research and post-graduate work.

4. National Association for Sport and Physical Education (NASPE) – a non-profit, professional membership organization that is the preeminent national authority on physical education. **Developed national standards for physical education.**

5. National Intramural Association

6. National Junior College Athletic Association

7. Phi Epsilon Kappa – fraternity for people pursuing careers in health, physical education, recreation, or safety.

CURRENT PROFESSIONAL LITERATURE, RESEARCH, AND OTHER SOURCES OF INFORMATION THAT ENHANCE PROFESSIONAL GROWTH

1. AAU Publication Amateur Athlete Yearbook, AAU News (monthly)

2. American Academy of PE – position papers, studies for and by the academy.

3. Journal of PE, Recreation, and Dance

4. Research Quarterly

5. School Health Review

6. The Foil - the official publication of Delta Psi Kappa, newsletter The Psi Kappa Shield.

7. NEA - Today's Education

8. National Jr. College Athletic Association

9. Journal of PE – published bi-monthly.

10. YMCA Magazine – public affairs news.

SKILL 5.2 Demonstrate knowledge of current state and national standards for physical education.

SEE ALSO Domain 1, Skill 3.2

NASPE FEDERAL CONTENT STANDARDS

The goal of physical education is to impart the knowledge, skills, and confidence necessary for students to enjoy a life of healthful physical activity. The National Association for Sport and Physical Education identifies six content standards for physical education:

- **Standard 1:** Demonstrates competency in motor skills and movement patterns needed to perform a variety of physical activities.

- **Standard 2:** Demonstrates understanding of movement concepts, principles, strategies, and tactics as they apply to the learning and performance of physical activities.

- **Standard 3:** Participates regularly in physical activity.

- **Standard 4:** Achieves and maintains a health-enhancing level of physical fitness.

- **Standard 5:** Exhibits responsible personal and social behavior that respects self and others in physical activity settings.

- **Standard 6:** Values physical activity for health, enjoyment, challenge, self-expression, and/or social interaction.

(Source: National Association for Sport & Physical Education)

A comprehensive physical education curriculum emphasizes the importance of physical activity and nutrition to lifelong wellness. In addition, physical education should introduce students to various activities that promote healthy living. Finally, physical education should provide students with strategies to maintain proper nutrition and activity and design personal fitness programs.

COMPETENCY 6.0 RELATIONSHIP BETWEEN HUMAN MOVEMENT ACTIVITIES AND VALUES

SKILL 6.1 Demonstrate an understanding of human movement activities as instruments for maintaining traditional values and/or for examining and changing traditional values.

Physical education activities can promote positive social behaviors, traits, and values in a number of different ways. Instructors can foster improved relations with adults and peers by making students active partners in the learning process and delegating responsibilities within the class environment to students. Giving students leadership positions (e.g. team captain) can give them a heightened understanding of the responsibilities and challenges facing educators.

Team-based physical activities like team sports promote collaboration and cooperation. In such activities, students learn to work together, both pooling their talents and minimizing the weaknesses of different team members, in order to achieve a common goal. The experience of functioning as a team can be very productive for development of loyalty between children, and seeing their peers in stressful situations that they can relate to can promote a more compassionate and considerate attitude among students. Similarly, the need to maximize the strengths of each student on a team (who can complement each other and compensate for weaknesses) is a powerful lesson about valuing and respecting diversity and individual differences. Varying students between leading and following positions in a team hierarchy are good ways to help students gain a comfort level being both followers and leaders.

Fairness is another trait that physical activities, especially rules-based sports, can foster and strengthen. Children are by nature very rules-oriented, and have a keen sense of what they believe is and isn't fair. Fair play, teamwork, and sportsmanship are all values that stem from proper practice of the spirit of physical education classes. Of course, a pleasurable physical education experience goes a long way towards promoting an understanding of the innate value of physical activity throughout the life cycle.

SOCIOLOGICAL BENEFITS of physical activity include the opportunity to spend time with family and friend, making new friends, the opportunity to be part of a team, the opportunity to participate in competitive experiences; the opportunity to experience the thrill of victories.

SKILL 6.2 Analyze the role of physical education in promoting equity for diverse groups.

Physical education and physical activity promote equity for diverse groups in three key ways:

- **Human Growth and Development** – Movement activities promote personal growth and development physically, by way of stimulating muscular development, and emotionally, by raising personal confidence levels among children and by allowing them to explore concepts of inter-group equity that may at first seem threatening. To the insecure child, the concept that another group may be equal to his own may seem to 'demote' his group and the child by extension.

- **Psychology** – Observation and interaction with the behavior of children from diverse backgrounds in a training environment (where the training activities tend to focus more on 'doing', which feels more genuine to children than the classroom setting of raising hands and answering questions) allows the child to see in others the same sorts of behavioral reasoning processes that he sees in himself. This humanizes others from diverse backgrounds, and promotes concepts of equity among diverse groups.

- **Aesthetics** – Human movement activities create an opportunity for individual participation in activities with intrinsic aesthetic qualities. A gymnastic technique or a perfectly executed swing of a baseball bat relies on both physical training and a level of intuitive action. This is an artistic form of expression that is readily accessible to children. Recognizing beauty in the activities and performances of others (in some cases from groups different from that of the viewing student) is a humanizing experience.

DOMAIN 2. GROWTH, MOTOR DEVELOPMENT, AND MOTOR LEARNING

COMPETENCY 1.0 INDIVIDUAL DIFFERENCES

SKILL 1.1 Demonstrate knowledge of individual motor and physical fitness variables such as agility, balance, coordination, strength, and speed.

SKILL RELATED COMPONENTS OF PHYSICAL FITNESS – IDENTIFICATION AND ASSESSMENT

The skill-related components of physical fitness include **agility, balance, coordination, power, reaction time, speed, and strength.** A student's natural ability in these areas greatly affects performance in fitness and athletic activities. While heredity plays a major role in each student's level of skill-related components, practice and coaching can improve performance. The following are examples of tests to assess skill related components of fitness.

Agility tests – Illinois Agility Run.

Balance tests – Bass Test of Dynamic Balance (lengthwise and crosswise), Johnson Modification of the Bass Test of Dynamic Balance, modified sideward leap, and balance beam walk.

Coordination tests – Stick test of Coordination.

Power tests – vertical jump.

Speed tests – 50-yard dash.

Muscle strength tests – dynamometers (hand, back, and leg), cable tensiometer, the 1-RM Test (repetition maximum: bench press, standing press, arm curl, and leg press), bench-squat, sit-ups (one sit up holding a weight plate behind the neck), and lateral pull-down.

Flexibility tests – sit and reach, Kraus-Webber Floor Touch Test, trunk extension, forward bend of trunk, Leighton Flexometer, shoulder rotation/flexion, and goniometer.

SKILL 1.2   Analyze individual physical changes and their impact on mechanical and physiological aspects of motor performance.

Recognizing individual students' physical changes helps with understanding how their physiques affect motor performance. The child's physique has a definite affect on their motor performance.

Somatype, another term for body type, deals with how fat, muscular, and linear your body is. The three body types are endomorph, mesomorph, and ectomorph. Everyone is some combination of the three types, with one classification usually prevailing over the others. You cannot change your body type but you can modify it through your eating habits and level of physical exercise, which in turn affects your body-fat percentage. Certain body types are more suited for certain sports, but it doesn't mean you won't be successful if your somatype is different from what's mentioned. Somatype classification is important because it shows how children differ in body physique and how vital it is that instruction accommodates individual differences.

Endomorphs are naturally "large" or "big boned" with a pear-shaped bodies and a slow metabolism. Endomorphs are often very strong, but have little speed. They experience difficulty at most sports, including both aerobic and anaerobic activities. Individual sports such as shot or discus throwing in track, wrestling, and judo are activities well suited for endomorphs.

Mesomorphs are "muscular" with an hourglass figure, broad shoulders, small waist, strong thighs, fast metabolism, and little body fat. Often called "natural athletes," they participate with ease and look forward to physical competition of any sort. These children perform best in team sports that require strength, speed, and agility such as football and baseball, or individual sports such as swimming.

Ectomorphs, often called "skinny," are extremely thin, with very little body fat, little or no muscle development, and an ultra fast metabolism. Ectomorphs have difficulty gaining weight or muscle mass. Because they lack power and strength, they are better suited for aerobic endurance activities such as cross-country running, many track and field events such as the high or long jump, sprints, relays, and middle-distance running.

COMPETENCY 2.0   PERCEPTUAL-MOTOR DEVELOPMENT

SKILL 2.1   Know components of perceptual-motor development such as visual, auditory, tactile, and kinesthetic discrimination and how they relate to skill acquisition and performance.

PERCEPTUAL ABILITIES - Activities that involve interpreting auditory, visual, and tactile stimuli in order to coordinate adjustments.

Perceptual-motor development refers to one's ability to receive, interpret, and respond successfully to sensory signals coming from the environment. Because many of the skills acquired in school rely on the child's knowledge of his body and its relationship to the surroundings, good motor development leads directly to perceptual skill development. Development of gross motor skills lead to successful development of fine motor skills, which in turn help with learning, reading, and writing. Adolescents with perceptual-motor coordination problems are at risk for poor school performance, low self-esteem, and inadequate physical activity participation. Without a successful intervention, these adolescents are likely to continue avoiding physical activity and experience frustration and teasing from their peers. Children with weak perceptual-motor skills may be easily distracted or have difficulty with tasks requiring coordination. They spend much of their energy trying to control their bodies, exhausting them so much that they physically cannot concentrate on a teacher-led lesson. Unfortunately, perceptual-motor coordination problems do not just go away and they don't self-repair. Practice and maturity are necessary for children to develop greater coordination and spatial awareness. Physical education lessons should emphasize activities that children enjoy doing, are sequential, and require seeing, hearing, and/or touching. Discussing with students the actual steps involved in performing a fundamental skill is a great benefit. Activities and skills that can be broken down and taught in incremental steps include running, dribbling, catching or hitting a ball, making a basket in basketball, and setting a volleyball. Recommended strategies include introducing the skill, practicing in a variety of settings with an assortment of equipment, implementing lead-up games modified to ensure practice of the necessary skills, and incorporating students into an actual game situation.

COMPETENCY 3.0   PHYSICAL AND DEVELOPMENTAL CHANGES

SKILL 3.1   Demonstrate an understanding of physical changes that occur with growth, development, and age, and analyze their impact on mechanical and physiological aspects of motor performance.

PHYSICAL DEVELOPMENT

Small children (ages 3-5) have a propensity for engaging in periods of a great deal of physical activity, punctuated by a need for a lot of rest. Children at this stage lack fine motor skills and cannot focus on small objects for very long. Their bones are still developing. At this age, girls tend to be better coordinated, and boys tend to be stronger.

The lag in fine motor skills continues during the early elementary school years (ages 6-8).

Pre-adolescent children (ages 9-11) become stronger, leaner, and taller. Their motor skills improve, and they are able to sit still and focus for longer periods of time. Growth during this period is constant. This is also the time when gender physical predispositions will begin to manifest. Pre-adolescents are at risk of obesity without proper nutritional and adequate activity.

Young adolescents (ages 12-14) experience drastic physical growth (girls earlier than boys do), and are highly preoccupied with their physical appearance.

As children proceed to the later stages of adolescence (ages 15-17), girls will reach their full height, while boys will still have some growth remaining. The increase in hormone levels will cause acne, which coincides with a slight decrease of preoccupation with physical appearance. At this age, children may begin to initiate sexual activity (boys generally more motivated by hormones, and girls more by peer pressure). There is a risk of teen pregnancy and sexually transmitted diseases.

RELATIONSHIP OF MOTOR DEVELOPMENT TO PHYSICAL, COGNITIVE, SOCIAL, AND EMOTIONAL DEVELOPMENT

Studies show that physical activity leads to improved motor development in children. Physical activity also enables various other progressions that shape the mind and personality of an individual. Such developments, which are the result of physical activity, include cognitive, psychosocial, and emotional growth.

Very often, we ignore the close relationship shared by motor development and the other aspects of development. Motor development, which starts with the proper nutrition, deeply affects the other aspects of development in an individual. Children acquire a vast range of motor development skills such as grasping, crawling, walking, running, and even speaking during the early stages of their lives. Gradually, such motor skills further develop leading to participation in sport and play activities that promote confidence in children and allow them to develop responsibility, deep emotions, and social etiquette. Through participation in sports, children learn to cooperate and develop competitive skills that will aid them in adulthood.

Studies reveal that the different types of play in childhood link motor development with the other aspects of development. Different kinds of play or physical activity such as cognitive play, social play, physical play, and emotional play, help in the overall development of a child.

Simple motor skills such as repeatedly hitting the ground with a shovel or building sand castles help in developing thinking and cognitive skills. Social play helps children to play with their peers cooperatively, to develop their motor skills, and to develop a sense of social togetherness. Motor activities greatly influence physical development as well. They help in providing the foundation for a normal and healthy physical education program suitable for all children. Research also shows that free play among peers leads to significant cognitive developments (such as improvement of reasoning abilities).

The manner in which children hop, jump, skip, run, climb, and play greatly facilitates their motor and physical development and helps to build other aspects of their personality. Children accomplish this development through their constant interaction with surrounding elements, environments, and persons.

Thus, motor skill development, which encompasses all motor movements by children, is strongly related to the physical, social, and emotional development of children.

ADOLESCENCE

Understanding the rate of the developmental growth process that occurs during adolescence will help educators understand growth and development norms and identify early or late maturing students. The age when the puberty growth spurt occurs and the speed with which adolescents experience puberty vary greatly within each gender and may affect participation in physical activity and sports. If the instructor pays attention to the varying body sizes and maturity stages, forming teams in co-educational classes can easily accommodate the needs of both genders' changing maturities. Starting in middle school and continuing into high school, it is perfectly acceptable for boys and girls to participate in non-contact physical activities together that rely on lower-body strength and agility (e.g. capture the flag, ultimate Frisbee, running). In more physical activities that require upper body strength, coaches should form teams based on individual skill levels to prevent injury. Matching teams evenly based on skill and maturity is important so that individual skill level deficiencies are not as apparent and the activity remains fun for all participants. Teachers need to monitor and adjust physical activities as needed to ensure a positive, competitive experience. Appropriate activities would include individual or partner badminton or tennis matches and team competitions in flag football.

COMPETENCY 4.0   MOTOR LEARNING

Skill 4.1   **Relate classical and current theories and models of motor learning to fundamental concepts underlying skill acquisition such as transfer, feedback, retention, practice, readiness, and observational learning.**

Motor-development learning theories that pertain to a general skill, activity, or age level are important and necessary teacher background information for effective lesson planning. Motor-skill learning is unique to each individual but does follow a general sequential skill pattern, starting with general gross motor movements and ending with specific or fine motor skills. Teachers must begin instruction at a level where all children are successful and proceed through the activity to the point where frustration for the majority is hindering performance. Students must learn the fundamentals of a skill, or subsequent learning of more advanced skills becomes extremely difficult. Instructors must spend enough time on beginning skills so they become second nature. Teaching in small groups with enough equipment for everyone is essential. Practice sessions that are too long or too demanding can cause physical and/or mental burnout. Teaching skills over a longer period of time, but with slightly different approaches, helps keep students' attentive and involved as they internalize the skill. The instructor can then teach more difficult skills while continuing to review the basics. If the skill is challenging for most students, allow plenty of practice time so they retain it due to learning in depth before having to use it in a game situation.

Visualizing and breaking the skill down mentally is another way to enhance the learning of motor movements. Instructors can teach students to "picture" the steps involved and see themselves executing the skill. An example is teaching dribbling in basketball. Start teaching the skill with a demonstration of the steps involved in dribbling. Starting with the first skill, introduce key language terms and have students visualize themselves performing the skill. A sample-progression lesson plan to teach dribbling could begin with students practicing while standing still. Next, add movement while dribbling. Finally, introduce how to control dribbling while being guarded by another student.

PRACTICE

Frequent, structured practice of motor skills enhances skill development in children. Without practice and instruction, natural ability and talent dictates the extent of motor skill development.

FEEDBACK

Feedback, or input from the tutor or educator, forms an extremely vital part of any learning process. Just as positive feedback works as a motivator enabling an athlete to improve and surge ahead with renewed interest, negative feedback also helps an athlete recognize and correct his or her mistakes.

When performers learn a skill, the skill goes into their short-term memory and receives positive feedback. The skill may eventually go into their long-term memory, creating memory that is more permanent. That is how positive feedback works to encourage the performer and helps in making the performer remember every aspect of the performance.

Negative feedback helps athletes, whether novice or experienced, become conscious of their mistakes. They can use this negative feedback to improve their shortcomings. Without feedback, an athlete is not likely to improve their technique and they will lose motivation.

There are different types of feedback and it is always important for the performer to receive the right type. Some examples of feedback include the following:

Intrinsic feedback – information received by the athlete as a direct result of producing a movement through the kinesthetic senses – e.g. feeling from muscles, joints, and balance.

Extrinsic feedback – information not inherent in the movement itself but which improves intrinsic feedback (this is also known as augmented feedback). There are two main categories: knowledge of performance and information about the technique and performance. The coach can provide extrinsic feedback verbally or visually via video. Extrinsic feedback enables the athlete to establish a kinesthetic reference for the correct movement.

Research also indicates that the stage when an athlete receives feedback is as important as the content of the feedback. Negative feedback might be boring for the beginner. However, if a performer is elite, then knowledge of results is very important. In addition, during the cognitive stage, positive feedback is essential to make sure that the athlete learns a skill successfully. Thus, feedback plays an extremely important role in any learning process, as it facilitates learning to a great extent.

READINESS

Students must be physically and psychologically ready to learn physical activities and skills successfully. No amount of instruction can teach a child who is not strong enough to shoot a basketball into a basket at regulation height. In such a situation, the instructor should first use a very low basket to allow the child to develop proper form. This adaptation addresses the problem of physical unreadiness. In addition to physical limitations, psychological obstacles may limit a child's readiness. For example, a young child who has the strength and coordination to cross the monkey bars may not want to because of a fear of falling. In such cases, the instructor should not force the child to perform the task.

OBSERVATIONAL LEARNING

Many physical education instructors believe that observational learning is the most effective method of learning motor skills. Visual observation of proper skill performance by an instructor or peer is generally more effective in promoting skill development than verbal instructions.

Skill 4.2 **Apply knowledge of motor task analysis as it relates to motor development, enabling students to select or design motor tasks that are appropriate to the process of learning movement skills.**

Children develop motor skills progressively. Motor tasks consist of distinct parts that the student must develop and practice to complete the task successfully. When teaching motor tasks, instructors should start with simple skills and gradually introduce more complex movements. Closed skills are skills performed in stable and predictable environments. Instructors should start with closed skills when introducing a new concept. Open skills are skills performed in a changing and unpredictable environment. Open skills are more difficult and require greater skill mastery. When teaching students to hit a baseball, for example, the lesson should start with students practicing the closed skill of hitting a ball off a tee. The next progression is hitting a ball on a string that moves slightly. Next, the instructor introduces the open skill of hitting a softly tossed ball. Finally, the instructor increases the pace and varies the direction of the pitch.

Skill assessment helps instructors identify student strengths and weaknesses. The following are examples of skill assessments that help instructors and students design and select appropriate motor tasks.

SKILL ASSESSMENT IN THE EVALUATION OF STUDENT PERFORMANCE

A. General Skills:

1. **Iowa Brace Test** – measures motor educability.

2. **AAHPERD Youth Fitness Test** – measures motor capacity.

3. **AAHPERD Health Related Physical Fitness Test** – measures physical capacity.

4. **McCloy's General Motor Ability and Capacity Test** – measures motor ability and motor efficiency.

5. **Rodgers Strength Test** – measures muscular strength.

6. **Texas PE Test** – measures motor ability.

7. **Skills tests for accuracy** – involve kicking, throwing, or striking an object toward a goal; activities include volleyball serves, basketball free throws, badminton short serves, and basketball passing (e.g. AAHPERD Basketball Passing Test for Accuracy).

8. **Skills test for total bodily movement** – requires performing a test course with movements similar to the sport (e.g. AAHPERD Basketball Control Test).

9. **Wall Volley Test** - measures the number of consecutive successful time/trials to pass, kick, throw, or strike an object at a wall in a given time (e.g. AAHPERD Basketball Passing Test).

10. **Skills Tests for Power or Distance** - involve kicks, throws, or strokes to measure the ability to kick, throw, or strike an object (e.g. Badminton Drive for Distance, Cornish Handball Power Test).

11. **Combination Tests** - composed of previous groupings to assess speed and accuracy.

B. Teacher Ratings: instructors create a numerical scale from one to five and rank performance based on specific, observable movements. An example is evaluating the use of space, use of focus, and variety of movements in a creative movement class.

C. Student Progress: score improvements (e.g. archery, badminton) and charting (e.g. basketball shots missed).

Instructors can administer skills tests for specific sports in one of two ways. First, rate individual performance based on a specified number of trials. Alternatively, evaluate skills using norm-referenced scales for a specific grade level.
Two problems with skill tests are that they take too much time to administer and the reliability is suspect.

SKILL 4.3 Analyze conditions that affect growth, motor development, and motor learning such as diseases, disabilities, and social, emotional, and environmental factors.

A variety of influences affects a student's motor development and fitness level:

Societal – We cannot separate students from the societies in which they live. The general perceptions around them about the importance of fitness activities will necessarily have an effect on their own choice regarding physical activity. We should consider the "playground to PlayStation" phenomenon and the rising levels of obesity among Americans negative societal influences on motor development and fitness.

Psychological – Psychological influences on motor development and fitness include a student's mental well-being, perceptions of fitness activities, and level of comfort in a fitness-training environment (both alone and within a group). Students experiencing psychological difficulties, such as depression, will tend to be apathetic and lack both the energy and inclination to participate in fitness activities. As a result, their motor development and fitness levels will suffer. Factors like the student's confidence level and comfort within a group environment, related to both the student's level of popularity within the group and the student's own personal insecurities, are also significant. It is noteworthy, though, that in the case of psychological influences on motor development and fitness levels, there is a more reciprocal relationship than with other influences. While a student's psychology may negatively affect their fitness levels, proper fitness training has the potential to positively affect the student psychologically, thereby reversing a negative cycle.

Cultural – Culture is a significant and sometimes overlooked influence on a student's motor development and fitness, especially in the case of students belonging to minority groups. Students may not feel motivated to participate in certain physical activities, either because they are not associated with the student's sense of identity or because the student's culture discourages these activities. For example, students from cultures with strict dress codes may not be comfortable with swimming activities. On the same note, students (especially older children) may be uncomfortable with physical activities in inter-gender situations. Educators must keep such cultural considerations in mind when planning physical education curricula.

Economic – The economic situation of students can affect their motor development and fitness because lack of resources can detract from the ability of parents to provide access to extra-curricular activities that promote development, proper fitness training equipment (ranging from complex exercise machines to team sport uniforms to something as simple as a basketball hoop), and even adequate nutrition.

Familial – Familial factors that can influence motor development and fitness relate to the student's home climate concerning physical activity. A student's own feelings toward physical activity often reflect the degree to which caregivers and role models (like older siblings) are athletically inclined and have a positive attitude towards physical activity. It isn't necessary for the parents to be athletically inclined, so much as it is important for them to encourage their child to explore fitness activities that could suit them.

Environmental and Health – Genetic make-up (i.e. age, gender, ethnicity) has a big influence on growth and development. Various physical and environmental factors directly affect one's personal health and fitness. Poor habits, living conditions, and afflictions such as disease or disability can affect a person in a negative manner. A healthy lifestyle with adequate conditions and minimal physical or mental stresses will enable a person to develop towards a positive, healthy existence. A highly agreed upon motor development theory is the relationship between one's own heredity and environmental factors.

Instructors should place students in rich learning situations, regardless of previous experience or personal factors, which provide plenty of positive opportunities to participate in physical activity. For example, prior to playing a game of softball, have students practice throwing by tossing the ball to themselves, progress to the underhand toss, and later to the overhand toss.

Skill 4.4   Demonstrate an understanding of developmental differences in motor learning and factors that affect motor skills acquisition for individuals with disabilities.

APPROPRIATE ACTIVITIES AND ADAPTATIONS FOR STUDENTS WITH LIMITATIONS

Appropriate activities are those activities in which handicapped students can successfully participate.

Adaptations include individualized instruction and modified rules, modified environments, and modified tasks. As needs warrant, instructors can move participants to less restrictive environments. Instructors can also initiate periodic assessments to advance a student's placement, review progress, and determine what the least restrictive environment is for each participant (including changing services to produce future optimum progress). However, the most appropriate placement depends on meeting the physical education needs, both educational and social, of the handicapped student.

FUNCTIONAL ADAPTATIONS

Instructors can provide blind students with auditory or tactile clues to help them find objects or to position their bodies in the activity area. Blind students also can learn the patterns of movement by manually mimicking the correct patterns or by verbal instructions.

Deaf students can read lips or learn signing to communicate and understand instructions.

Physically challenged students may have to use crutches to enable them to move.

Asthmatics can play goalie or similar positions requiring less cardio-respiratory demands.

Simplifying rules can accommodate a retarded participant's limited comprehension.

ADAPTING SELECTED ACTIVITIES

Walking: adapt distance, distance over time, and number of steps in specified distance; provide handrails for support; change slope for incline walking; and change width of walking pathway.

Stair climbing: change pathway, pace of climbing, and number and height of steps.

Running: change distance over time, use an incline-changing slope (distance over time), and form a maze (distance over time).

Jumping: change distance and height of jump, change distance in a series and from a platform, change participants' arm positions.

Hopping: change distance for one and two hops (using preferred and non-preferred leg) and distance through obstacle course.

Galloping: change number of gallops over distance, change distance covered in number of gallops, and widen pathway.

Skipping: change number of errorless skips, change distance covered in number of skips, change number of skips in distance, and add music for skipping in rhythm.

Leaping: change distance and height of leaps.

Bouncing balls: change size of ball (larger), have participant use two hands, reduce number of dribbles, bounce ball higher, have participant stand stationary and perform bounces one at a time.

Catching: use larger balls and have participant catch balls thrown at chest level from a lower height of release, shorten catching distance, have participant stop and then catch ball (easier than moving and catching).

ADAPTING FOR PROBLEMS WITH STRENGTH, ENDURANCE, AND POWER ACTIVITIES

1. Lower basketball goals or nets; increase size of target.

2. Decrease throwing distance between partners, serving distance, and distance between bases.

3. Reduce size or weight of projectiles.

4. Shorten length and/or reduce weight of bat or other striking apparatus.

5. Play games in lying or sitting positions to lower center of gravity.

6. Select a "slow ball" (one that will not get away too fast), deflate ball in case it gets away, or attach a string to the ball for recovery.

7. Reduce playing time and lower number of points to win.

8. Use more frequent rest periods.

9. Rotate often or use frequent substitution when needed.

10. Use mobilization alternatives, such as using scooter boards one inning/period and feet for one inning/period.

ADAPTING FOR BALANCE AND AGILITY PROBLEMS

1. Verify if balance problem is due to medication (you may have to consult physician).

2. Use chairs, tables, or bars to help with stability.

3. Have participants learn to utilize eyes optimally for balance skills.

4. Teach various ways to fall and incorporate dramatics into fall activities.

5. Use carpeted surfaces.

6. Lower center of gravity.

7. Have participant extend arms or provide a lightweight pole.

8. Have participant keep as much of his/her body in contact with the surface.

9. Widen base of support (distance between feet).

10. Increase width of walking parameters.

ADAPTING FOR COORDINATION AND ACCURACY

Throwing Activities: use beanbags, yarn or nerf balls, and/or smaller-sized balls.

Catching and Striking Activities: use larger, softer, and lighter balls; throw balls to mid-line; shorten distance; and reduce speed of balls.

Striking/Kicking Activities: enlarge striking surface, choke up on bats, begin with participant successfully striking stationary objects and then progress to striking with movement, and increase target size.

EXERCISE PHYSIOLOGY ADAPTATIONS

Decrease the amount of weight, amount of reps/sets, pace, and/or distance of exercise; increase the amount of intervals; and combine together any of the previous modifications.

DOMAIN 3. THE SCIENCE OF HUMAN MOVEMENT

COMPETENCY 1.0 BODY SYSTEMS

Skill 1.1 Demonstrate knowledge of the skeletal system, the general organization of the nervous system, the actions of muscles and major muscle groups, and the interaction of these systems with one another and with the external environment in producing motion.

STRUCTURES, LOCATIONS, AND FUNCTIONS OF THE THREE TYPES OF MUSCULAR TISSUE

The main function of the muscular system is movement. There are three types of muscle tissue: skeletal, cardiac, and smooth.

Skeletal muscle is voluntary. These muscles are attached to bones and are responsible for their movement. Skeletal muscle consists of long fibers and is striated due to the repeating patterns of the myofilaments (made of the proteins actin and myosin) that make up the fibers.

Cardiac muscle is found in the heart. Cardiac muscle is striated like skeletal muscle, but differs in that the plasma membrane of the cardiac muscle causes the muscle to beat even when away from the heart. The action potentials of cardiac and skeletal muscles also differ.

Smooth muscle is involuntary. It is found in organs and enables functions such as digestion and respiration. Unlike skeletal and cardiac muscle, smooth muscle is not striated. Smooth muscle has less myosin and does not generate as much tension as skeletal muscle.

MECHANISM OF SKELETAL MUSCLE CONTRACTION

A nerve impulse strikes a muscle fiber. This causes calcium ions to flood the sarcomere. Calcium ions allow ATP to expend energy. The myosin fibers creep along the actin, causing the muscle to contract. Once the nerve impulse has passed, calcium is pumped out and the contraction ends.

MOVEMENT OF BODY JOINTS

The axial skeleton consists of the bones of the skull and vertebrae. The appendicular skeleton consists of the bones of the legs, arms and tail, and shoulder girdle. Bone is a connective tissue. Parts of the bone include compact bone that gives strength, spongy bone that contains red marrow to make blood cells and yellow marrow in the center of long bones to store fat cells, and the periosteum that is the protective covering on the outside of the bone.

A joint is a place where two bones meet. Joints enable movement. Ligaments attach bone to bone. Tendons attach bone to muscle. Joints allow great flexibility in movement. There are three types of joints:

1. Ball and socket – allows for rotational movement. An example is the joint between the shoulder and the humerus. Ball and socket joints allow humans to move their arms and legs in many different ways.

2. Hinge – movement is restricted to a single plane. An example is the joint between the humerus and the ulna.

3. Pivot – allows for the rotation of the forearm at the elbow and the hands at the wrist.

MAJOR MUSCLES AND BONES

Muscles

Shoulder
    Deltoids – Military/Shoulder Press

Arms
    Biceps Brachii – Front of upper arm - Curls
    Triceps Brachii – Back of upper arm - Triceps Extension

Legs
    Quadriceps – Front of upper leg – Leg Extensions
    Hamstrings – Back of upper leg – Leg Curls
    Gastrocnemius – Back of lower leg (calves) – Calf Raises
    Gluteus Maximus – Buttocks – Squats

Chest
    Pectoralis Major – Bench Press

Back
    Latissimus Dorsi – Chin-ups, Pull-ups

Waist
    Rectus Abdominis – Stomach/Abdominals – Sit-ups

Bones

Skull – comprised of cranium (head) and facial bones

Vertebral column – backbone
- seven cervical vertebrae (neck)
- twelve thoracic vertebrae (middle back)
- five lumbar vertebrae (lower back)

Shoulder
    Clavicle – collar bone
    Scapula – Shoulder socket located on this bone

Thorax
    Sternum – breastbone
    Ribs – twelve pairs, each attaching to the twelve thoracic vertebrae

Arm
    Humerus – upper arm; attaches to scapula to form shoulder joint
    Ulna and Radius – forearm

Legs
    Femur – upper leg; largest bone in body
    Tibia and Fibula – lower leg
    Patella – knee

Hip
    Ilium, Ischium, and Pubis

BODY SYSTEMS

HUMAN NERVOUS AND ENDOCRINE SYSTEMS

The **central nervous system (CNS)** consists of the brain and spinal cord. The CNS is responsible for the body's response to environmental stimuli. The spinal cord is located inside the spine. It sends out motor commands for movement in response to stimuli. The brain is where responses to more complex stimuli occur. The meninges are the connective tissues that protect the CNS. The CNS contains fluid filled spaces called ventricles. These ventricles are filled when cerebrospinal fluid which is formed in the brain. This fluid cushions the brain and circulates nutrients, white blood cells, and hormones. The CNS's response to stimuli is a reflex. A reflex is an unconscious, automatic response.

The **peripheral nervous system (PNS)** consists of the nerves that connect the CNS to the rest of the body. The sensory division brings information to the CNS from sensory receptors and the motor division sends signals from the CNS to effector cells. The motor division consists of somatic nervous system and the autonomic nervous system. The body consciously controls the somatic nervous system in response to external stimuli. The hypothalamus in the brain unconsciously controls the autonomic nervous system to regulate the internal environment. This system is responsible for the movement of smooth muscles, cardiac muscles, and the muscles of other organ systems.

Understand the major endocrine glands and the function of their hormones

The function of the **endocrine system** is to manufacture proteins called hormones. **Hormones** circulate in the bloodstream and stimulate actions when they interact with target tissue. There are two classes of hormones, steroid and peptide. Steroid hormones come from cholesterol and include the sex hormones. Amino acids are the source of peptide hormones. Hormones are specific and fit receptors on the target tissue cell surface. The receptor activates an enzyme that converts ATP to cyclic AMP. Cyclic AMP (cAMP) is a second messenger from the cell membrane to the nucleus. The genes found in the nucleus turn on or off to cause a specific response.

Endocrine cells, which make up endocrine glands, secrete hormones. The major endocrine glands and their hormones include:

Hypothalamus – located in the lower brain; signals the pituitary gland.

Pituitary gland – located at the base of the hypothalamus; releases growth hormones and antidiuretic hormone (retention of water in kidneys).

Thyroid gland – located on the trachea; lowers blood calcium levels (calcitonin) and maintains metabolic processes (thyroxine).

Gonads – located in the testes of the male and the ovaries of the female; testes release androgens to support sperm formation and ovaries release estrogens to stimulate uterine lining growth and progesterone to promote uterine lining growth.

Pancreas – secretes insulin to lower blood glucose levels and glucagon to raise blood glucose levels.

ROLE OF NERVE IMPULSES AND NEURONS

The **neuron** is the basic unit of the nervous system. It consists of an axon, which carries impulses away from the cell body to the tip of the neuron; the dendrite, which carries impulses toward the cell body; and the cell body, which contains the nucleus. Synapses are spaces between neurons. Chemicals called neurotransmitters are found close to the synapse. The myelin sheath, composed of Schwann cells, covers the neurons and provides insulation.

Nerve action depends on depolarization and an imbalance of electrical charges across the neuron. A polarized nerve has a positive charge outside the neuron. A depolarized nerve has a negative charge outside the neuron. Neurotransmitters turn off the sodium pump which results in depolarization of the membrane. This wave of depolarization (as it moves from neuron to neuron) carries an electrical impulse. This is actually a wave of opening and closing gates that allows for the flow of ions across the synapse. Nerves have an action potential. There is a threshold of the level of chemicals that must be met or exceeded in order for muscles to respond. This is the "all or nothing" response.

STRUCTURE AND FUNCTION OF THE SKIN

The skin consists of two distinct layers, the epidermis and the dermis. The epidermis is the thinner outer layer and the dermis is the thicker inner layer. Layers of tightly packed epithelial cells make up the epidermis. The tight packaging of the epithelial cells supports the skin's function as a protective barrier against infection.

The top layer of the epidermis consists of dead skin cells and contains keratin, a waterproofing protein. The dermis layer consists of connective tissue. It contains blood vessels, hair follicles, sweat glands, and sebaceous glands. The body releases an oily secretion called sebum, produced by the sebaceous gland, to the outer epidermis through the hair follicles. Sebum maintains the pH of the skin between 3 and 5, which inhibits most microorganism growth.

The skin also plays a role in thermoregulation. Increased body temperature causes skin blood vessels to dilate, causing heat to radiate from the skin's surface. Increased temperature also activates sweat glands, increasing evaporative cooling. Decreased body temperature causes skin blood vessels to constrict. This results in blood from the skin diverting to deeper tissues and reduces heat loss from the surface of the skin.

HUMAN RESPIRATORY AND EXCRETORY SYSTEMS

Surface area, volume, and function of the respiratory and excretory systems

The lungs are the respiratory surface of the human respiratory system. A dense net of capillaries contained just beneath the epithelium form the respiratory surface. The surface area of the epithelium is about 100m^2 in humans. Based on the surface area, the volume of air inhaled and exhaled is the tidal volume. This is normally about 500mL in adults. Vital capacity is the maximum volume the lungs can inhale and exhale. This is usually around 3400mL.

The kidneys are the primary organ in the excretory system. Each of the two kidneys in humans is about 10cm long. Despite their small size, they receive about 20% of the blood pumped with each heartbeat. The function of the excretory system is to rid the body of nitrogenous wastes in the form of urea.

Knowledge of process of breathing and gas exchange

The respiratory system functions in the gas exchange of oxygen and carbon dioxide waste. It delivers oxygen to the bloodstream and picks up carbon dioxide for release from the body. Air enters the mouth and nose, where it is warmed, moistened and filtered of dust and particles. Cilia in the trachea trap and expel unwanted material in mucus. The trachea splits into two bronchial tubes and the bronchial tubes divide into smaller and smaller bronchioles in the lungs. The internal surface of the lung is composed of alveoli, which are thin walled air sacs. These allow for a large surface area for gas exchange. Capillaries line the alveoli. Oxygen diffuses into the bloodstream and carbon dioxide diffuses out of the capillaries and is exhaled from the lungs due to partial pressure. Hemoglobin, a protein containing iron, carries the oxygenated blood to the heart and all parts of the body.

The thoracic cavity holds the lungs. The diaphragm muscle below the lungs is an adaptation that makes inhalation possible. As the volume of the thoracic cavity increases, the diaphragm muscle flattens out and inhalation occurs. When the diaphragm relaxes, exhalation occurs.

HUMAN CIRCULATORY AND IMMUNE SYSTEMS

Structure, function, and regulation of the heart

The function of the closed circulatory system (**cardiovascular system**) is to carry oxygenated blood and nutrients to all cells of the body and return carbon dioxide waste to the lungs for expulsion. The heart, blood vessels, and blood make up the cardiovascular system. The following diagram shows the structure of the heart:

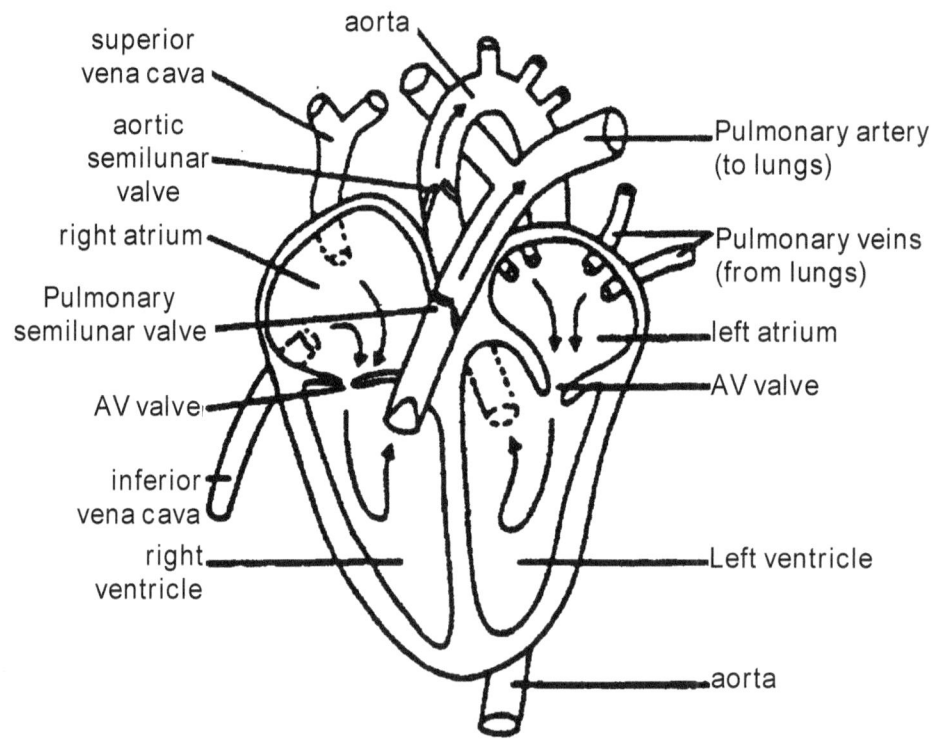

The atria are the chambers that receive blood returning to the heart and the ventricles are the chambers that pump blood out of the heart. There are four valves, two atrioventricular (AV) valves and two semilunar valves. The AV valves are located between each atrium and ventricle. The contraction of the ventricles closes the AV valve to keep blood from flowing back into the atria. The semilunar valves are located where the aorta leaves the left ventricle and the pulmonary artery leaves the right ventricle. Ventricular contraction opens the semilunar valves, pumping blood out into the arteries, and ventricular relaxation closes the valves.

The cardiac output is the volume of blood per minute that the left ventricle pumps. This output depends on the heart rate and stroke volume. The **heart rate** is the number of times the heart beats per minute and the **stroke volume** is the amount of blood pumped by the left ventricle each time it contracts. Humans have an average cardiac output of about 5.25 L/min. Heavy exercise can increase cardiac output up to five times. Epinephrine and increased body temperature also increase heart rate and, thus, the cardiac output.
Cardiac muscle can contract without any signal from the nervous system. The sinoatrial node is the pacemaker of the heart. It is located on the wall of the right atrium and generates electrical impulses that make the cardiac muscle cells contract in unison. The atrioventricular node briefly delays the electrical impulse to ensure the atria empty before the ventricles contract.

Structure, function, and regulation of the immune system

The immune system is responsible for defending the body against foreign invaders. There are two defense mechanisms: non-specific and specific.

The **non-specific** immune mechanism has two lines of defense. The first line of defense is the physical barriers of the body. These include the skin and mucous membranes. The skin prevents the penetration of bacteria and viruses as long as there are no abrasions on the skin. Mucous membranes form a protective barrier around the digestive, respiratory, and genitourinary tracts. In addition, the pH of the skin and mucous membranes inhibit the growth of many microbes. Mucous secretions (tears and saliva) wash away many microbes and contain lysozyme that kills microbes.

The second line of defense includes white blood cells and the inflammatory response. **Phagocytosis** is the ingestion of foreign particles. Neutrophils make up about seventy percent of all white blood cells. Monocytes mature to become macrophages, which are the largest phagocytic cells. Eosinophils are also phagocytic. Natural killer cells destroy the body's own infected cells instead of the invading the microbe directly.

The other second line of defense is the inflammatory response. The blood supply to the injured area increases, causing redness and heat. Swelling also typically occurs with inflammation. Basophils and mast cells release histamine in response to cell injury. This triggers the inflammatory response.

The **specific** immune mechanism recognizes specific foreign material and responds by destroying the invader. These mechanisms are specific and diverse. They are able to recognize individual pathogens. An **antigen** is any foreign particle that elicits an immune response. The body manufactures **antibodies** that recognize and latch onto antigens, hopefully destroying them. They also discriminate between foreign material versus self material. Memory of the invaders provides immunity upon further exposure.

Immunity is the body's ability to recognize and destroy an antigen before it causes harm. Active immunity develops after recovery from an infectious disease (e.g. chicken pox) or after a vaccination (e.g. mumps, measles, rubella). Passive immunity may be passed from one individual to another and is not permanent. A good example is the immunities passed from mother to nursing child. A baby's immune system is not well developed and the passive immunity they receive through nursing keeps them healthier.

There are two main responses made by the body after exposure to an antigen:

1. **Humoral response** - Free antigens activate this response and B cells (lymphocytes from bone marrow) give rise to plasma cells that secrete antibodies and memory cells that will recognize future exposures to the same antigen. The antibodies defend against extracellular pathogens by binding to the antigen and making them an easy target for phagocytes to engulf and destroy. Antibodies are in a class of proteins called immunoglobulins. There are five major classes of immunoglobulins (Ig) involved in the humoral response: IgM, IgG, IgA, IgD, and IgE.

2. **Cell mediated response** – Infected cells activate T cells (lymphocytes from the thymus). These activated T cells defend against pathogens in the cells or cancer cells by binding to the infected cell and destroying them along with the antigen. T cell receptors on the T helper cells recognize antigens bound to the body's own cells. T helper cells release IL-2, which stimulates other lymphocytes (cytotoxic T cells and B cells). Cytotoxic T cells kill infected host cells by recognizing specific antigens.

Vaccines are antigens given in very small amounts. They stimulate both humoral and cell mediated responses. After vaccination, memory cells recognize future exposure to the antigen so the body can produce antibodies much faster.

HUMAN DIGESTIVE SYSTEM

Roles of basic nutrients found in foods

The function of the digestive system is to break food down into nutrients, absorb them into the blood stream, and deliver them to all cells of the body for use in cellular respiration.

Essential nutrients are those nutrients that the body needs but cannot make. There are four groups of essential nutrients: essential amino acids, essential fatty acids, vitamins, and minerals.

There is about eight essential amino acids humans need. A lack of these amino acids results in protein deficiency. There are only a few essential fatty acids.

Vitamins are organic molecules essential for a nutritionally adequate diet. Scientists have identified thirteen vitamins essential to humans. There are two groups of vitamins: water-soluble (includes the vitamin B complex and vitamin C) and water insoluble (vitamins A, D and K). Vitamin deficiencies can cause severe problems.

Unlike vitamins, minerals are inorganic molecules. Calcium is important in bone construction and maintenance. Iron is important in cellular respiration and is a major component of hemoglobin.

Carbohydrates, fats, and proteins are fuel for the generation of ATP. Water is necessary to keep the body hydrated. We discussed the importance of water in previous sections.

Essential Amino Acids	Essential Vitamins
• Arginine	• Vitamin A
• Histidine	• Vitamin B complex (8 vitamins)
• Isoleucine	• Vitamin C
• Leucine	• Vitamin D
• Lysine	• Vitamin E
• Methionine	• Vitamin K
• Phenylalanine	
• Threonine	
• Tryptophan	
• Valine	

Mechanical and chemical digestion

The teeth and saliva begin digestion by breaking food down into smaller pieces and lubricating it to allow swallowing. The lips, cheeks, and tongue form a bolus or ball of food. The process of peristalsis (wave-like contractions) carries the food down the pharynx where it enters the stomach through the sphincter, which closes to keep food from going back up. In the stomach, pepsinogen and hydrochloric acid form pepsin, the enzyme that hydrolyzes proteins. This chemical action breaks the food down further and churns into a semifluid mass called acid chyme. The pyloric sphincter muscle opens to allow the food to enter the small intestine. Most nutrient absorption occurs in the small intestine. Its large surface area, resulting from its length and protrusions called villi and microvilli, allow for a great absorptive surface into the bloodstream. Neutralization of the chyme after arrival from the acidic stomach allows the local enzymes to function. Accessory organs function in the production of necessary enzymes and bile. The pancreas makes many enzymes to break down food in the small intestine. The liver makes bile, which breaks down and emulsifies fatty acids. Any food left after the trip through the small intestine enters the large intestine. The large intestine functions to reabsorb water and produce vitamin K. The feces, or remaining waste, pass out through the anus.

HUMAN REPRODUCTIVE SYSTEM

Hormone control and development and function of male and female reproductive systems

Hormones regulate sexual maturation in humans. Humans cannot reproduce until puberty, about the age of 8-14 depending on the individual. The hypothalamus begins secreting hormones that help mature the reproductive system and develop the secondary sex characteristics. Reproductive maturity in girls occurs with their first menstruation and occurs in boys with the first ejaculation of viable sperm.

Hormones also regulate reproduction. In males, the primary sex hormones are the androgens, testosterone being the most important. The testes produce androgens that dictate the primary and secondary sex characteristics of the male. Female hormone patterns are cyclic and complex. Most women have a reproductive cycle length of about 28 days. The menstrual cycle is specific to the changes in the uterus. The ovarian cycle results in ovulation and occurs in parallel with the menstrual cycle. Hormones regulate this parallelism. Five hormones participate in this regulation, most notably estrogen and progesterone. Estrogen and progesterone play an important role in signaling to the uterus and the development and maintenance of the endometrium. Estrogens also dictate the secondary sex characteristics of females.

Gametogenesis, fertilization, and birth control

Gametogenesis is the production of the sperm and egg cells.

Spermatogenesis begins at puberty in the male. One spermatogonia, the diploid precursor of sperm, produces four sperm. The sperm mature in the seminiferous tubules located in the testes. **Oogenesis**, the production of egg cells (ova), is usually complete by the birth of a female. Females do not release egg cells until menstruation begins at puberty. Meiosis forms one ovum with all the cytoplasm and three polar bodies that the body reabsorbs. The ovaries store the ovum and release them each month from puberty to menopause.

Seminiferous tubules in the testes house sperm, where they mature. The epididymis, located on top of the testes, contains mature sperm. After ejaculation, the sperm travel up the **vas deferens** where they mix with semen made in the prostate and seminal vesicles and travel out the urethra.

Ovulation releases the egg into the fallopian tubes where cilia move the egg along the length of the tubes. Fertilization of the egg by the sperm normally occurs in the fallopian tube. If pregnancy does not occur, the egg passes through the uterus and is expelled through the vagina during menstruation. Levels of progesterone and estrogen stimulate menstruation. Implantation of a fertilized egg downregulates the levels, stopping menstruation.

There are many methods of contraception (birth control) that affect different stages of fertilization. Chemical contraception (birth control pills) prevents ovulation by synthetic estrogen and progesterone. Several barrier methods of contraception are available. Male and female condoms block semen from contacting the egg. Sterilization is another method of birth control. Tubil ligation in women prevents eggs from entering the uterus. A vasectomy in men involves the cutting of the vas deferens. This prevents the sperm from entering the urethra. The most effective method of birth control is abstinence. Programs exist worldwide that promote abstinence, especially amongst teenagers.

COMPETENCY 2.0 BASIC KINEMATIC AND KINETIC PRINCIPLES OF MOTION

Skill 2.1 Apply knowledge of basic kinematics and kinetic principles of motion including, but not limited to, summation of forces of equilibrium, vectors, and force-velocity relationships.

CONCEPTS OF EQUILIBRIUM AND CENTER OF GRAVITY APPLIED TO MOVEMENT

When body segments move independently, body mass redistributes, changing the location of the body's center of gravity. Segments also move to change the body's base of support from one moment to the next to cope with imminent loss of balance.

The entire center of gravity of the body shifts in the same direction of movement of the body's segments. As long as the center of gravity remains over the base of support, the body will remain in a state of equilibrium. The more the center of gravity is situated over the base, the greater the stability. A wider base of support and/or a lower center of gravity enhances stability. To be effective, the base of support must widen in the direction of the force produced or opposed by the body. Shifting weight in the direction of the force in conjunction with widening the base of support further enhances stability.

Constant interaction of forces that move the body in the elected direction results in dynamic balance. The smooth transition of the center of gravity changing from one base of support to the next produces speed.

CONCEPT OF FORCE APPLIED TO MOVEMENT

Force is any influence that can change the state of motion of an object; we must consider the objective of movement.

Magnitude of Force – force must overcome the inertia of the object and any other resisting forces for movement to occur.

For linear movement, force applied close to the center of gravity requires a smaller magnitude of force to move the object than does force applied farther from the center of gravity.

For rotational movement, force applied farther from the center of gravity requires a smaller magnitude of force to rotate the object than does force applied closer to the center of gravity.

For objects with a fixed point, force applied anywhere other than through the point of fixation results in object rotation.

Energy – the capacity to do work. (The more energy a body has the greater the force with which it can move something [or change its shape] and/or the farther it can move it).

Movement (mechanical energy) has two types:

1. Potential energy (energy possessed by virtue of position, absolute location in space or change in shape).

> **A. Gravitational potential energy** - potential energy of an object that is in a position where gravity can act on it.

> **B. Elastic (strain) potential energy** - energy potential of an object to do work while recoiling (or reforming) after stretching, compressing, or twisting.

2. Kinetic energy (energy possessed by virtue of motion that increases with speed).

Force Absorption - maintaining equilibrium while receiving a moving object's kinetic energy without sustaining injury or without losing balance while rebounding. The force of impact is dependent on an object's weight and speed. The more abruptly kinetic energy is lost, the more likely injury or rebound occurs. Thus, **absorbing force requires gradually decelerating a moving mass by utilization of smaller forces over a longer period of time**. Stability is greater when the object receives the force closer to the center of gravity.

Striking resistive surfaces - the force of impact per unit area decreases when the moving object's area of surface making contact increases and the surface area that the object strikes increases.

Striking non-resistive surfaces - the force of impact decreases if the moving object's area of surface making contact decreases because it is more likely to penetrate.

The more time and distance that motion stops for a moving object to strike any surface, the more gradually the surface absorbs the force of impact, and the reaction forces acting upon the moving object decrease.

Equilibrium returns easily when the moving body (striking a resistive surface) aligns the center of gravity more vertically over the base of support.

Angular force against a body decreases when the distance between a contacting object and the body decreases and the contact occurs closer to the center of gravity. Also, widening the base of support in the direction of the moving object increases stability.

COMPETENCY 3.0 BIOMECHANICAL PRINCIPLES

Skill 3.1 Apply knowledge of biomechanical principles (e.g. Newton's laws of motion, center of gravity) to a broad range of movement activities.

SEE ALSO Domain 3, Skill 2.1

CONCEPT OF LEVERAGE APPLIED TO MOVEMENT

First-class lever - the axis is between the points of application of the force and the resistance.

Second-class lever - the force arm is longer than the resistance arm (operator applies resistance between the axis and the point of application of force).

Second-class lever systems

Third-class lever - the force works at a point between the axis and the resistance (resistance arm is always longer than the force arm).

Muscle force is applied where muscles insert on bones.

With a few exceptions, the body consists primarily of third-class levers, with bones functioning as the levers and contracting innervated muscles acting as the fulcrums or by gravity acting on various body masses. As a result, the human body favors speed and range of motion over force.

Because most human body levers are long, their distal ends can move rapidly. Thus, the body is capable of swift, wide movements at the expense of abundant muscle force.

The human body easily performs tasks involving rapid movement with light objects. Very heavy tasks require a device for the body to secure an advantage of force.

Sports instruments increase body levers, thereby increasing the speed of an object's impacting force. However, the use of sports instruments requires more muscle force.

The body's leverage rarely includes one part of the body (a simple, singular lever). Movement of the body is an outcome of a system of levers operating together. However, levers do function in sequence when the force produced by the system of levers is dependent on the speed at the extremity. Many levers function simultaneously for a heavy task (e.g. pushing).

NEWTON'S LAWS OF MOTION

Sir Isaac Newton developed three laws of motion that describe the movement of objects. Newton's three laws are as follows:

1. Concept of Inertia – an object in motion maintains its motion until an external force acts on it

2. $F = ma$ – The force applied to an object is equal to the mass of the object multiplied by the acceleration of the object.

3. For every action there is an equal and opposite reaction.

Newton's laws of motion are important to movement activities. The concept of inertia comes into play in any activity that involves a moving ball or other object. For example, when playing tennis, it is more difficult to hit a shot that changes the direction of the ball because you must overcome the ball's inertia. In other words, it is difficult to take a ball hit crosscourt and return it down the line, because you must factor in the ball's tendency to continue on its present path. Force and acceleration are important concepts in many sports, including striking sports, contact sports, and net/wall sports. Finally, action/reaction is an important concept in basic movement activities such as running and walking. The reactive force that occurs when a runner's foot strikes the ground helps propel the runner forward.

Skill 3.2 **Apply knowledge of biomechanical principles in relation to individual differences and to body mechanics for safe and efficient movement/motion.**

MECHANICAL PRINCIPLES OF MOTION APPLIED TO PHYSICAL EDUCATION ACTIVITIES

1. **Inertia** - tendency of a body or object to remain in its present state of motion; an object will stay in a prescribed straight path and will move at its given speed unless some force acts to change it.

2. **Projecting objects for vertical distance** - the forces of gravity and air resistance prevent vertically projected objects from continuing at their initial velocities. The downward, resistive force of gravity slows a projectile directed upward until it halts (at the peak of vertical path). At this point, the downward force of gravity becomes an incentive force that increases the speed of the object until it confronts another force (the earth or other external object) that slows the object until it stops. When the object stops ascending and begins to descend, gravity alters the object's direction of motion. Air resistance (of still air) always opposes the object's motion. Therefore, an ascending object's air resistance is downward and a descending object's air resistance is upward. An increase in velocity increases air-drag force that decreases the magnitude of the drag as the object moves upward, slowing in velocity. The magnitude of the drag increases as the object moves faster and faster downward. Moreover, the direction and magnitude of the object's acceleration, due to the force of gravity, are constant while direction and magnitude of changes, due to air resistance, are dependent on the object's speed and direction.

An object travels the highest when projected with the greatest velocity, and the object's weight affects neither gravity's upward deceleration nor its downward acceleration. The object's weight, however, is a factor in calculating the net force acting on the object's vertical movement through the air.

- **Projecting the body for vertical distance** - for these activities (e.g. vertical leaping), the height of reach of the hand from the ground is the significant factor. The following three factors determine the body's reach height: 1) the center of gravity's vertical velocity, 2) the center of gravity's height from the ground at takeoff, and 3) the vertical distance of the fingertips relative to the center of gravity at the peak of the jump.

- **Projecting for vertical distance with a horizontal component** - for these activities (e.g. high jumping), a running approach to the point of takeoff produces some horizontal velocity even with a 100% vertical takeoff.

- **Projecting for horizontal distance** - a body will continue to travel horizontally until an external force, usually the ground, halts it. Gravity stops vertical movement while ground friction eventually stops horizontal velocity, preventing any additional horizontal distance. "Air time" increases when the initial upward vertical velocity component is greater. There is a tradeoff between maximum "air time" (determined by vertical velocity) and maximum horizontal distance (determined by horizontal velocity).

- **Horizontal projections where takeoff and landing heights are equal** - maximum horizontal distance occurs when the projection angle is 45-degrees.

- **Horizontal projections where takeoff and landing heights are uneven** – the height of an object's center of gravity depends on a performer's height and his/her location in relation to the ground upon release or impact of the object. The greater the object's travel time forward, the farther the object's distance before landing. Hence, a taller performer has an automatic advantage over a shorter performer who throws with the same projection velocity. In addition, the greater the difference between takeoff and landing heights, the smaller the optimum angle of release - given equal projection velocities.

Projecting objects for accuracy:

- **Vertical plane targets** - accuracy is easiest when using a trajectory that is perpendicular to the target as it coincides with the target face. As projection distance increases, a more curved parabolic path is required.

- **Horizontal plane targets** - the more vertically the projectile arrives at the target (as close to 90 degrees as possible), the greater the likelihood of successfully hitting the target and preventing the object from rolling or sliding away from the target area.

Projecting the body for accuracy - for moving or positioning the body (or its segments) to achieve an ideal/model performance by body maneuvers, the performer projects his body's center of gravity to an imaginary target point in space.

Projecting objects for accuracy when speed may enhance the performance - the performer must increase the angle of projection for slower projection speeds (must consider participant's height).

- **Acceleration** - the movement response (acceleration) of a system depends not only on the net external force applied, but also depends on the resistance to movement change (inertia).

If an object's acceleration is proportional to the applied force, greater force produces greater acceleration. An object's acceleration is inversely proportional to its mass (the greater the mass, the less the acceleration).

- **Angular acceleration** (rate that an object's angular speed or direction changes) - angular acceleration is great when there is a large change in angular velocity in a short amount of time. A rigid body (or segment) encounters angular acceleration or deceleration only when a net external torque is applied. When torque stops, the body reaches and maintains a new velocity until another torque occurs. Acceleration is always in the direction of the acting torque, and the greater the torque, the greater the angular acceleration.

- **Linear acceleration** (time rate of change in velocity) - an object's magnitude of acceleration is significant if there is a large change of velocity in a small amount of time. When the same velocity changes over a longer period of time, acceleration is small. Acceleration occurs only when force is applied. When the force stops, the object/body reaches a new and the object/body continues at the new speed until that a force changes that speed or direction. In addition, the direction of acceleration is the same direction as the applied net force. A large force produces a large acceleration. A small force produces a modest acceleration.

- **Zero/Constant Acceleration** (constant velocity) - there is no change in a system's velocity when the object/body moves at a given velocity and encounters equal, opposing forces. Hence, velocity is constant since no force causes acceleration or deceleration.

- **Acceleration caused by gravity** - a falling object/body continues to accelerate at the rate of 9.8 m/sec. (32 ft/sec.) throughout its fall.

- **Radial acceleration (direction change caused by centripetal force)** - centripetal force is aimed along an illusory line (the circular path) at any instant. Therefore, it is the force responsible for change of direction. The bigger the mass, the greater the centripetal force required. A tighter turn magnifies direction change (radial acceleration), so friction must increase to offset the increased acceleration. Maximum friction (centrifugal force) reduces speed. A combination of the variables mass, radius of curvature, speed of travel, and centripetal force cause radial acceleration.

Action/Reaction - every action has an equal and opposite reaction.

- **Linear motion** - the larger the mass, the more it resists motion change initiated by an outside force.

Body segments exert forces against surfaces they contact. These forces and the reaction of the surfaces result in body movement. For example, a runner propels himself forward by exerting a force on the ground (as long as the surface has sufficient friction and resistance to slipping). The force of the contact of the runner's foot with the ground and the equal and opposite reaction of the ground produces movement. A canoe paddler or swimmer exerts a backward force by pushing the water backwards, causing a specific velocity that is dependent on the stroke's force - as well as the equal and opposite force made by the water pushing forward against the canoe paddle or arm moving the canoe or swimmer forward.

Every torque (angular motion) exerted by one body/object on another has another torque equal in magnitude and opposite direction exerted by the second body/object on the first. Changing angular momentum requires a force that is equal and opposite the change in momentum.

Performing actions in a standing position requires the counter pressure of the ground against the feet for accurate movement of one or more parts of the body.

COMPETENCY 4.0   MOVEMENT ANALYSIS

Skill 4.1   Apply knowledge of movement analysis to movement patterns, including technologies for movement analysis.

ERRORS IN SKILL PERFORMANCE

Because performing a skill has several components, determining why a participant is performing poorly may be difficult. Instructors may have to assess several components of a skill to determine the root cause of poor performance and appropriately correct errors. **An instructor should have the ability to identify performance errors by observing a student's mechanical principles of motion during the performance of a skill. Process assessment** is a subjective, observational approach to identify errors in the form, style, or mechanics of a skill.

APPROPRIATE OBJECTIVE MEASUREMENTS OF FUNDAMENTAL SKILLS

Instructors should use **product assessments**, quantitative measures of a movement's end result, to evaluate objectively fundamental skills. How far, how fast, how high, or how many are the quantitative measures of product assessments.

A **criterion-referenced test** (superior to a standardized test) or a **standardized norm-referenced test** can provide valid and reliable data for objectively measuring fundamental skills.

SKILL ASSESSMENT INFORMATION USED TO CORRECT ERRORS IN SKILL PERFORMANCE

Instructors can use criterion-referenced standards to diagnose weaknesses and correct errors in skill performance because such performance standards define appropriate levels of achievement. However, instructors can also use biomechanical instructional objectives. The following list describes the skill assessment criteria in several representative activities:

- Archery - measuring accuracy in shooting a standardized target from a specified place.

- Bowling - calculating the bowling average attained under standardized conditions.

- Golf - the score after several rounds.

- Swimming - counting the number of breaststrokes needed to swim 25 yards.

After assessing student skill performance, the instructor should design drills or tasks that will develop the weakest component of the student's performance. For example, an instructor notices that a group of students attempting to shoot basketball free throw shots cannot get the ball to the basket because they do not use their legs to add power to the shot. The instructor should use this observation to construct drills that encourage leg use and develop strength.

TECHNOLOGIES FOR MOVEMENT ANALYSIS

Physical educators can use various technological tools to analyze student performance, fitness, and performance. Two important and interrelated technological tools are videotape and movement analysis software.

Videotape

Videotaping students participating in skill performance and fitness activities allows students and teachers to analyze technique closely. Instructors can identify and point out errors in form to the students. This visual reinforcement enhances the learning process. In addition, periodic videotaping allows instructors to monitor progress in skill performance and fitness over time.

Movement analysis software

Movement analysis software helps students and instructors analyze movement patterns captured on digital video cameras in great detail. For example, movement analysis software can distill the individual characteristics of a person's gate. Such high detailed analysis allows instructors and students to study individual patterns of movement, individual movement styles, and strategies for peak performance. Movement analysis software helps identify key elements of a movement that need improvement and helps track progress in development, maturation, and error correction.

Skill 4.2   **Demonstrate knowledge of acute and chronic effects of exercise on body systems (e.g. pulmonary, cardiorespiratory, muscular, skeletal, neural, endocrine) and on energy systems utilized during exercise.**

SEE ALSO Domain 3, Skill 1.1

The structure and function of the human body adapts greatly to physical activity and exertion. When challenged with any physical task, the human body responds through a series of integrated changes in function that involve most, if not all, of its physiological systems. Movement requires activation and control of the musculoskeletal system. The cardiovascular and respiratory systems provide the ability to sustain this movement over extended periods. When the body engages in exercise training several times, each of these physiological systems undergoes specific adaptations that increase the body's efficiency and capacity.

When the body works, it makes great demand on every muscle of the body. Either the muscles have to 'shut down' or they have to do work. The heart beats faster during strenuous exercise so that it can pump more blood to the muscles, and the stomach shuts down during strenuous exercise so that it does not waste energy that the muscles need. Exercising makes the muscles work like a motor that use up energy in order to generate force. Muscles, also known as 'biochemical motors', use the chemical adenosine triphosphate (ATP) as an energy source.

Different types of systems, such as the glycogen-lactic acid system, help muscles perform. Such systems help in producing ATP, which is extremely vital to working muscles. Aerobic respiration, which also helps in releasing ATP, uses the fatty acids from fat reserves in muscle and helps produce ATP for a much longer period of time.

The following points summarize the process of bodily adaptation to exercise:

• Muscle cells use the ATP they have floating around in about 3 seconds.

• The phosphagen system kicks in and supplies energy for 8 to 10 seconds.

• If exercise continues longer, the glycogen-lactic acid system kicks in.

• Finally, if exercise continues, aerobic respiration takes over. This would occur in endurance events such as an 800-meter dash, marathon run, rowing, cross-country skiing, or distance skating.

Physical activity affects the cardiovascular and musculoskeletal systems the most. However, it also helps in proper functioning of metabolic, endocrine, and immune systems.

ENERGY SYSTEMS

In order to help muscles perform their duty, there are different types of systems such as the Glycogen-Lactic Acid System that provide energy. Such systems help in producing ATP, which is extremely vital for proper muscle function. Of the systems, aerobic respiration, which also helps in releasing ATP, uses the fatty acids from fat reserves in muscle and helps in producing ATP for the longest period of time.

ROLE OF EXERCISE IN HEALTH MAINTENANCE

The health risk factors improved by physical activity include cholesterol levels, blood pressure, stress related disorders, heart diseases, weight and obesity disorders, early death, certain types of cancer, musculoskeletal problems, mental health, and susceptibility to infectious diseases.

PHYSIOLOGICAL BENEFITS OF EXERCISE

Physiological benefits of physical activity include:

- improved cardio-respiratory fitness
- improved muscle strength
- improved muscle endurance
- improved flexibility
- more lean muscle mass and less body fat
- quicker rate of recovery
- improved ability of the body to utilize oxygen
- lower resting heart rate
- increased cardiac output
- improved venous return and peripheral circulation
- reduced risk of musculoskeletal injuries
- lower cholesterol levels
- increased bone mass
- cardiac hypertrophy and size and strength of blood vessels

PHYSICAL EDUCATION

- increased number of red cells
- improved blood-sugar regulation
- improved efficiency of thyroid gland
- improved energy regulation
- increased life expectancy

IDENTIFY THE HEALTH- AND SKILL-RELATED COMPONENTS OF PHYSICAL FITNESS DEVELOPED BY SELECTED ACTIVITIES

The following is a list of physical activities that may reduce specific health risks, improve overall health, and develop skill-related components of physical activity.

1. **Aerobic Dance**:
Health-related components of fitness = *cardio-respiratory, body composition.*
Skill-related components of fitness = *agility, coordination.*

2. **Bicycling**:
Health-related components of fitness = *cardio-respiratory, muscle strength, muscle endurance, body composition.*
Skill-related components of fitness = *balance.*

3. **Calisthenics**:
Health-related components of fitness = *cardio-respiratory, muscle strength, muscle endurance, flexibility, body composition.*
Skill-related components of fitness = *agility.*

4. **Circuit Training**:
Health-related components of fitness = *cardio-respiratory, muscle strength, muscle endurance, body composition.*
Skill-related components of fitness = *power.*

5. **Cross Country Skiing**:
Health-related component of fitness = *cardio-respiratory, muscle strength, muscle endurance, body composition.*
Skill-related components of fitness = *agility, coordination, power.*

6. **Jogging/Running**:
Health-related components of fitness = *cardio-respiratory, body composition.*

7. **Rope Jumping**:
Health-related components of fitness = *cardio-respiratory, body composition.*
Skill-related components of fitness = *agility, coordination, reaction time, speed.*

8. **Rowing:**
Health-related components of fitness = *cardio-respiratory, muscle strength, muscle endurance, body composition.*
Skill-related components of fitness = *agility, coordination, power.*

9. **Skating:**
Health-related components of fitness = *cardio-respiratory, body composition.*
Skill-related components of fitness = *agility, balance, coordination, speed.*

10. **Swimming/Water Exercises**:
Health-related components of fitness = *cardio-respiratory, muscle strength, muscle endurance, flexibility, body composition.*
Skill related components of fitness = *agility, coordination.*

11. **Walking (brisk):**
Health-related components of fitness = *cardio-respiratory, body composition.*

COMPETENCY 5.0 COMPONENTS OF WELLNESS

Skill 5.1 Demonstrate an understanding of components of wellness, such as nutrition, stress management, cardiorespiratory risk reduction, and physical fitness (i.e. cardiorespiratory endurance, flexibility, muscular strength and endurance, and body composition).

WELLNESS

Wellness has two major components: understanding the basic human body functions and how to care for and maintain personal fitness, and developing an awareness and knowledge of how certain everyday factors, stresses, and personal decisions can affect one's health. Teaching fitness needs to go along with skill and activity instruction. Life-long fitness and the benefits of a healthy lifestyle need to be part of every P.E. teacher's curriculum. Cross-discipline teaching and teaching thematically with other subject matter in classrooms would be the ideal method to teach health to adolescents.

Incorporating wellness into the P.E. teacher's lesson plan doesn't need to take that much time or effort. For example, have students understand the idea that if you put more calories in your body than what you burn, you will gain weight. Teaching nutrition and the caloric content of foods in P.E. can be as simple as learning the amount of calories burned when participating in different sports for a set amount of time. To teach a more sophisticated lesson on nutrition that can have students understand the relationship between caloric intake and caloric expenditure, students could keep a food diary, tabulating the caloric content of their own diets while comparing it to an exercise diary that keeps track of the calories they've burned.

Another example of incorporating wellness into the P.E. curriculum would be when participating in endurance running activities. Having students run a set distance and then giving them a finish time rewards the faster students and defeats the slower students. In addition to a final time, teach students a more beneficial way of measuring one's cardiovascular fitness by understanding pulse rate.

Teach students how to take their own pulse, how pulse rates vary at different stages of exercise (i.e. resting pulse, target pulse, recovery pulse, etc.), how pulse rates can differ between boys and girls, and encourage them to keep track of their own figures. As students gather their data, teacher-led discussions amongst classmates about similarities, differences and patterns that are developing would teach students how to monitor effectively and easily their own vital signs.

NUTRITION AND WEIGHT CONTROL

Identify the components of nutrition

The components of nutrition are **carbohydrates, proteins, fats, vitamins, minerals, and water.**

Carbohydrates – the main source of energy (glucose) in the human diet. The two types of carbohydrates are simple and complex. Complex carbohydrates have greater nutritional value because they take longer to digest, contain dietary fiber, and do not excessively elevate blood sugar levels. Common sources of carbohydrates are fruits, vegetables, grains, dairy products, and legumes.

Proteins – are necessary for growth, development, and cellular function. The body breaks down consumed protein into component amino acids for future use. Major sources of protein are meat, poultry, fish, legumes, eggs, dairy products, grains, and legumes.

Fats – a concentrated energy source and important component of the human body. The different types of fats are saturated, monounsaturated, and polyunsaturated. Polyunsaturated fats are the healthiest because they may lower cholesterol levels, while saturated fats increase cholesterol levels. Common sources of saturated fats include dairy products, meat, coconut oil, and palm oil. Common sources of unsaturated fats include nuts, most vegetable oils, and fish.

Vitamins and minerals – organic substances that the body requires in small quantities for proper functioning. People acquire vitamins and minerals in their diets and in supplements. Important vitamins include A, B, C, D, E, and K. Important minerals include calcium, phosphorus, magnesium, potassium, sodium, chlorine, and sulfur.

Water – makes up 55 – 75% of the human body. Essential for most bodily functions. Attained through foods and liquids.

Determine the adequacy of diets in meeting the nutritional needs of students

Nutritional requirements *vary from person-to-person.* General guidelines for meeting adequate nutritional needs are: *no more than 30% total caloric intake from fats* (preferably 10% from saturated fats, 10% from monounsaturated fats, 10% from polyunsaturated fats), *no more than 15% total caloric intake from protein* (complete), *and at least 55% of caloric intake from carbohydrates* (mainly complex carbohydrates).

Exercise and diet help maintain proper body weight by equalizing caloric intake and caloric output.

Fallacies and dangers underlying selected diet plans

High Carbohydrate diets (i.e. Pritikin, Bloomingdale's) can produce rapid or gradual weight loss, depending on caloric intake. Usually requires vitamin and mineral supplements because protein intake is low. These diets may or may not recommend exercising or permanent lifestyle changes, which are necessary to maintain one's weight.

High-Protein Diets promote the same myths, fallacies, and results as high carbohydrate diets. High-protein diets also require vitamin and mineral supplements. In addition, these diets are usually high in saturated fats and cholesterol because of the emphasis on meat products.

Liquid Formulas that are physician/hospital run (i.e. Medifast, Optifast) provide 800 or fewer calories a day consumed in liquid form. Dieters forgo food intake for 12 to 16 weeks in lieu of the protein supplement. Liquid diets require vitamin and mineral supplements and close medical supervision. Dieters should gradually reintroduce food after the initial fast. These diets can result in severe and/or dangerous metabolic problems in addition to an irregular heartbeat, kidney infections and failure, hair loss, and sensations of feeling cold and/or cold intolerance. These diets are very expensive and have a high rate of failure.

Over-The-Counter Liquid Diets (i.e. Slimfast) are liquid/food bar supplements taken in place of one or more meals per day. Such diets advocate an intake of 1,000 calories daily. Carbohydrate, protein, vitamin, and mineral intake may be so low that the diet can be as dangerous as the medically supervised liquid diets when relied on for the only source of nutrition. Because of the lack of medical supervision, the side effects can be even more dangerous.

Over-The-Counter Diet Pills/Aids and Prescription Diet Pills (appetite suppressants) have as their main ingredient phenyl propanolamine hydrochloride [PPA]. Keeping weight off by the use of these products is difficult. Dizziness, sleeplessness, high blood pressure, palpitation, headaches, and tachycardia are potential side effects of these products. Moreover, prescription diet pills can be addictive.

Low Calorie Diets (caloric restricted) are the most misunderstood method of weight loss. However, restricting the intake of calories is the way most people choose to lose weight. All the focus is on food, creating anxiety over the restriction of food - especially favorite foods. These diets are also difficult to maintain and have a high failure rate. Like the other diets, once the diet is over, dieters regain weight quickly because they fail to make permanent behavioral changes. Side effects of caloric restriction include diarrhea, constipation, Ketosis, a lower basal metabolic rate, blood-sugar imbalances, loss of lean body tissue, fatigue, weakness, and emotional problems. Low calorie diets require dietary supplements. Those who choose **fasting** (complete caloric restriction) to lose weight can deplete enough of the body's energy stores to cause death.

PHYSICAL ACTIVITY, DIET, AND HEALTH RISK FACTORS

Exercise and diet maintain proper body weight by equalizing caloric intake to caloric output.

Nutrition and exercise are closely related concepts important to student health. An important responsibility of physical education instructors is to teach students about proper nutrition and exercise and how they relate to each other. The two key components of a healthy lifestyle are consumption of a balanced diet and regular physical activity. Nutrition can affect physical performance. Proper nutrition produces high energy levels and allows for peak performance. Inadequate or improper nutrition can impair physical performance and lead to short-term and long-term health problems (e.g. depressed immune system and heart disease, respectively). Regular exercise improves overall health. Benefits of regular exercise include a stronger immune system, stronger muscles, bones, and joints, reduced risk of premature death, reduced risk of heart disease, improved psychological well-being, and weight management.

STRESS MANAGEMENT

General stress management principles of interest to physical education instructors include regular physical activity, exercise, physical play, and proper nutrition. Proper nutrition refers to the consumption of a balanced diet, consisting of adequate amounts of lean protein, complex carbohydrates, fruits, vegetables, and unsaturated fats.

Stress management and good nutrition are among the cornerstones of healthy living. Physical education instructors can introduce students to these important concepts through development of individualized fitness and wellness plans. Fitness and wellness plans should include a concrete exercise plan and a detailed nutritional plan.

HEALTH-RELATED COMPONENTS OF PHYSICAL FITNESS

There are five health related components of physical fitness: **cardio-respiratory or cardiovascular endurance, muscle strength, muscle endurance, flexibility, and body composition.**

Cardiovascular endurance – the ability of the body to sustain aerobic activities (activities requiring oxygen utilization) for extended periods.

Muscle strength – the ability of muscle groups to contract and support a given amount of weight.

Muscle endurance – the ability of muscle groups to contract continually over a period of time and support a given amount of weight.

Flexibility – the ability of muscle groups to stretch and bend.

Body composition – an essential measure of health and fitness. The most important aspects of body composition are body fat percentage and ratio of body fat to muscle.

Flexibility is the range of motion around a joint or muscle. Flexibility has two major components: static and dynamic. Static flexibility is the range of motion without a consideration for speed of movement. Dynamic flexibility is the use of the desired range of motion at a desired velocity. These movements are useful for most athletes.

Good flexibility can help prevent injuries during all stages of life and can keep an athlete safe. To improve flexibility, you can lengthen muscles through activities such as swimming, a basic stretching program, or Pilates. These activities all improve your muscles' range of motion. While joints also consist of ligaments and tendons, muscles are the main target of flexibility training. Muscles are the most elastic component of joints while ligaments and tendons are less elastic and resist elongation. Overstretching tendons and ligaments can weaken joint stability and lead to injury.

Coaches, athletes and sports medicine personnel use stretching methods as part of their training routine for athletes. They help the body to relax and to warm-up for more intense fitness activities.

COMPONENTS OF FLEXIBILITY

Muscles – Muscle is the body's contractile tissue. Its function is to produce force and cause motion (movement within the internal organs and, especially for our purposes, locomotion). Muscles are generally split into Type I (slow twitch) which carries more oxygen and sustains aerobic activity, and Type II (fast twitch), which carries less oxygen and powers anaerobic activity. Muscles that are too short can limit flexibility, and failing to stretch after resistance training can cause the muscles to shorten. The stretch reflex, whereby the opposing muscle will contract in order to prevent over-expansion, can also curtail flexibility (this contraction is generally premature, and part of flexibility training is to re-train the opposing muscle not to contract as quickly).

Joints – Joints are the locations at which two bones make contact. Their construction allows movement and provides functional mechanical support. We can classify joints as fibrous (connected by collagen), cartilaginous (connected by cartilage), or synovial (capped by cartilage, supported by ligaments, enveloped by the synovial membrane, and filled with synovial fluid). The limits of its range of motion, imposed by the joint's physical structure or, more often, by lack of flexibility of the muscles, ligaments and tendons, define a joint's flexibility.

Ligaments – A ligament is a short band of tough fibrous connective tissue composed mainly of long, stringy collagen fibers. They connect bones to other bones to form a joint. Ligaments can limit the mobility of a joint or prevent certain movements altogether. Ligaments are slightly elastic and under tension, they will gradually lengthen. Ligaments that are too short may curtail flexibility by limiting a joint's range of motion.

Tendons – A tendon (or sinew) is a tough band of fibrous connective tissue (similar in structure to ligaments) that connects muscle to bone or muscle to muscle. Tendons are composed mainly of water, type-I collagen, and cells called tenocytes. Most of the strength of tendons stems from the parallel, hierarchical arrangement of densely packed collagen fibrils, which have great strength, little extensibility, and no ability to contract.

EVALUATING FLEXIBILITY

Standard methods of evaluating flexibility include the sit and reach test and having students try to touch their hands behind their backs. Instructors can devise additional flexibility tests to evaluate the range of motion of specific joints. In these cases, the tests should reflect practical function.

TARGET HEART RATE ZONE AND HEART RATE MONITORS

The target heart rate (THR) zone is another common measure of aerobic exercise intensity. Participants find their THR and attempt to raise their heart rate to the desired level for a certain period of time. Students can use electronic heart rate monitors that constantly track heart rate during physical activity. Such monitors often alert students when they enter and leave their THR, allowing for adjustment of activity level. There are three ways to calculate the target heart rate.

1. METs (maximum oxygen uptake), which is 60% to 90% of functional capacity.

2. Karvonean Formula = [Maximum heart rate (MHR) – Resting heart rate (RHR)] x intensity + RHR.   MHR= 220 - Age
Intensity = Target Heart Range (which is 60% - 80% of MHR - RHR + RHR).

THR = (MHR - RHR) x .60 + RHR to (MHR - RHR) x .80 + RHR

3. Cooper's Formula to determine target heart range is:
THR = (220 - AGE) x .60 to (220 - AGE) x .80.

Skill 5.2   Analyze the effects of factors such as gender, age, disability, environment, and substance abuse on physical performance.

OVERVIEW

The effect of factors such as gender, age, environment, nutrition, heredity and substance abuse is also crucial in understanding adolescent fitness performance. Girls mature earlier than boys do, but boys quickly catch up and grow larger and stronger. Age, combined with maturity level, influences a child's physical strength, flexibility, and coordination. Good nutrition positively influences the quality of a child's physical activity level, while poor nutrition has the opposite effect. Adverse environmental conditions such as high heat or poor air quality strongly affect activity level. Students that inherit favorable physical characteristics will perform better and with more ease than those who aren't so fortunate. Substance abuse of any sort – alcohol, tobacco, or drugs – is a detriment to physical performance.

Dealing with factors that are out of the teacher's control requires both structure and flexibility. When necessary, make adjustments amongst the students and/or the activity. For example, when teaching how to throw a softball, don't hesitate to pair girls with boys if their maturity and strength levels are similar. If the distance is too far for some pairs, move them closer. If some pairs are more advanced, challenge them by increasing the partner's distance while continuing to work on accuracy and speed. Add a personal challenge to see how many times they can toss without dropping the ball. Finally, having more advanced students teach their peers that aren't as competent will benefit all students.

BIOLOGICAL AND ENVIRONMENTAL INFLUENCES ON GENDER DIFFERENCES IN MOTOR PERFORMANCES

The differences between males and females in motor performance result from certain biological and environmental influences. Generally, people perceive the males as stronger, faster, and more active than females. This higher activity level can stem from childhood behaviors influenced by certain environmental factors and superior motor performance results largely from the biological make up of males versus females.

In most cases, the male body contains less fat mass and more muscle mass than the female body. In addition, the type of muscle differs between males and females. Males have more fast-twitch muscle fibers allowing for more short duration, high intensity movements such as jumping and sprinting. In addition, males generally, but not always, display better coordination. Females have proved their superiority at certain activities, such as skipping, and tend to display better fine movements, such as neater handwriting.

Certain environmental factors also contribute to the gender differences in motor performance. As children, boys tend to be more physically active. Society expects boys to participate in sports and play games that involve running around, such as tag and foot races. On the other hand, society expects girls to be more social and less active. They participate in activities such as playing with dolls. In addition, parents rarely ask girls to perform tasks involving manual labor.

While these sedentary tasks have value, it is important for both males and females to participate in an adequate amount of physical activity each day. If children develop this type of active lifestyle early in life, they are more likely to maintain it throughout adulthood.

RELATIONSHIP BETWEEN HUMAN GROWTH AND DEVELOPMENT AND APPROPRIATE PHYSICAL ACTIVITY

Understanding the rate of the developmental growth process that occurs during adolescence will help educators understand growth and development norms and identify early or late maturing students. The age when the puberty growth spurt occurs and the speed with which adolescents experience puberty vary greatly within each gender and may affect participation in physical activity and sports. If the instructor pays attention to the varying body sizes and maturity stages, forming teams in co-educational classes can easily accommodate the needs of both genders' changing maturities. Starting in middle school and continuing into high school, it is perfectly acceptable for boys and girls to participate in non-contact physical activities together that rely on lower-body strength and agility (e.g. capture the flag, ultimate Frisbee, running). In more physical activities that require upper body strength, coaches should form teams based on individual skill levels to prevent injury. Matching teams evenly based on skill and maturity is important so that individual skill level deficiencies are not as apparent and the activity remains fun for all participants. Teachers need to monitor and adjust physical activities as needed to ensure a positive, competitive experience. Appropriate activities would include individual or partner badminton or tennis matches and team competitions in flag football.

SUBSTANCE ABUSE

Substance abuse can lead to adverse behaviors and increased risk of injury and disease. Any substance affecting the normal functions of the body, illegal or not, is potentially dangerous and students and athletes should avoid them completely.

Anabolic steroids – The alleged benefit is an increase in muscle mass and strength. However, this substance is illegal and produces harmful side effects. Premature closure of growth plates in bones can occur if abused by a teenager, limiting adult height. Other effects include bloody cysts in the liver, increased risk of cardiovascular disease, increased blood pressure, and dysfunction of the reproductive system.

Alcohol – This is a legal substance for adults but is very commonly abused. Moderate to excessive consumption can lead to an increased risk of cardiovascular disease, nutritional deficiencies, and dehydration. Alcohol also causes ill effects on various aspects of performance such as reaction time, coordination, accuracy, balance, and strength.

Nicotine – Another legal but often abused substance that can increase the risk of cardiovascular disease, pulmonary disease, and cancers of the mouth. Nicotine consumption through smoking severely hinders athletic performance by compromising lung function. Smoking especially affects performance in endurance activities.

Marijuana – This is the most commonly abused illegal substance. Adverse effects include a loss of focus and motivation, decreased coordination, and lack of concentration.

Cocaine – Another illegal and somewhat commonly abused substance. Effects include increased alertness and excitability. This drug can give the user a sense of over confidence and invincibility, leading to a false sense of one's ability to perform certain activities. A high heart rate is associated with the use of cocaine, leading to an increased risk of heart attack, stroke, potentially deadly arrhythmias, and seizures.

COMPETENCY 6.0 PHYSICAL FITNESS TESTING AND PRESCRIPTION

Skill 6.1 Demonstrate knowledge of physical fitness testing, exercise prescription, and fitness programs for all individuals, including those with disabilities, as well as the components of health-related fitness and technologies for fitness testing and training.

Instructors should compare assessment data to grade equivalency norms to determine where each child is relative to where he should be. However, the instructor should place the most emphasis on evaluating the child relative to past performance. Progress is more important than current achievement. A learning-disabled child might display below average levels of achievement despite having made a great deal of progress, while a gifted child might be above grade equivalency norms despite stagnation.

SPECIFIC PHYSICAL FITNESS APPRAISALS

The following is a list of tests that instructors can use to assess the physical fitness of students.

Cardio-respiratory fitness tests – maximal stress test, sub maximal stress test, Bruce Protocol, Balke Protocol, Astrand and Rhyming Test, PWC Test, Bench Step Test, Rockport Walking Fitness Test, and Cooper 1.5 Mile Run/Walk Fitness Test.

Muscle endurance tests – squat-thrust, pull-ups, sit-ups, lateral pull-down, bench-press, arm curl, push-ups, and dips.

Body Composition determination – Hydrostatic weighing, skin fold measurements, limb/girth circumference, and body mass index.

Agility tests – Illinois Agility Run.

Coordination tests – Stick test of Coordination.

Power tests – vertical jump.

Speed tests – 50-yard dash.

ANALYZING THE COMPONENTS OF FITNESS

Data from physical fitness assessments can diagnose an individual's level of fitness and identify the components of fitness (i.e. cardio-respiratory endurance, muscle strength, muscle endurance, flexibility, and body composition) requiring improvement. We compare data to norms.

Cardio-respiratory data identifies an individual's functional aerobic capacity by the predicted maximum oxygen consumption. This can partially explain natural leanness, running ability, and motivation.

Muscle strength data identifies an individual's ability to execute some basic skills, ability to exercise continually for an extended period, potential for injury, potential to develop musculoskeletal problems, and potential to cope with life threatening situations.

Flexibility data identifies an individual's potential of motor skill performance, potential of developing musculoskeletal problems (including poor posture), and potential of performing activities of daily living.

Body composition data is an indicator of an individual's health status and potential to participate in physical activities.

FITNESS PRESCRIPTIONS

Physical fitness assessments are an important tool for physical education instructors and students. Instructors must be careful not to overemphasize fitness assessments, as students that score poorly may become discouraged and students that perform well may become complacent. When used correctly, however, the results of fitness assessments are valuable tools in the development of exercise prescriptions. For example, an instructor can use the results of a multi-faceted fitness assessment to determine the fitness strengths and weaknesses of each student and the areas that each student needs to improve.

Simple exercises to improve aerobic endurance include walking, jogging, and bicycling. Exercises to improve muscular strength and endurance include push-ups, pull-ups, sit-ups, and weight lifting. Exercises to improve flexibility are stretches for various parts of the body. The exercises that help improve aerobic endurance, muscular strength, and muscular endurance also help improve body composition.

PHYSICAL FITNESS PROGRAMS INCORPORATING THE HEALTH-RELATED COMPONENTS TO MEET THE NEEDS OF STUDENTS

Instructors design fitness programs incorporating: mode, frequency, intensity, time, and progression.

The following is an example of a **cardio-respiratory fitness** program design:

- **mode:** aerobic activities (e.g. walking, jogging, swimming, cycling, rowing)
- **frequency:** 3 to 5 days/week

- **intensity:** 60% to 90% of maximum oxygen uptake or 60% to 80% THR

- **time:** 20 to 60 minutes of continuous or interval (non-continuous) activity (time depends on intensity level)

- **progression:** instructor adjusts prescription according to an individual's fitness level and conditioning effects.

The following is an example of a **muscle strength** program design:

- **mode:** weight training (isotonic/dynamic)

- **frequency:** minimum 3 days/week to a maximum of every other day

- **intensity:** 60% to 90% of maximum muscle strength (1-RM)

- **time:** 3 sets with 3 to 8 reps and a 60 second rest interval

- **progression:** increase workload (overload) when individual can perform 15 reps at 10 RM level

The following is an example of a **muscle endurance** program design:

- **mode:** weight training

- **frequency:** minimum 3 days/week up to every other day

- **intensity:** 30% to 60% of maximum muscle strength (1-RM)

- **time:** 3 sets with 12 to 20 reps, or until point of muscle fatigue with a 15 to 60 second rest interval

- **progression:** increase workload (overload) periodically based on number of continuous repetitions

The following is an example of a **flexibility** program design:

- **mode:** stretching

- **frequency:** 3 to 7 days/week

- **intensity:** just below individual's threshold of pain

- **time:** 3 sets with 3 reps holding stretches 15 to 30 seconds, with a 60 rest interval between sets

The following is an example of a **body composition** program design:

- **mode:** combining aerobic exercise and weight training and a moderate reduction of caloric intake

- **frequency:** minimum of 3 days/week; however, daily is best

- **intensity:** low intensity, long duration

- **time:** 45 to 60 minutes of aerobic activity; 3 sets with a minimum of 6 reps for weights every other day

- **progression:** periodically increase as individual improves

ASSESSMENT APPLICATIONS

After assessing an individual's fitness level, a personal fitness trainer or instructor can prescribe a training program. Prescription of a fitness program begins with:

1. Identifying the components of fitness that need changing (via assessment)

2. Establishing short-term goals

3. Developing a plan to meet the established goals

4. Keeping records to record progress

5. Evaluating progress of goals and making changes based on success or failure

For successful programs, the instructor and student should formulate new goals and change the personal fitness program to accomplish the new goals.

For unsuccessful programs, changing the goals, particularly if the goals were too unrealistic, is an appropriate response. Adjusting goals allows individuals to make progress and succeed. In addition, analyzing positive and negative results may identify barriers preventing an individual's success in her personal fitness program. Incorporating periodic, positive rewards for advancing can provide positive reinforcement and encouragement.

COMPETENCY 7.0 FACTORS AFFECTING PHYSICAL PERFORMANCE

Skill 7.1 Analyze the effects of factors such as gender, age, disability, environment, and substance abuse on physical performance.

SEE Domain 3, Skill 5.2

TEACHER CERTIFICATION STUDY GUIDE

COMPETENCY 8.0   SAFETY, INJURY PREVENTION, AND FIRST AID

Skill 8.1   Demonstrate an understanding of safety-related topics such as the prevention and care of injuries, cardiopulmonary resuscitation (CPR), and first aid.

STRATEGIES FOR INJURY PREVENTION

Participant screenings – evaluate injury history, anticipate and prevent potential injuries, watch for hidden injuries and reoccurrence of an injury, and maintain communication.

Standards and discipline – ensure that athletes obey rules of sportsmanship, supervision, and biomechanics.

Education and knowledge – stay current in knowledge of first aid, sports medicine, sport technique, and injury prevention through clinics, workshops, and communication with staff and trainers.

Conditioning – programs should be yearlong and participants should have access to conditioning facilities in and out of season to produce more fit and knowledgeable athletes that are less prone to injury.

Equipment – perform regular inspections; ensure proper fit and proper use.

Facilities – maintain standards and use safe equipment.

Field care – establish emergency procedures for serious injury.

Rehabilitation – use objective measures such as power output on an isokinetic dynamometer.

PREVENTION OF COMMON ATHLETIC INJURIES

Foot – start with good footwear, foot exercises.

Ankle – use high top shoes and tape support; strengthen plantar (calf), dorsiflexor (shin), and ankle eversion (ankle outward).

Shin splints – strengthen ankle dorsiflexors.

Achilles tendon – stretch dorsiflexion and strengthen plantar flexion (heel raises).

Knee – increase strength and flexibility of calf and thigh muscles.

Back – use proper body mechanics.

Tennis elbow – lateral epicondylitis caused by bent elbow, hitting late, not stepping into the ball, heavy rackets, and rackets with strings that are too tight.

PHYSICAL EDUCATION

Head and neck injuries – avoid dangerous techniques (i.e. grabbing facemask) and carefully supervise dangerous activities like the trampoline.

School officials and instructors should base **equipment selection** on quality and safety; goals of physical education and athletics; participants interests, age, sex, skills, and limitations; and trends in athletic equipment and uniforms. Knowledgeable personnel should select equipment; keeping in mind continuous service and replacement considerations (i.e. what's best in year of selection may not be best the following year). One final consideration is the possibility of reconditioning versus the purchase new equipment.

ACTIONS THAT PROMOTE SAFETY AND INJURY PREVENTION

The following is a list of practices that promote safety in all types of physical education and athletic activities.

1. Having an instructor who is properly trained and qualified.

2. Organizing the class by size, activity, and conditions of the class.

3. Inspecting buildings and other facilities regularly and immediately giving notice of any hazards.

4. Avoiding overcrowding.

5. Using adequate lighting.

6. Ensuring that students dress in appropriate clothing and shoes.

7. Presenting organized activities.

8. Inspecting all equipment regularly.

9. Adhering to building codes and fire regulations.

10. Using protective equipment.

11. Using spotters.

12. Eliminating hazards.

13. Teaching students correct ways of performing skills and activities.

14. Teaching students how to use the equipment properly and safely.

IDENTIFYING EXERCISE EQUIPMENT AS EITHER SOUND OR UNSOUND USING PHYSIOLOGICAL PRINCIPLES

Rolling machines, vibrating belts, vibrating tables and pillows, massaging devices, electrical muscle stimulators, weighted belts, motor-driven cycles and rowing machines, saunas, and plastic or rubberized sweat and sauna suits **are all ineffective exercise equipment because they produce passive movement** (no voluntary muscle contractions).

Sound exercise equipment produces active movement resulting from the participant initiating the movement of the equipment or the participant voluntarily producing muscle contractions.

The more you analyze exercise equipment on the market the more you may wonder who is actually creating it. For example, equipment that has weight increments measured as light, medium, or difficult, is unsound. Such ambiguous labeling depends on who is using the equipment and their level of proficiency.

Some advertisements claim that their equipment uses all muscle groups at once. Just three minutes a day is as good as a total gym workout. Such claims are certainly false.

But what is good equipment? Good equipment uses a safe range of motion, safe increments of weight progression, and is structurally sound. The components of good equipment are reliable and not likely to cause injury. Safe equipment can consist of a combination of pieces that, when used correctly, improve physiological processes by guiding range of motion.

INJURY TREATMENT AND FIRST AID

Immediate treatment tips

When a student endures a physical injury, the first priority is to avoid further damage. Following an injury the teacher should look for the obvious cause of the accident (i.e., ill-fitting equipment, improper sliding technique, a missed step while running). The next step is to reduce swelling. The primary means of accomplishing this is a sequence of treatments (rest, ice, compression, elevation) known as **R.I.C.E.** It is vital to implement this procedure following an injury since swelling causes pain and a loss of motion.

Steps for the immediate treatment of an injury

1. Stop the activity immediately
2. Wrap the injured part in a compression bandage (i.e., an ACE bandage).
3. Apply ice to the injured part (crushed ice or frozen vegetables are ideal) for no more than 15 minutes at a time. You should allow the area to warm periodically.
4. Elevate the injured part.
5. For a proper diagnosis, send the injured student to the school's nurse or, for more serious injuries, to a physician.

Treating specific illnesses

Diabetes

Most children with diabetes suffer from Type 1 (insulin-dependent or juvenile) diabetes. Type 1 diabetes limits the pancreas' ability to produce insulin, a hormone vital to life. Without insulin, the body cannot use the sugar found in blood. In order to stay alive, an individual suffering from Type 1 diabetes must take one or more injections of insulin daily.

Diabetics control their disease by keeping the level of sugar (glucose) in the blood as close to normal as possible. The means to achieve diabetes control include proper nutrition, exercise, and insulin. Most children with diabetes self-monitor blood glucose levels to track their condition and respond to changes.

Some rules of thumb to keep in mind when dealing with a diabetic child are:

- Food makes the glucose level rise
- Exercise and insulin make the glucose level fall
- Hypoglycemia occurs when the blood sugar level is low
- Hyperglycemia occurs when the blood sugar level is high

Low Blood Sugar (Hypoglycemia)

This is the diabetic emergency most likely to occur. Low blood sugar may result from eating too little, engaging in too much physical activity without eating, or by injecting too much insulin.

Symptoms:
- Headache
- Sweating
- Shakiness
- Pale, moist skin
- Fatigue/Weakness
- Loss of coordination

Treatment:

Provide sugar immediately. You may give the student ½ cup of fruit juice, non-diet soda, or two to four glucose tablets. The child should feel better within the next 10 minutes. If so, the child should eat some additional food (e.g. half a peanut butter, meat, or cheese sandwich). If the child's status does not improve, treat the reaction again.

High Blood Sugar (Hyperglycemia)

Hyperglycemia can result from eating too much, engaging in too little physical activity, not injecting enough insulin, or illness. You can confirm high blood sugar levels by testing with a glucose meter.

Symptoms:
- Increased thirst
- Weakness/Fatigue
- Blurred vision
- Frequent urination
- Loss of appetite

Treatment:

If hyperglycemia occurs, the instructor should contact the student's parent or guardian immediately.

Dehydration

Dehydration occurs when a person loses more fluids than he/she takes in. The amount of water present in the body subsequently drops below the level needed for normal body functions. The two main causes of dehydration are gastrointestinal illness (vomiting, diarrhea) and sports. It is essential to replace fluids lost by sweating to prevent dehydration, especially on a hot day.

Symptoms:
- Thirst
- Dizziness
- Dry mouth
- Producing less/darker urine

Prevention/Treatment:
- Drink lots of fluids. Water is usually the best choice.
- Dress appropriately (i.e., loose-fitting clothes and a hat).
- If you begin to feel thirsty/dizzy, take a break and sit in the shade.
- Drink fluids prior to physical activity and then in 20-minute intervals after activity commences.
- Play sports or train in the early morning or late afternoon. You will avoid the hottest part of the day.

CPR BASICS

Cardiopulmonary resuscitation (CPR) is a first-aid technique used to keep victims of cardiac arrest alive. It is also prevents brain damage while the individual is unconscious and more advanced medical help is on the way. CPR keeps blood flowing through the body and in and out of the lungs.

CPR Steps
- Step 1 – Call 911
- Step 2 – Tilt head, lift chin, check breathing
- Step 3 – Give two breaths
- Step 4 – Position hands in the center of chest
- Step 5 – Firmly push down two inches on the chest 15 times

Continue with two breaths and 15 pumps until help arrives. The American Heart Association and the American Red Cross both offer classes to train individuals in CPR.

3. Muscle endurance:

Overloading for muscle endurance:

- **Frequency** = every other day
- **Intensity** = 30% to 60% of assessed muscle strength
- **Time** = 3 sets of 12 - 20 reps (low resistance with a high number of repetitions)

Progression for muscle endurance:

- begin 3 days/week and work up to every other day
- begin at 20% to 30% of muscle strength and work up to no more than 60% of muscle strength
- begin with 1 set with 12 reps and work up to 3 sets with 20 reps

Specificity for muscle endurance:

- same as muscle strength

4. Flexibility:

Overloading for flexibility:

- **Frequency**: 3 to 7 days/week
- **Intensity**: stretch muscle beyond its normal length
- **Time**: 3 sets of 3 reps holding stretch 15 to 60 seconds

Progression for flexibility:

- begin 3 days/week and work up to every day
- begin stretching with slow movement as far as possible without pain, holding at the end of the range of motion (ROM) and work up to stretching no more than 10% beyond the normal ROM
- begin with 1 set with 1 rep, holding stretches 15 seconds, and work up to 3 sets with 3 reps, holding stretches for 60 seconds

Specificity for flexibility:

- ROM is joint specific

5. Body composition:

Overloading to improve body composition:

- **Frequency**: daily aerobic exercise
- **Intensity**: low
- **Time**: approximately one hour

Progression to improve body composition:

- begin daily
- begin a low aerobic intensity and work up to a longer duration (see cardio-respiratory progression)
- begin low-intensity aerobic exercise for 30 minutes and work up to 60 minutes

Specificity to improve body composition:

increase aerobic exercise and decrease caloric intake

TECHNIQUES AND BENEFITS OF WARMING UP AND COOLING DOWN

Warming up should consist of a 5 to 10 minute aerobic activity in which the participant uses the muscles needed in the activity to follow (similar movements at a lower activity). Warm-ups also include stretching of major muscle groups after the gradual warm-up.

The benefits of warming up are:

- preparing the body for physical activity
- reducing the risk of musculoskeletal injuries
- releasing oxygen from myoglobin
- warming the body's inner core
- increasing the reaction of muscles
- bringing the heart rate to an aerobic conditioning level

Cooling down is similar to warming up - a moderate to light tapering-off vigorous activity at the end of an exercise session.

The benefits of cooling down are:

- redistributing circulation of the blood throughout the body to prevent pooling of blood

- preventing dizziness

- facilitating the removal of lactic acid

APPLICATIONS

One of the most important tasks for physical education instructors is to introduce students to strategies to incorporate physical activity into everyday situations. For example, instructors can recommend that students walk or ride a bike to school, rather than drive or ride the bus. In addition, there are a number of everyday activities that promote fitness including yard work, sports and games, walking, and climbing stairs. Beyond these everyday activities, physical education instructors must also be able to design physical fitness programs to meet the needs of students.

DOMAIN 4. THE SOCIOLOGY AND PSYCHOLOGY OF HUMAN MOVEMENT

COMPETENCY 1.0 PERSONAL DEVELOPMENT

Skill 1.1 Analyze the relationship of movement to the development of individual identity, including the development of self-awareness, self-concept, self-discipline, self-expression, and body image.

For most people, the development of social roles and appropriate social behaviors occurs during childhood. Physical play between parents and children, as well as between siblings and peers, serves as a strong regulator in the developmental process. Chasing games, roughhousing, wrestling, or practicing sport skills such as jumping, throwing, catching, and striking, are some examples of childhood play. These activities may be competitive or non-competitive and are important for promoting social and moral development of both boys and girls. Unfortunately, fathers will often engage in this sort of activity more with their sons than their daughters. Regardless of the sex of the child, both boys and girls enjoy these types of activities.

Physical play during infancy and early childhood is central to the development of social and emotional competence. Research shows that children who engage in play that is more physical with their parents, particularly with parents who are sensitive and responsive to the child, exhibited greater enjoyment during the play sessions and were more popular with their peers. Likewise, these early interactions with parents, siblings, and peers are important in helping children become more aware of their emotions and to learn to monitor and regulate their own emotional responses. Children learn quickly through watching the responses of their parents which behaviors make their parents smile and laugh and which behaviors cause their parents to frown and disengage from the activity.

If children want the fun to continue, they engage in the behaviors that please others. As children near adolescence, they learn through rough-and-tumble play that there are limits to how far they can go before hurting someone (physically or emotionally), which results in termination of the activity or later rejection of the child by peers. These early interactions with parents and siblings are important in helping children learn appropriate behavior in the social situations of sport and physical activity.

Children learn to assess their social competence (i.e., ability to get along with and acceptance by peers, family members, teachers and coaches) in sport through the feedback received from parents and coaches. Initially, authority figures teach children, "You can't do that because I said so." As children approach school age, parents begin the process of explaining why a behavior is right or wrong because children continuously ask, "why?"

Similarly, when children engage in sports, they learn about taking turns with their teammates, sharing playing time, and valuing rules. They understand that rules are important for everyone and without these regulations, the game would become unfair. The learning of social competence is continuous as we expand our social arena and learn about different cultures. A constant in the learning process is the role of feedback as we assess the responses of others to our behaviors and comments.

In addition to the development of social competence, sport participation can help youth develop other forms of self-competence. Most important among these self-competencies is self-esteem. Self-esteem is how we judge our worth and indicates the extent to which an individual believes he is capable, significant, successful and worthy. Educators have suggested that one of the biggest barriers to success in the classroom today is low self-esteem.

Children develop self-esteem by evaluating abilities and by evaluating the responses of others. Children actively observe parents' and coaches' responses to their performances, looking for signs of approval or disapproval of their behavior. Children often interpret feedback and criticism as either a negative or a positive response to the behavior. In sports, research shows that the coach is a critical source of information that influences the self-esteem of children.

Little League baseball players whose coaches use a "positive approach" to coaching (e.g. more frequent encouragement, positive reinforcement for effort and corrective, instructional feedback), had significantly higher self-esteem ratings over the course of a season than children whose coaches used these techniques less frequently. The most compelling evidence supporting the importance of coaches' feedback was found for those children who started the season with the lowest self-esteem ratings and increased considerably their self-assessment and self-worth. In addition to evaluating themselves more positively, low self-esteem children evaluated their coaches more positively than did children with higher self-esteem who played for coaches who used the "positive approach." Moreover, studies show that 95 percent of children who played for coaches trained to use the positive approach signed up to play baseball the next year, compared with 75 percent of the youth who played for untrained adult coaches.

We cannot overlook the importance of enhanced self-esteem on future participation. A major part of the development of high self-esteem is the pride and joy that children experience as their physical skills improve. Children will feel good about themselves as long as their skills are improving. If children feel that their performance during a game or practice is not as good as that of others, or as good as they think mom and dad would want, they often experience shame and disappointment.

Some children will view mistakes made during a game as a failure and will look for ways to avoid participating in the task if they receive no encouragement to continue. At this point, it is critical that adults (e.g., parents and coaches) intervene to help children to interpret the mistake or "failure." We must teach children that a mistake is not synonymous with failure. Rather, a mistake shows us that we need a new strategy, more practice, and/or greater effort to succeed at the task.

FACTORS RELATED TO DEVELOPMENT OF INDIVIDUAL IDENTITY AND PHYSICAL ACTIVITY

Body Image

Expectations relating to body image influence the development of self-concept by creating a benchmark of assumed correlations between body image and other traits. For example, a slight and skinny (ectomorphic) student may see himself as unathletic, even though students with ectomorphic body types often excel at endurance sports. Students are also likely to generalize from body image to perceived ability to master new physical skills (for example, an athletic child might expect to be better at a new sport than less athletic children, even if the sport is new to both of them).

Physical Appearance

Expectations relating to physical appearance influence the development of self-concept by virtue of assumptions correlating physical appearance with likeability. In fact, the relationship is reciprocal, and stronger in the opposite direction (students that are popular will tend to develop a more positive self-concept about their physical appearance).

Skill Level

Expectations relating to skill level influence the development of self-concept by setting the baseline for the performance that students will expect to deliver, both when attempting tasks that they are familiar with and new tasks (students with a high skill level will expect to do well, and students who are good at several things will expect to be good at other, new things).

Media

Media-based expectations influence the development of self-concept by setting media-based role models as the benchmarks against which students will measure their traits. Self-concept is a set of statements describing the child's own cognitive, physical, emotional, and social self-assessment. These statements will usually tend to be fairly objective ("good at baseball" or "has red hair"), media-based expectations can change the statements to be measurements against role models ("athletic like this actor" or "tall like that pop star").

Culture

Cultural expectations influence the development of self-concept by suggesting to the child traits they should include in their personal self-assessment. For example, students from a very warm and energetic cultural background, where there is a strong emphasis on family life, may develop self-concepts that incorporate those traits into their personal self-description. Cultural gender roles may also express themselves in this way.

Enjoyment and Personal Expression

In addition to the previously discussed achievement benefits of physical activity, physical activity also provides many people with pure enjoyment and the opportunity for personal expression. Exercise promotes a sense of well-being and usually improves a person's mood. Sports also provide a venue for social interaction and enjoyment of nature. Finally, many sports and activities, especially freestyle activities like skateboarding, figure skating, dance, and surfing, allow for a high level of personal expression.

Benefits of Physical Education in the Cognitive Domain

- contributes to academic achievement
- promotes higher thought processes via motor activity
- contributes to knowledge of exercise, health and disease
- contributes to an understanding of the human body
- contributes to an understanding of the role of physical activity and sport in American culture
- contributes to the knowledgeable consumption of goods and services

Benefits of Physical Education in the Affective Domain

- contributes to self-actualization, self-esteem, and a healthy response to physical activity
- contributes to an appreciation of beauty
- contributes to directing one's life toward worthy goals
- emphasizes humanism
- affords individuals the chance to enjoy rich social experiences through play
- promotes cooperative play with others
- teaches courtesy, fair play, and good sportsmanship
- contributes to humanitarianism

Benefits of Physical Education in the Psychomotor Domain

- develops movement skills for participation in sports and other physical activities
- develops skills to utilize leisure hours in mental and cultural pursuits develops skills necessary to the preservation of the natural environment

DEVELOPMENTAL CHARACTERISTICS

Cognitive development – Language development is the most important aspect of cognitive development in small children (ages 3-5). Allowing successes, rewarding mature behavior, and allowing the child to explore can improve confidence and self-esteem at this age.

Early elementary school children (Ages 6-8) are eager to learn and love to talk. Children at this age have a very literal understanding of rules and verbal instructions and must develop strong listening skills.

Pre-adolescent children (ages 9-11) display increased logical thought, but their knowledge or beliefs may be unusual or surprising. Differences in cognitive styles develop at this age (e.g. field dependant or independent preferences).
In early adolescence (ages 12-14), boys tend to score higher on mechanical/spatial reasoning, and girls on spelling, language, and clerical tasks. Boys are better with mental imagery, and girls have better access and retrieval of information from memory. Self-efficacy (the ability to self-evaluate) becomes very important at this stage.

In later adolescence (ages 15-17), children are capable of formal thought, but don't always apply it. Conflicts between teens' and parents' opinions and worldviews will arise. Children at this age may become interested in advanced political thinking.

Social development – Small children (ages 3-5) are socially flexible. Different children will prefer solitary play, parallel play, or cooperative play. Frequent minor quarrels will occur between children, and boys will tend to be more aggressive (children at these ages are already aware of gender roles).

Early elementary school children (ages 6-8) are increasingly selective of friends (usually of the same sex). Children at this age enjoy playing games, but are excessively preoccupied by the rules. Verbal aggression becomes more common than physical aggression, and adults should encourage children of this age to solve their own conflicts.

Pre-adolescent children (ages 9-11) place great importance on the (perceived) opinions of their peers and of their social stature, and will go to great lengths to 'fit in'. Friendships at this age are very selective, and usually of the same sex.

Young adolescents (ages 12-14) develop greater understanding of the emotions of others, which results in increased emotional sensitivity and impacts peer relationships. Children at this age develop an increased need to perform.

In the later stages of adolescence (ages 15-17), peers are still the primary influence on day-to-day decisions, but parents will have increasing influence on long-term goals. Girls' friendships tend to be close and intimate, whereas boys' friendships are based on competition and similar interests. Many children this age will work part-time, and educators should be alert to signs of potential school dropouts.

Emotional development – Small children (ages 3-5) express emotion freely and have a limited ability to learn how emotions influence behavior. Jealousy at this age is common.

Early elementary school children (ages 6-8) have easily bruised feelings and are just beginning to recognize the feelings of others. Children this age will want to please teachers and other adults.

Pre-adolescent children (ages 9-11) develop a global and stable self-image (self-concept and self-esteem). Comparisons to their peers and the opinions of their peers are important. An unstable home environment at this age contributes to an increased risk of delinquency.

Young adolescence (ages 12-14) can be a stormy and stressful time for children, but, in reality, this is only the case for roughly 20% of teens. Boys will have trouble controlling their anger and will display impulsive behavior. Girls may suffer depression. Young adolescents are very egocentric and concerned with appearance, and will feel very strongly that "adults don't understand."

In later stages of adolescence (ages 15-17), educators should be alert to signs of surfacing mental healthy problems (e.g. eating disorders, substance abuse, schizophrenia, depression, and suicide).

Skill 1.2 **Demonstrate an understanding of contemporary theories such as attribution, social learning, competence, learned helplessness, self-efficacy, and other social/psychological theories as they relate to motivation in physical activities.**

Motivation is essential to student learning in physical education and all academic disciplines. Physical education instructors should recognize and understand the important elements of student motivation. Important theories and concepts in student motivation include attribution theory, social learning theory, learned helplessness, and self-efficacy.

Attribution theory describes how people make causal explanations and how they answer questions beginning with 'Why?' The theory deals with the information people use in making causal inferences and with how they utilize this information to answer causal questions. For instance, a student's aggressively competitive behavior may reflect her personality, or it may be a response to situational pressures. Attribution theory describes the processes of explaining events and the behavioral and emotional consequences of those explanations. Attribution theory also claims that students' perceptions of their educational experience affect their motivation more than the experience itself.

Social learning theory focuses on the learning that occurs within a social context. It emphasizes that people learn from one another and includes such concepts as observational learning, imitation, and modeling. Social learning theory asserts that people can learn by observing the behavior of others and the outcomes of those behaviors. It further states that learning can occur without a permanent change in behavior. Physical education instructors should also be note that cognition plays an important role in learning. Awareness and expectations of future rewards or punishments can have a major effect on the behaviors that people exhibit. Thus, socialization and reward/punishment can motivate students to learn.

Learned helplessness occurs in situations where continued failure may inhibit somebody from trying again and can also lead to many forms of depression. Thus, it is very important how physical education instructors respond to children's failures and successes. If a student feels as though he cannot control his environment, this lack of control will impair learning in certain situations. That is, learned helplessness often occurs in environments where people experience events in which they have, or feel as though they have, no control over what happens to them.

Self-efficacy describes a person's belief about his/her capability to produce designated levels of performance that exercise influence over events that affect their lives. Self-efficacy beliefs determine how people feel, think, motivate themselves, and behave. Such beliefs produce these diverse effects through cognitive, motivational, affective, and selection processes. A strong sense of efficacy enhances human accomplishment and personal well-being in many ways. People with high assurance in their capabilities view difficult tasks as challenges rather than threats. A student with high self-efficacy will be highly motivated to participate in sports and game related activities. To build efficacy, the instructor must not only raise the student's belief in his/her capabilities, but also structure situations that breed success and limit repeated failure. Students with high self-efficacy measure success in terms of self-improvement rather than by triumphs over others.

Competence is the ability to perform some task. However, competence is also an outcome and does not describe the learning process. In order to measure reliably someone's ability to do something, there must be clearly defined and widely accessible standards that instructors can use to measure and evaluate performance. In addition, we must also take into consideration that competence is a measure of what someone can do at a particular point in time. Therefore, a person may be competent at one task, sport or game, and not another or may also be able to do well at one point and either better or worse at another.

COMPETENCY 2.0 SOCIAL DEVELOPMENT

Skill 2.1 Analyze the relationship of movement to social interaction and the development of group member identity through physical education activities.

Physical fitness activities incorporate group processes, group dynamics, and a wide range of cooperation and competition. Ranging from team sports (which are both competitive and cooperative in nature) to individual competitive sports (like racing), to cooperative team activities without a winner and loser (like a gymnastics team working together to create a human pyramid), there is a great deal of room for the development of mutual respect and support among the students, safe cooperative participation, and analytical, problem solving, teamwork, and leadership skills.

Teamwork situations are beneficial to students because they create opportunities for them to see classmates with whom they might not generally socialize, and with whom they may not even get along, in a new light. It also creates opportunities for students to develop reliance on each other and practice interdependence. Cooperation and competition can also offer opportunities for children to practice group work. These situations provide good opportunities to practice analytical thinking and problem solving in a practical setting.

The social skills and values gained from participation in physical activities include:

- The ability to make adjustments to both self and others by an integration of the individual to society and the environment.

- The ability to make judgments in a group situation.

- Learning to communicate with others and be cooperative.

- The development of the social phases of personality, attitudes, and values in order to become a functioning member of society such as being considerate.

- The development of a sense of belonging and acceptance by society.

- The development of positive personality traits.

- Learning for constructive use of leisure time.

- A development of attitude that reflects good moral character.

- Respect of school rules and property.

TEACHER CERTIFICATION STUDY GUIDE

ACTIVITIES THAT ENHANCE SOCIALIZATION

At the junior high level, students indicate a desire to play on a team. They also emphasize that they want to learn activities that would prove useful in their leisure hours.

The senior high level students desire to play harmoniously with others and to participate in team play. Students view activities such as dance and sports as a place to learn respect for their fellow students. The change of pace that physical education classes from academic offerings provides opportunities for enhanced socialization.

Basketball, baseball, football, soccer, and volleyball are social, team activities. Tennis and golf are social activities that are useful in leisure hours.

Skill 2.2 **Identify strategies and activities for promoting appropriate skills and behaviors for cooperation, competition, problem solving, trust building, and risk taking.**

COOPERATION AND COMPETITION

Cooperation refers to the practice of students working together with agreed-upon goals and possibly methods, instead of working separately in competition. Hence, cooperation is the opposite of competition. Competition is the act of striving against another force for the purpose of achieving dominance or attaining a reward or goal. The need or desire to compete with others is a very common impetus that motivates individuals to organize into a group and cooperate with each other in order to form a stronger competitive force. Therefore, in a game of football, we would encourage cooperation and a team spirit and perhaps in track we would encourage competition to be the fastest person.

PROBLEM SOLVING

Problem solving is a higher-order cognitive process that requires the modulation and control of more routine or fundamental skills. It is the ability to solve a problem. We would have the students call upon their problem-solving skills during a game of chess. Alternatively, they could strategize during a timeout in the last few seconds of a basketball game where their team is down by two points. Development of adequate problem solving skills also provides the student with self-confidence and a sense of accomplishment.

TRUST BUILDING

Trust building activities can break down barriers and build deep feelings of trust and reliance between individuals and within small groups of students. However, the power of these activities is a double-edged sword and instructors must use caution in selecting and conducting trust-based activities. If instructors introduce trust activities too early or too fast, emotional and/or physical harm can occur, with trust broken rather than built. For example, a common trust building activity involves blindfolding a person and having another member of the group guide. It is vital to demonstrate and actively encourage a high level of care and responsibility towards people in these exercises who take the risk of trusting. It is not ok to have a blindfolded and trusting person walk into a wall or low bench. For example, we could use the circle of trust game where a group of students form a circle around a blindfolded student or a student with her eyes closed. The blindfolded student keeps her entire body stiff and leans/falls forward or backward. The other students, keeping hands raised the entire time, keep her from falling. This is an exercise requiring both diligence and vigilance in keeping the blindfolded student safe, but the trust building rewards are worth it.

RISK TAKING

Healthy risk taking is a positive tool in an adolescent's life for discovering, developing, and consolidating his or her identity. It is important to remember that learning how to assess risks is a process that we work on throughout our lives. Children and adolescents need support, tools, and practice in order to do this. Teachers can help support students by encouraging a student to participate in something that may stretch his abilities, but not to the point where his limitations place him in a dangerous situation. For example, participation in an unfamiliar sport where the other students welcoming and supportive provides a degree of satisfaction for the student. A bad example would be putting a student on a team of large football players when he is either small-framed, inexperienced, or both.

You can observe the styles of risk taking by the way a student handles a new social situation. Although there are many styles, we can observe certain patterns, such as the cautious risk taker, the middle-of-the-roader, the adventurer or high-end risk taker, and the social risk taker whose boldness increases when he or she is with friends. It is also important to note that some children may be risk takers in one area – social, physical, intellectual, artistic – and not in others.

COMPETENCY 3.0   ROLE OF MOVEMENT ACTIVITIES IN SOCIETY

Skill 3.1   Demonstrate knowledge of the role of movement activities in society and the relationship of movement activities to social norms, ethics, values, and institutions.

Movement activities are joyful ways for children to explore movement through music, develop physical skills, channel energy, stimulate imagination, and promote creativity. It also provides children with opportunities for non-competitive, success-oriented, and creative experiences. Creative movement is a way for children to know themselves and to see connections with the rest of the world. This is a way for them to understand themselves and their relationship with the world. Instructors can use these activities to enhance all areas of learning and growth. Social norms are the rules that a group uses for values, beliefs, attitudes, and behaviors. Ethics is the determination of right and wrong. In any game or movement activity, there are rules that determine whether doing something is right or wrong. Values are ideals that guide or qualify your personal conduct and interaction with others. Movement activities require students to remember values and personal conduct. Like morals and ethics, they help you to distinguish what is right from what is wrong and help you to conduct your life in a meaningful way. Institutions are structures of social order and cooperation with a social purpose. They transcend individual lives and intentions with the making and enforcing of rules governing cooperative human behavior. We often apply institutions to customs and behavior patterns important to a society. The critical skills necessary for purposeful and self-directed living include realizing one's own uniqueness, recognizing and appreciating the uniqueness of others, and expressing personal feelings and cooperating within a social structure in accordance with that society's norms and values. Ultimately, this will help define and create one's self. Creative movement and other movement activities are rich with opportunities to fulfill these kinds of experiences successfully. It encourages an interactive environment where children share space as they explore movement together. They move their own way and gradually learn to observe different responses to movement ideas. The possibility of creating movements together becomes more appealing. Here they realize also that the institution (group) is more important than the individual is.

Skill 3.2 Demonstrate knowledge of the role of movement activities in the development of social interaction skills, a sense of group identity, and a sense of productive participation with others.

SEE ALSO Domain 4, Skill 2.2

POSITIVE AND NEGATIVE INFLUENCES OF PARTICIPATION IN PHYSICAL ACTIVITY ON PSYCHO-SOCIAL FACTORS

Physical activity can influence psycho-social development both positively and negatively. Thus, physical education instructors must create an environment that maximizes the benefits of physical activity and minimizes the potential negative aspects.

Positive Individual Influences:

Reduces tension and depression; provides means of affiliation with others; provides exhilarating experiences; provides aesthetic experiences; creates positive body image; controls aggression, provides relaxation and a change of pace from long hours of work, study, or other stresses; provides challenge and sense of accomplishment; provides a way to be healthy and fit; improves self-esteem through skill mastery; provides creative experiences; creates positive addiction to exercise in contrast to negative addiction to substances.

Positive Group Influences:

Development of cooperation skills; acceptance of and respect for all persons regardless of race, creed or origin; assimilation of the group attitude; opportunity to develop a group relationships; development of a spirit of fairness; development of traits of good citizenship; development of leadership and following skills; development of self-discipline; additional avenues for social acquaintances; development of social poise and self-understanding; development of a social consciousness with an accompanying sense of values; and individual and social development.

Negative influences:

Ego-centered athletes; winning at all costs; false values; harmful pressures; loss of identity; role conflict; aggression and violence; compulsiveness; over-competitiveness; addiction to exercise, where commitment to exercise has a higher priority than commitments to family, interpersonal relationships, work, and medical advice; escape or avoidance of problems; exacerbation of anorexia nervosa; exercise deprivation effects; fatigue; overexertion; poor eating habits; self-centeredness; preoccupation with fitness, diet, and body image.

Skill 3.3 **Demonstrate knowledge of the role of movement activities in promoting positive social behaviors and traits (e.g. loyalty; compassion; fairness; understanding and appreciation of similarities, differences, and abilities).**

SEE ALSO Domain 1, Skill 6.1

Through movement activities, children learn about their bodies, the space around them, and their relationships with each other. These activities should encourage all children, both boys and girls, to participate. All children can benefit, including children with communication, sensory, developmental, or physical deficiencies. Experiences in creative movement can help children respect the working space of others, as they learn about "personal space" and "shared space". Students realize what they have in common with others. They also learn to recognize, appreciate, and respect differences in the people with whom they come in contact. Children learn and respect the fact that all bodies come in various sizes and shapes. They also learn to respect these differences in their peers.

When everyone participates as a group in an activity, the focus is on the activity or movement rather than on the individual and individual differences. Students can transfer this mindset into their everyday experiences. They also learn loyalty to the group because their attendance and participation is crucial to the success of the activity. Thus, their commitment to the event is important. Self-esteem is also an invaluable benefit from incorporating movement into any curriculum. As children learn more and develop new skills, their self-esteem increases. When a child exclaims, 'I did it!' or 'I know that!' they are showing the power they feel in their own competence. Successful participation in and contribution to team activities enhance a child's self-esteem. Children can also develop compassion and empathy for those who are having difficulty learning a particular game or movement. Those who are more knowledgeable can assist others who are not as proficient. Students also learn to be fair and impartial to others in the group as well as themselves, because everyone has to abide by the same rules. Once again, they can apply this impartiality to everyday life situations.

FAIRNESS, EQUITY, DIVERSITY

Physical activity and related games can introduce children to the concepts of equity and fairness. In addition, physical activity provides a venue for the interaction of diverse groups of people, allowing participants to observe and appreciate cultural differences and similarities.

- **Human Growth and Development** – Movement activities promote personal growth and development physically, by way of stimulating muscular development, and emotionally, by raising personal confidence levels among children and by allowing them to explore concepts of inter-group equity that may at first seem threatening. To the insecure child, the concept that another group may be equal to his own may seem to 'demote' his group and the child by extension.

- **Psychology** – Observation and interaction with the behavior of children from diverse backgrounds in a training environment (where the training activities tend to focus more on 'doing', which feels more genuine to children than the classroom setting of raising hands and answering questions) allows the child to see in others the same sorts of behavioral reasoning processes that he sees in himself. This humanizes others from diverse backgrounds, and promotes concepts of equity among diverse groups.

- **Aesthetics** – Human movement activities create an opportunity for individual participation in activities with intrinsic aesthetic qualities. A gymnastic technique or a perfectly executed swing of a baseball bat relies on both physical training and a level of intuitive action. This is an artistic form of expression that is readily accessible to children. Recognizing beauty in the activities and performances of others (in some cases from groups different from that of the viewing student) is a humanizing experience.

COMPETENCY 4.0   FACTORS INFLUENCING ACTIVITY CHOICES

Skill 4.1   Analyze factors that influence an individual's activity choices (e.g. gender, age, ethnicity, culture, disability).

Many factors influence a student's participation in a particular activity. For instance, a boy may not wish to participate in a ballet dance because he perceives ballet dancing to be something for girls only. Or his cultural or ethnic norms may dictate that boys are too "macho" for that kind of dance (or any kind of dance for that matter). Similarly, a girl may not be interested in playing football because she believes football is a sport only boys play. Or perhaps her background and culture may suggest that any participation in sports or game is inappropriate for females. She may also think that she is not strong or big enough to participate in football. She may have been told that girls should play non-contact sports like tennis or participate in a dance group. The fact that only men play organized football at the highest levels reinforces the perception that women cannot play football. Perhaps contact sports are sports that her older brother(s) play and, even if she (or a boy) were interested, she (or he) is too young to participate.

In any of the above cases, the emphasis should be impartiality in terms of requirements for participation regardless of age, gender, ethnicity, and disability. We should also note that everyone is good at something and that nobody is good at everything. Those who are disabled may believe that they cannot play anything at all because of their disability. For those disabled students, many games and sports are strictly prohibited. However, instructors can modify many others to a point where the disabled student may participate and gain satisfaction.

DOMAIN 5. MOVEMENT CONCEPTS AND FORMS

COMPETENCY 1.0 FUNDAMENTAL AND CREATIVE MOVEMENT SKILLS

Skill 1.1 Demonstrate knowledge of fundamental movement skills such as basic locomotor and non-locomotor skills, movement patterns, manipulative skills, and basic rhythmic movement, as well as knowledge of elements and qualities of movement (e.g. space, time, force, flow, level).

LOCOMOTOR SKILLS

Locomotor skills move an individual from one point to another.

1. **Crawling** - A form of locomotion where the person moves in a prone position with the body resting on or close to the ground or on the hands and knees.

2. **Creeping** - A slightly more advanced form of locomotion in which the person moves on the hands and knees.

3. **Walking** - with one foot contacting the surface at all times, walking shifts one's weight from one foot to the other while legs swing alternately in front of the body.

4. **Running** - an extension of walking that has a phase where the body is propelled with no base of support (speed is faster, stride is longer, and arms add power).

5. **Jumping** - projectile movements that momentarily suspend the body in midair.

6. **Vaulting** - coordinated movements that allow one to spring over an obstacle.

7. **Leaping** - similar to running, but leaping has greater height, flight, and distance.

8. **Hopping** - using the same foot to take off from a surface and land.

9. **Galloping** - forward or backward advanced elongation of walking combined and coordinated with a leap.

10. **Sliding** - sideward stepping pattern that is uneven, long, or short.

11. **Body Rolling** - moving across a surface by rocking back and forth, by turning over and over, or by shaping the body into a revolving mass.

12. **Climbing** - ascending or descending using the hands and feet with the upper body exerting the most control.

NONLOCOMOTOR SKILLS

Nonlocomotor skills are stability skills where the movement requires little or no movement of one's base of support and does not result in change of position.

1. **Bending** - movement around a joint where two body parts meet.

2. **Dodging** - sharp change of direction from original line of movement such as away from a person or object.

3. **Stretching** - extending/hyper-extending joints to make body parts as straight or as long as possible.

4. **Twisting** - rotating body/body parts around an axis with a stationary base.

5. **Turning** - circular moving the body through space releasing the base of support.

6. **Swinging** - circular/pendular movements of the body/body parts below an axis.

7. **Swaying** - same as swinging but movement is above an axis.

8. **Pushing** - applying force against an object or person to move it away from one's body or to move one's body away from the object or person.

9. **Pulling** - executing force to cause objects/people to move toward one's body.

RHYTHMIC SKILLS

Rhythmic skills include responding and moving the body in time with the beat, tempo, or pitch of music. To develop rhythmic skills, instructors can ask students to clap their hands or stomp their feet to the beat of the music. Dancing and gymnastics requires high levels of rhythmic competency. As with all physical skills, development of rhythmic skills is a sequential process.

MANIPULATIVE SKILLS

Manipulative skills use body parts to propel or receive an object, controlling objects primarily with the hands and feet. Two types of manipulative skills are receptive (catch + trap) and propulsive (throw, strike, kick).

1. **Bouncing/Dribbling** - projecting a ball downwards.

2. **Catching** - stopping momentum of an object (for control) using the hands.

3. **Kicking** - striking an object with the foot.

4. **Rolling** - initiating force to an object to instill contact with a surface.

5. **Striking** - giving impetus to an object with the use of the hands or an object.

6. **Throwing** - using one or both arms to project an object into midair away from the body.

7. **Trapping** - without the use of the hands, receiving and controlling a ball.

CONCEPT OF BODY AWARENESS APPLIED TO PHYSICAL EDUCATION ACTIVITIES

Body awareness is a person's understanding of his or her own body parts and their capability of movement.

Instructors can assess body awareness by playing and watching a game of "Simon Says" and asking the students to touch different body parts. You can also instruct students to make their bodies into various shapes, from straight to round to twisted, and varying sizes, to fit into different sized spaces.

In addition, you can instruct children to touch one part of their body to another and to use various body parts to stamp their feet, twist their neck, clap their hands, nod their heads, wiggle their noses, snap their fingers, open their mouths, shrug their shoulders, bend their knees, close their eyes, bend their elbows, or wiggle their toes.

CONCEPT OF SPATIAL AWARENESS APPLIED TO PHYSICAL EDUCATION ACTIVITIES

Spatial awareness is the ability to make decisions about an object's positional changes in space (i.e. awareness of three-dimensional space position changes). Developing spatial awareness requires two sequential phases: 1) identifying the location of objects in relation to one's own body in space, and 2) locating more than one object in relation to each object and independent of one's own body. Plan activities using different size balls, boxes, or hoops and have children move towards and away; under and over; in front of and behind; and inside, outside, and beside the objects.

CONCEPT OF EFFORT QUALITIES APPLIED TO PHYSICAL EDUCATION

Effort qualities are the qualities of movement that apply the mechanical principles of balance, time, and force).

Balance - activities for balance include having children move on their hands and feet, lean, move on lines, and balance and hold shapes while moving.

Time - activities using the concept of time can include having children move as fast as they can and as slow as they can in specified, timed movement patterns.

Force - activities using the concept of force can include having students use their bodies to produce enough force to move them through space. They can also paddle balls against walls and jump over objects of various heights.

ANALYSIS OF BASIC MOVEMENT PATTERNS: OVERHAND THROW, UNDERHAND THROW, KICK

Overhand Throw

The overhand throw consists of a sequence of four movements: a stride, hip rotation, trunk rotation, and forward arm movement. The thrower should align his body sideways to the target (with opposite shoulder pointing towards the target). The overhand throw begins with a step or stride with the opposite foot (i.e. left foot for a right-handed thrower). As the stride foot contacts the ground, the pivot foot braces against the ground and provides stability for the subsequent movements. Hip rotation is the natural turning of the hips toward the target. Trunk rotation follows hip rotation. The hips should rotate before the trunk because the stretching of the torso muscles allows for stronger muscle contraction during trunk rotation. Following trunk rotation, the arm moves forward in two phases. In the first phase the elbow is bent. In the second phase, the elbow joint straightens and the thrower releases the ball.

Development of the overhand throwing motion in children occurs in three stages: elementary, mature, and advanced. In the elementary stage, the child throws mainly with the arm and does not incorporate the other body movements. The signature characteristic of this stage is striding with the foot on the same side of the body as the throwing arm (i.e. placing the right foot in front when throwing with the right hand). In the mature stage, the thrower brings the arm backward in preparation for the throw. Use of body rotation is still limited. Children in the advanced stage incorporate all the elements of the overhand throw. The thrower displays an obvious stride and body rotation.

Underhand Throw

The thrower places the object in the dominant hand. When drawing the arm back the triceps straighten the elbow and, depending on the amount of power behind the throw, the shoulder extends or hyperextends using the posterior deltoid, latissimus dorsi, and the teres major. At the time of drawback, the thrower takes a step forward with the leg opposite of the throwing arm. When coming back down, the thrower moves the shoulder muscles (primarily the anterior deltoid) into flexion. When the object in hand moves in front of the body, the thrower releases the ball. The wrist may be firm or slightly flexed. The thrower releases the object shortly after the planting the foot and the biceps muscle contracts, moving the elbow into flexion during follow through.

Kick

In executing a kick, the object needs to be in front of the body and in front of the dominant leg. The kicker steps and plants with the opposite leg while drawing the kicking leg back. During draw back, the hamstring muscle group flexes the knee. When the kicker plants the opposite foot, the hips swing forward for power and the knee moves into extension using the quadriceps muscle group. The contact point is approximately even with the plant foot and a comfortable follow through completes the action.

Skill 1.2   Demonstrate knowledge of creative movement such as exploration, improvisation, and problem solving.

SEE ALSO Domain 4, Skill 2.2

Creative dance is one technique for applying fundamental concepts. A social benefit of creative dance is that it encourages an interactive environment where children share space as they explore movement together in their own way. Gradually, opportunities arise for children to observe different responses to movement ideas and the possibility of creating movements together becomes more appealing. The children can explore different scenarios and improvise to describe what happens along the way. The teacher can assign the starting place (e.g. a zoo) and the children can choose an animal and move like that animal across the floor. Music adds flavor and children are also able to work on tempo and beat while moving like their favorite animal. They can also add props of their choice. For example, after a group experienced a free flow snow dance with white streamers moving up, down, and around in the air, some of the children improvised a solid ice castle of connected body shapes. In addition, after stomping around in a friendly dinosaur dance, some of the children decided to line up and take big steps together while dragging the last child along lying flat, as the tail!

The instructor can asked the children to solve a particular problem between two animals – perhaps a dog and a cat – that cannot seem to get along. One seems to want to eat the others food all the time. One child can play the cat, which eats most of his food and leaves some for the dog to taste and vice versa. Other students can take turns playing different animals that can solve their problems, work together, and still be friends. They can also move across the floor playing different colors, shapes, or other objects. This freedom to explore and create is a joyful and freeing experience for children of all ages.

TEACHER CERTIFICATION STUDY GUIDE

COMPETENCY 2.0 DANCE CONCEPTS AND FORMS

Skill 2.1 Demonstrate knowledge of skills used in rhythmic activities, creative dance, and structured dance forms (e.g. modern, ballet, jazz, tap, social, folk, country, ethnic, classical).

DANCE CONCEPTS AND FORMS – OVERVIEW

Students of dance acquire many skills during their course of study. The student identifies and demonstrates movement elements in dance performance and uses correct body alignment, strength, flexibility, and stamina (for more demanding performances). Crucial to any form of dance is the concept of coordination in the performance of technical movements. Technical movements must look as though they are easy to perform. The dancer must perform technical dance skills with artistic expression including musicality and rhythm. As the student progresses, he or she will perform more extended movement sequences and rhythmic patterns. The student will then have enough experience to introduce his or her own stylistic nuance into the performance. The student will also be able to use improvisation to solve movement problems and adjust choices based on the movement responses of other dancers in the ensemble. Through continued experience, he or she will become a skillful, seasoned dancer whose technique and ability will transcend any form of dance.

Instructors can create rhythmic activities by putting on music with a strong beat and asking students to dance to the beat. Tell the students to listen to the beat and move accordingly (e.g. stomping their feet or clapping their hands in time with the beat). It's important for children to learn to move to various sounds and use their bodies to mimic the beat. Another idea is to have the students take turns beating on a coffee can while trying to keep movements in sync with the rhythm. In more structured dance forms, technique or skill comes into play. For instance, in ballet, dancers must have good flexibility, body control, and coordination. Ballet dancers must also have a sense of rhythm, an understanding of music, good turnout and alignment, and a sense of balance and counterbalance. These skills take many years to acquire and, once acquired, take many more years to master and maintain. Ballet dancing may express a mood, tell a story, or simply reflect a piece of music and is the most classical of all dance forms. Other types of music may have similar requirements in terms of a sense of musicality and rhythm. For example, tap dance requires a greater degree of footwork and modern is comparable to ballet, but more flowing and less rigid.

DANCE CONCEPTS, FORMS, AND BASIC VOCABULARY – JAZZ AND BALLET

There are several forms of dance including modern, ballet, jazz, country, ballroom, and hip-hop. Though essentially very different from each other, they all have similarities. A sense of musicality is the one constant required for each of the dance forms. Along with that, we can add timing, coordination, flexibility, and, needless to say, an interest in the concept of dance itself. We all know that we will probably experience greater success when we engage in activities that we are interested in and enjoy. Understanding of most dance forms requires knowledge of basic vocabulary. For example, in jazz, turns or kick ball turns; in tap dance, the shuffle or the flap, etc. Ballet has more specialized vocabulary than any other dance form. For example, plie, to bend; tendu, to stretch; degage, to disengage; fouette, to whip; fondu, to melt; ronde jambe, circle of the leg; pirouette, to turn on one leg; port de bras, movement of the arms; and assemble, to assemble.

Integral to dance and particularly ballet are the concepts of balance and counterbalance, pull-up and turnout, weight distribution and alignment, including shoulders down, hips square, legs turned out, and chest lifted.

In ballet, there are many different dance forms and techniques that a dancer can follow. Three of the larger ones are the Cecchetti, Russian Vaganova, and Royal Academy of Dance, (RAD), programmes. They all have levels for all dancers from beginner to advanced and they all have their advantages and disadvantages. The Cecchetti Society developed the Cecchetti technique from the teachings of the great ballet master Enrico Cecchetti. It is a full syllabus designed to train dancers for professional work. One notable emphasis in the Cecchetti syllabus is that the arms flow and blend from position to position more than any other technique. The Cecchetti technique has formed the core of the program at the National Ballet School of Canada. The Russian Vaganova technique derives and takes its name from the teachings of Agrippina Vaganova, who was the artistic director of the Kirov Ballet for many years. In the Vaganova method, the dancers bring attention to their hands. The hands do not flow invisibly from one position to the, as in the Cecchetti method, rather they are left behind and turn at the last moment. This is where the "flapping" look comes from that many dancers make with their hands. Unlike the RAD method, the Vaganova method does not have formally established exercises for each level. Each teacher choreographs his own class according to specialized guidelines and the students dance that class in their examinations. The Vaganova method forms the core of the program at the Royal Winnipeg Ballet School. The RAD syllabus is very common. It is well suited to dance classes in community dance schools where the students usually do no more than an average of one class per day. If you go to the ballet school in your community, there is a good chance they will use the RAD method. The American School of Ballet teaches the Balanchine method. Created by George Balanchine in the American School of Ballet, the Balanchine method allows dancers to dance Balanchine's choreography much more easily than other dancers can. In the Balanchine method the hands are held differently again from any of the other systems.

DANCE CONCEPTS, FORMS, AND BASIC VOCABULARY – FOLK AND TAP

Folk dance is a term used to describe a large number of dances that originated in Europe and share several common characteristics. Most folk dances practiced today were created before the 20th century, and were practiced by people with little or no training. For this reason, a spontaneous style, adaptable movements, and culturally distinctive steps representative of the dance's country of origin usually characterize folk dances. Types of folk dancing include the contra dance, English country-dance, and Maypole dance.

Contra dance is a term used to describe folk dances in which couples dance in two facing lines. A pair of such lines is a set, and these sets generally run the length of a long hall. The head of a set is the end of the line closest to the band and caller. At contra dance events where dancers perform several different folk dances, the caller or dance leader teaches the movements of an individual dance to the dancers during the "walk through," a short period of time before the next type of dance begins. During the walk through, all dancers mark the movements following the caller's instructions. At contra dance events in North America, contra dancers traditionally change partners for every dance, while in the United Kingdom, dancers remain with the same partner for the entire evening.

Square dance refers to a type of folk dance in which four couples begin and end each sequence in a square formation. When four couples align themselves in such a manner, the formation is "sets-in-order," and we call dances that use such formations "quadrilles." Similar to folk dance, American square dance steps are based on traditional European dances. At every square dance event, the dance caller prompts participants through a sequence of steps to the beat throughout the entirety of each dance, but does not usually participate in the dancing. Steps common to many square dances include allemande left and allemande right, where couples face, take hands, and circle around one another; promenade, where partners cross hands and walk to a counter-clockwise position; and circle right and circle left, where all dancers grasp hands and move round in a circle. Traditionally, the caller explains the steps to each individual square dance at the beginning of a session.

Tap is a form of dance born in the United States during the 19th century in which the dancer sounds out the rhythm by clicking taps on the toes and heels of his shoes. This form of percussive music and dance evolved from a fusion of Irish and African Shuffle in New York City during the 1830s. One common characteristic of modern tap dance is "syncopation," where choreographies generally begin on the eighth music beat. Learning to tap dance is a cumulative process in which new information builds on previously learned steps and terms. To teach tap dance successfully, instructors must first teach simple steps that make up the foundation of tap before introducing complex movements. The most basic steps of tap include the walk, step, heel, step-heel, stamp, ball-change, brush, toe tap, shuffle, side shuffle, back shuffle, and cramp roll. Dance instructors can combine these steps to form simple routines for beginners. Once students have mastered these steps, dancers can move on to attempt movements such as the buffalo, Maxi Ford, Cincinnati, pullback, wings, toe clips, and riffs.

Skill 2.2 **Demonstrate an understanding of the use of dance to express perceptions, feelings, images, and thoughts.**

Dancing requires many physical skills, but, just as importantly, it also calls on our mental and emotional states to convey messages. In dance whether in a full-length classical ballet, such as *The Nutcracker* or *Giselle*, or a peppy tap number, internal feelings are an integral part of any performance. In Romeo and Juliet, when Romeo thinks that Juliet is dead, his thoughts of suicide are clear. How do actors express seemingly intangible emotions on stage? Actors express emotions through movement; the highs, the lows, the hanging head, the slow gait, the arms thrown up in the air and, of course, the music. Dance requires expression of feelings of anger, sadness, joy, or happiness. The tempo of the music, the number of people turning in succession, costumes, and smiles can all express happiness. Conversely, all of these elements (except smiles) can convey sadness.

Dancing is also acting and, as such, it often requires a full spectrum of emotion. Dancers express feelings and moods as a result of emotion coming from the material. Dancers do not just arbitrarily "put on" feelings, rather they form from the inside and transform to the outside. One often may not realize that, though a dancer is far away on stage, spectators throughout the theatre can see his expression. When a dancer looks out into the audience, perhaps he ponders the arrival of a loved one. Perhaps as a dancer waits for the arrival of his lover, he laughs as he thinks of a funny moment that they shared together earlier. Dancing, like acting, transports us to another place; one where we can completely submerge ourselves in the expressions of the dancer and perhaps ourselves. Dancing conveys a message and the dancer's talent often determines the degree of success in conveying that message.

Skill 2.3 **Demonstrate an understanding of dance concepts, forms, and basic vocabulary.**

SEE Domain 5, Skill 2.1

COMPETENCY 3.0 GYMNASTICS MOVEMENTS

Skill 3.1 Demonstrate knowledge of gymnastic forms such as rhythmic gymnastics and educational gymnastics.

Rhythmic gymnastics is a sport, which combines dance and gymnastics with the use of balls, hoops, ribbons, ropes, and clubs. Gymnasts perform on a carpet to music either individually or in a group of five. In competition, gymnasts perform leaps, pivots, balances, and other elements to demonstrate flexibility and coordination. The gymnast must completely integrate the apparatus into the routine and perform specific moves with each apparatus. Individual routines last from 1 minute and 15 seconds to 1 minute and 30 seconds, while group routines last from 2 minutes 15 seconds to 2 minutes and 30 seconds. The main difference between rhythmic and artistic gymnastics is that rhythmic gymnasts cannot incorporate acrobatic skill. In fact, judges penalize gymnasts for incorporating acrobatic skill into their routines. However, gymnasts may perform pre-acrobatic elements such as forward and backward shoulder rolls, fish-flops, and tah-dahs. In addition, the new Code of Points permits walkovers and cartwheels. Originality and risk are integral parts of this sport, and no two routines are ever the same.

In educational gymnastics, students learn to use and manage their bodies in safe, efficient and creative ways. Educational gymnastics can utilize certain fixed equipment such as mats, bars, ropes, and boxes and is also know as "body management" because the activities provide opportunities for students to learn to manage their own bodies. Instead of a series of gymnastics stunts, they select, refine and perform the six Basic Movement Patterns of Landings, Locomotions, Statics, Rotations, Swings, and Springs in a variety of contexts and environments. Emphasis is on challenges and problem solving. Instructors use the Movement Variables of Body, Space, Effort, and Relationships to design movement-learning experiences. Students work individually, in pairs, and in groups to create movement sequences and structures.

Elaborate facilities are not required in this approach. In fact, many good educational gymnastics programs take place out-of-doors in natural settings. While large-scale gymnastics equipment is not essential for providing students with quality movement-learning experiences, such equipment is certainly advantageous. Another advantage of educational gymnastics is that it provides for the development of the upper body. It is much easier and more common to develop strength in the lower body than in the upper body. Many everyday events such as walking and running and jumping enhance lower body strength. Most team games and sports emphasize lower body strength and tend to neglect upper body development. Gymnastics also help to build overall muscular strength and flexibility. There is also equal development of both left and right sides of the body because most gymnastics activities involve simultaneous use of both arms (e.g. rolls, hangs, swings, supports) or both legs (e.g. springs, tumbling). In contrast, many game activities that involve the use of an implement (e.g., bat, racquet, stick) or object (e.g., beanbag, ball, Frisbee) tend to favor the development of one side of the body more than the other does.

Finally, if educational gymnastics experiences are to be truly "educational," then we must ask in what ways are they educational? In short, these experiences are educational because they start with the needs of students. The instructor presents the students with movement problems , which the students must solve, asks questions to gain the cognitive involvement of students, offers various solutions in the form of movement sequences, and guides students to reflect upon and synthesize their experiences. Students gain knowledge and understandings of the mechanical principles associated with the Basic Movement Patterns of gymnastics and they increase their ability to apply these principles.

Skill 3.2   **Demonstrate knowledge of gymnastic movements such as stunts, tumbling, apparatus work, and floor exercise.**

Gymnastics is a sport involving the performance of sequences of movements requiring physical strength, flexibility, and kinesthetic awareness (e.g. handsprings, handstands, and forward rolls). Its roots lie in the fitness and beauty practices of ancient Greeks, including skills for mounting and dismounting a horse and circus performance skills. In ancient times the term implied exercise taken by men in a gymnasium, a venue for intellectual and physical education. It is often considered a dangerous sport, as the difficult acrobatic maneuvers often performed on equipment high above the ground puts the athlete at risk of serious injury.

Proper stretching and strength building exercises are necessary for gymnastics. A useful, brief warm-up can consist of push-ups, sit-ups, and flexibility exercises for hamstrings, back, ankles, neck, wrists, and shoulders. An aerial is one example of a stunt (i.e. difficult physical feat) in which the gymnast turns completely over in the air without touching the apparatus with his or her hands. Floor exercise and tumbling can include somersaults, backward and frontward rolls, cartwheels, forward straddle rolls, back tucks, back handsprings, and handstands. Gymnasts perform apparatus work on the vaulting horse, balance beam, and uneven bars. A strong run, dynamism, power, and precision in the rotations are characteristics of an efficient vault. The main characteristics for the beam are a well-developed sense of balance and great power of concentration. The uneven bars demand strength as well as concentration, courage, coordination, precision, and split-second timing.

TEACHER CERTIFICATION STUDY GUIDE

COMPETENCY 4.0 AQUATIC SKILLS

Skill 4.1 Demonstrate knowledge of aquatic skills such as water safety, swimming strokes, diving, and water fitness activities and games.

Water safety issues include student familiarity with appropriate medical responses to life-threatening situations. Students should recognize signs that someone needs medical attention (e.g. not moving, not breathing, etc.) and have knowledge of the proper response (e.g. who to contact and where to find them). With older children, the instructor can introduce rudimentary first aid. The instructor must also ensure that students are aware and observant of safety rules (e.g. no running near the water, no chewing gum while swimming, no swimming without a lifeguard, no roughhousing near or in the water, etc.).

Swimming strokes include Butterfly, Breast Stroke, Crawl, Sidestroke, Trudgen, Freestyle, Backstroke, and Dog Paddle. When teaching children how to dive, instructors should emphasize form (arm and body alignment) and safety procedures (e.g. no diving in the shallow end, no pushing students into the water).

Water fitness activities and games should place emphasis on generating a lot of movement in the pool (gross motor activities), and may also incorporate activities that require more coordinated manipulations, like catching a ball (fine motor). Sample games include:

- **Water Tag** – Children can attempt to catch each other in the pool. When someone is caught, he becomes 'it'. Variations include freeze tag (where a caught student isn't allowed to move until someone swims between their legs to free them) and base tag (where some sections of the pool, for example the ladders or the walls, are a safe 'base' – rules must be in place limiting the time that a student can spend on the base). Water tag emphasizes gross motor activities. Safety issue: students may not hold other students or grab other students in the water.

- **Water Dodgeball** – Students divide into two teams, one on either side of the pool. They play dodgeball, throwing a ball from one side to the other. The opposing team captures a student by hitting him with the ball, but if the targeted player catches the ball, the opposition captures the thrower instead. Safety issue: students may not throw the ball at another student's head at close range.

PHYSICAL EDUCATION

- **Relay Races** – Students divide into teams and perform relay races (i.e. one student swims the length of the pool and back, when he returns the next one does the same, repeating until the whole team has completed the task). This can incorporate various swimming strokes; either all team members use the same stroke or each team member uses a different stroke.

WATER SAFETY BASICS

- Get a partner. Even experienced swimmers get tired or get muscle cramps. When swimming with a partner you can help each other or go for help in case of an emergency.
- Learn some life-saving techniques (e.g. CPR).
- Know your limits. If you're a novice swimmer, don't go in water that is so deep that you're unable to touch the bottom. Also, don't try to keep up with advanced swimmers.
- Swim only in places with lifeguard supervision.
- When swimming in an open body of water, don't fight the current, swim with it, gradually trying to make your way to shore.
- Dive only in areas that are safe for diving.
- Watch the sun and reapply sunscreen often.
- Drink plenty of fluids to prevent dehydration from the sun.
- Don't stay in cool waters for too long. This can lower your body temperature. Get out of the water if you feel your muscles cramp or you begin to shiver.
- Never mix alcohol and swimming.

TEACHER CERTIFICATION STUDY GUIDE

COMPETENCY 5.0 INDIVIDUAL, DUAL, AND TEAM SPORTS AND GAMES

Skill 5.1 Demonstrate knowledge of techniques, skills, critical elements, scientific principles, and equipment for individual, dual, and team sports.

TARGET SPORTS – OVERVIEW

Golf – The most fundamental skills for students to learn when studying golf include the correct way to execute a golf swing with proper posture and how to judge distance for shot selection correctly. Further, students should learn specific shots and their names (e.g. tee shot, fairway shot, bunker shot, putt).

Strategy in golf centers on properly gauging distances and required force to control the ball to the best extent possible.

Safety practices in golf, especially with students, involve ensuring that the course is clear and there are no students nearby when players are swinging. Instructors should also remind students that golf clubs are not toys, and that misuse can result in injury.

Equipment necessary for a golf class includes a proper set of clubs and golf balls (a golf course or open area for hitting balls is also necessary).

Archery – Skills that students study in archery classes include proper care for their equipment, properly stringing the bow, drawing, and shooting with accuracy (including compensating for distance, angle, and wind).

Safety practices in archery include respectful handling of the equipment (which is potentially dangerous) and ensuring that students only draw bows when pointed at a (non-living) target. Finally, instructors should keep students away from the path between firing students and their targets at all times.

Proper equipment for archery classes include a bow and arrows, which can vary greatly in technical complexity and cost, and a target.

Bowling – Skills that students will learn in bowling classes include learning to select a ball of comfortable weight and appropriate for the shot they need to make, properly controlling the ball so it hits the pins they are aiming for, and learning the dynamics of pin interaction to plan the proper angle of entry for the ball.

Safety practices in bowling include wearing proper footwear, handling the balls cautiously, and preventing horseplay (to avoid situations where a heavy bowling ball may drop inopportunely and cause injury).

Equipment needed for a bowling class include proper footwear, a bowling ball, pins, and a lane.

Frisbee Golf – Skills that students will acquire in a Frisbee golf class include methods of throwing the Frisbee (primarily forehand, side arm, and backhand throws). Students will also gain an intuitive sense for the physics governing the movement of the Frisbee (e.g. stability and speed range).

Frisbee golf strategy focuses on gauging distances and the amount of force and angle of throw required to land the disc in the target.

Frisbee golf safety practices involve ensuring that students don't wander in areas where a disc is in play, as this may result in injury. Instructors should also instruct students to remain alert and not throw the disc if they perceive there is a possibility that they might hit an individual.

Equipment needed for Frisbee golf include a proper disc (though you can substitute a regular Frisbee for school purposes), target nets, and a playing area large enough to accommodate the game without excessive risk of the Frisbee flying irretrievably out of bounds.

Shuffleboard – Depending on whether students are playing deck shuffleboard or table shuffleboard, they will learn to manipulate the discs, either with or without sticks.

Strategy requires students to properly gauge and apply the force needed to propel the disc accurately to a particular spot on the playing area.

Safety practices in shuffleboard include properly instructing and monitoring students to avoid horseplay, which may result in injury caused by the playing equipment.

Equipment needed for a shuffleboard class include a disc with which to play, the equipment to manipulate the disc (this will vary depending on whether the shuffleboard game is played on a deck or on a table), and the appropriate playing area.

Bocce ball – Requires a flat, level playing surface (packed dirt, gravel or grass are ideal). The instructor divides students into two teams of one, two, or four players each. Each team gets four balls, divided equally among the players. A player from the starting team stands behind the foul line (10 feet from the throwing end of the court) and throws the small ball ("pallina") toward the opposite end of the playing surface. The player then throws one of the larger balls ("boccia"), trying to get it as close to the pallina as possible without touching it. Players from the opposing team take turns throwing their balls until one of the balls stops closer to the pallina than the starting player's ball. If they fail to do so, the starting team tries to outdo its first attempt. Teams continue to take turns in this manner until they have thrown all the balls. The team with closest ball gets a point. This game emphasizes throwing skills (coordination, gross and fine motor skills).

TARGET SPORTS – TERMINOLOGY

Archery Terminology:

- Addressing the target – standing ready to shoot with a proper shooting stance.

- Anchor point – specific location on the archer's face to which index finger comes while holding and aiming.

- Archery golf (adaptation of golf to archery) – players shoot for holes, scoring according to the number of shots required to hit the target.

- Arm guard – a piece of leather or plastic worn on the inside of the forearm, protecting the arm from the bowstring.

- Arrow plate – a protective piece of hard material set into the bow where the arrow crosses it.

- Arrow rest – a small projection at the top of the bow handle where the arrow rests.

- Back – the side of the bow away from the shooter.

- Bow arm – the arm that holds the bow.

- Bow sight – a device attached to the bow through which the archer sights when aiming.

- Bow weight – designates the amount of effort needed to pull a bowstring a specific distance.

- Cant – shooting while holding the bow slightly turned or tilted.

- Cast – the distance a bow can shoot an arrow.

- Clout shooting – a type of shooting using a target 48 feet in diameter laid on the ground at a distance of 180 yards for men and 120 or 140 yards for women. Participants usually shoot 36 arrows per round.

- Cock/Index feather – the feather that is set at a right angle to the arrow nock; differently colored than the other two feathers.

- Creeping – letting the drawing hand move forward at the release.

- Crest – the archer's identifying marks located just below the fletchings.

- Draw – pulling the bowstring back into the anchor position.

- End – a specific number of arrows shot at one time or from one position before retrieval of arrows.

- Face – the part of the bow facing the shooter.

- Finger tab – a leather flap worn on the drawing hand protecting the fingers and providing a smooth release of the bowstring.

- Fletchings – the feathers of the arrow that give guidance to its flight.

- Flight shooting – shooting an arrow the farthest possible distance.

- Handle – the grip at the midsection of the bow.

- Hen feathers – the two feathers that are not set at right angles to the arrow nock.

- Instinctive shooting – aiming and shooting instinctively rather than using a bow sight or point-of-aim method.

- Limbs – upper and lower parts of the bow divided by the handle.

- Nock – the groove in the arrow's end where the string is placed.

- Nocking point – the point on the string where the arrow is placed.

- Notch – the grooves of the upper and lower tips of the limbs where the bowstring is fitted.

- Over bow – using too strong a bow that is too powerful to pull a bowstring the proper distance.

- Overdraw – drawing the bow so that the pile of the arrow is inside the bow.

- Petticoat – the part of the target face outside the white ring.

- Pile/point – the arrow's pointed, metal tip.

- Plucking – jerking the drawing hand laterally away from the face on the release causing the arrow's flight to veer to the left.

- Point-blank range – the distance from the target where the point of aim is right on the bull's eye.

- Point-of-aim – a method of aiming that aligns the pile of the arrow with the target.

- Quiver – a receptacle for carrying or holding arrows.

- Recurve bow – a bow curved on the ends.

- Release – the act of letting the bowstring slip off the fingertips.

- Round – the term used to indicate shooting a specified number of arrows at a designated distance or distances.

- Roving – an outdoor archery game that uses natural targets (trees, bushes, stumps, etc.) for competition.

- Serving – the thread wrapped around the bowstring at the nocking point.

- Shaft – the long, body part of the arrow.

- Spine – the rigidity and flexibility characteristics of an arrow.

- Tackle – archery equipment referred to in its entirety.

- Target face – the painted front of a target.

- Trajectory – the flight path of the arrow.

- Vane – an arrow's plastic feather.

Bowling Terminology:

- Anchor – the teammate who shoots last.

- Baby split – the 1-7 or 3-10 pin railroads.

- Backup – a reverse hook rotating to the right for a right-handed bowler.
- Bed posts – the 7-10 railroad.
- Blow – an error or missing a spare that is not split.
- Box – a frame.
- Brooklyn – a crossover ball striking the 1-2 pocket.
- Bucket – the 2-4-5-8 or 3-5-6-9 leaves.
- Cherry – chopping off the front pin on a spare.
- Double – two consecutive strikes.
- Double pinochle – the 7-6 and 4-10 split.
- Crossover – same as a Brooklyn.
- Dutch 200 (Dutchman) – a score of 200 made by alternating strikes and spares for the entire game.
- Error – same as a "blow."
- Foul – touching or going beyond the foul line in delivering the ball.
- Frame – the box where scores are entered.
- Gutter ball – a ball that falls into either gutter.
- Handicap – awarding an individual or team a bonus score or score adjustment based on averages.
- Head pin – the number one pin.
- Hook – a ball that breaks to the left for a right-handed bowler and breaks to the right for a left-handed bowler.
- Jersey side – same as a Brooklyn.
- Kegler – synonym for a bowler.
- Lane – a bowling alley.
- Leave – pin or pins left standing after a throw.
- Light hit – hitting the head pin lightly to the right or left side.

- Line – a complete game as recorded on the score sheet.

- Mark – getting a strike or spare.

- Open frame – a frame in which no mark is made, leaving at least one pin standing after rolling both balls in a frame.

- Pocket – space between the head pin and pins on either side.

- Railroad – synonym for a split.

- Sleeper – a pin hidden from view.

- Spare – knocking all pins down with two balls.

- Split – a leave, after throwing the first ball, in which the number one pin plus a second pin are down, and when seven pins remain standing.

- Spot – a bowler's point of aim on the alley.

- Striking out – obtaining three strikes in the last frame.

- Tap – a pin that remains standing after an apparently perfect hit.

- Turkey – three consecutive strikes.

STRIKING/FIELDING SPORTS – OVERVIEW

Softball – Skills students in softball classes will acquire include accurate throwing and catching, and the correct way to swing and hit with a softball bat.

Softball is similar in strategy to baseball. Defensive strategy focuses on the pitcher, who is responsible for trying to strike out the team that is at bat. Offensive strategy centers on batting, and attempting to turn batters into runners.

Safety practices in softball are also similar to baseball. Enforcing discipline and maintaining student attentiveness to prevent the chance of injury is of utmost importance. Instructors must also emphasize to the students that they should not swing the bat when other students are in the area.

Equipment required for softball practice includes a softball bat and softball, fielding gloves, appropriate protective gear, and base markers of some sort.

Baseball – Skills that students studying baseball will acquire include accurate throwing and catching, and the correct way to swing and hit with a baseball bat.

Defensive strategy in baseball focuses on the actions of the pitcher, who is responsible for trying to strike out the team that is at bat. Offensive strategy in baseball centers on batting, and attempting to turn batters into runners.

Safety practices in baseball include maintaining discipline among the students, as horseplay and lack of attentiveness can lead to injury (e.g. a ball could hit a student who isn't paying attention). In addition, instructors should remind students the baseball bat is not a toy, and they should handle it with care and not swing it near other students.

Equipment required for baseball practice includes baseball bats, baseballs, baseball gloves (though for some educational situations, the gloves are not necessary), base markers of some kind, and protective padding for the catcher.

Cricket – Skills that students in cricket class will acquire include accurate throwing and catching, swinging the bat correctly, and the proper form for the execution of an effective pitch.
Unlike baseball and softball, where pitching controls the game, in cricket batting controls the game. Since in cricket the batter can hit in any direction around him, he will focus on weak spots in the opposing team's field deployment, and the defensive strategy of the opposing team will focus on minimizing weak spots for the batter to exploit.

Safety practices in cricket are similar to baseball and softball; enforcing discipline and maximizing attentiveness to prevent the chance of injury, and reminding students that they should not swing the bat when other students are in the vicinity.

Equipment required for cricket practice includes cricket bats, cricket balls, appropriate protective gear, and base markers.

Field hockey – Skills that students of field hockey will acquire include running, tactical thinking on the field, and the ability to manipulate the ball with the stick (including running with the ball and different types of shots).

Offensive strategy in field hockey focuses on maneuvering the ball between team members to prevent the opposing team from intercepting, in order to get close enough to the opposing team's net to score a goal. Defensive strategy will strive to create solid coverage of the advancing team, to enable interception of the ball.

Safety practices include emphasizing mindfulness on the part of the students to prevent accidents, and reinforcing the safety regulations of the game concerning legal use of the hockey stick.

Equipment needed for the practice of field hockey with students includes an appropriate ball, sticks for the students, and appropriate protective gear.

NET/WALL SPORTS – OVERVIEW

Badminton – Students in a badminton class will have to master the strokes as basic skills and should learn at least some of them by name (e.g. types of serves, net shot, net kills, drive, push, lift). Students should also know which strokes are appropriate from which areas of the court.

Handball – Skills that students will learn in a handball class will include catching and accurately throwing the ball, taking steps while bouncing it (similar to basketball's dribble), and quick analysis of the playing situation to determine who the best target is for a pass.

Strategy in handball centers on staying one step ahead of the opposing team. Keep them guessing and have multiple contingencies for given situations, so that gameplay doesn't become predictable (and easier to counter). Specific tactics can include types of shots that are harder for the opponent to hit, and shots that will put the ball out of play (when it is advantageous to do so).

Pickleball – Skills that students will learn in pickleball classes include manipulation of the ball with the racket and the variety of strokes.

Pickleball strategy is similar to tennis. Students should learn to vary their strokes to keep their opponents guessing, with the goal of reaching the frontcourt in a net volley position first. This places the students in the best position to win the point.

Table Tennis (Ping Pong) – Skills that students will study when learning table tennis include the variety of grips (e.g. penhold, shakehand, V-grip), and the various types of offensive and defensive strokes. Students will also learn to gauge the force needed to manipulate the ball properly.

Strategies for success in table tennis involve manipulating and minimizing the opponent's ability to return a shot – this includes learning to hit to the opponent's weak side, putting a spin on the ball so as to make its movement less predictable, and setting the opponent up to receive a shot that he cannot return.

Tennis – Skills that students will learn when studying tennis include the proper grips of the racket and stroke techniques, which they should know by name (e.g. flat serve, topspin serve, twist serve, forehand, backhand, volley, overhead).

Volleyball – Students studying volleyball should master six basic skills: the serve, pass, set, attack, block, and dig. Each of these skills comprises a number of specific techniques that are standard volleyball practice.

SAFETY PRACTICES AND EQUIPMENT – NET/WALL SPORTS

In addition to the general safety procedures discussed in the previous skill, there are several specific safety considerations for net/wall sports. First, because most of these sports involve swinging a racket or paddle and hitting a ball with a great deal of force, monitoring the area of play is very important. Instructors must ensure that students only swing rackets and hit balls at appropriate times. Second, instructors and students must keep the playing area clear of stray balls and other obstacles to prevent injuries. Finally, some of the net/wall sports, such as handball, require use of protective eyewear.

The following is a list of sport-specific equipment for net/wall sports:

- Badminton – rackets, nets, shuttlecocks
- Handball – a wall, handballs, protective eyewear
- Pickleball – wood paddle rackets, plastic balls, nets, a paved surface
- Table Tennis – paddles, balls, table, nets
- Tennis – court, nets, rackets, tennis balls
- Volleyball – nets, volleyballs

TERMINOLOGY OF VARIOUS NET/WALL SPORTS

Badminton Terminology:

- Alley – the area on each side of the court used for doubles that is 1.5 feet wide.

- Around the head stroke – an overhead stroke used to hit a forehand-like overhead stroke that is on the backhand side of the body.

- Back alley – the area between the baseline and the doubles long service line.

- Backcourt – the back third of the court.

- Backhand – a stroke made on the non-racket side of the body.

- Baseline – the back boundary line of the court.

- Bird – another name for the shuttlecock/shuttle.

- Block – a soft shot used mainly to defend a smash; intercepting opponent's smash and returning it back over the net.

- Carry/Throw – a call when the shuttle remains on the racket during a stroke. It is legal if the racket follows the intended line of flight.

- Centerline – the mid-line separating the service courts.

- Clear – a high shot that goes over the opponent's head and lands close to the baseline.

- Combination alignment – partners playing both up-and-back and side-by-side during doubles games and/or volleys.

- Crosscourt – a diagonal shot hit into the opposite court.

- Defense – the team or player hitting the shuttle upwards.

- Double hit – an illegal shot where the player contacts the shuttle twice with the racket in one swing.

- Doubles service court – the short, wide area to which the server must serve in doubles play.

- Down the line shot – a straight-ahead shot (usually down the sideline).

- Drive – a hard, driven shot traveling parallel to the floor (clears net but does not have enough height for opponent to smash).

- Drop – a shot just clearing the net and then falling close to it.

- Face – the racket's string area.

- Fault – an infraction of the rules resulting in loss of serve or a point awarded to the server.

- First serve – a term used in doubles play to indicate that the server is the "first server" during an inning.

- Foot fault – Illegal movement/position of the feet by either the server or receiver.

- Forecourt – the front area of the court (between the net and the short service line).

- Forehand – a stroke made on the racket side of the body.

- Game point – the point, if won, that allows the server to win the game.

- Hand in – a term indicating that the server retains the serve.

- Hand out – the term used in doubles to denote that one player has lost the service.

- Home base – a center court position where a player can best play any shot hit by an opponent.

- Inning – the period a player or team holds service.

- Let – stopping the point because of some type of outside interference. Players replay the point.

- Lifting the shuttle – stroking the shuttle underhanded and hitting it upward.

- Long serve – a high, deep serve landing near the long service line in doubles or the back boundary line in singles.

- Love – the term used to indicate a zero score.

- Match – a series of games. Winning two out of three games wins the match.

- Match point – the point, if won by the server, which makes that person the winner of the match.

- Midcourt – the middle-third of the court (between short service line and long service line for doubles).

- Net shot – a shot taken near the net.

- Non-racket side – the opposite side of the hand holding the racket.

- Offense – the team or player that is stroking the shuttle downward.

- Overhead – a motion used to strike the shuttle when it is above the head.

- Racket foot or leg – the foot or leg on the same side as the hand holding the racket.

- Ready position – the position a player assumes to be ready to move in any direction.

- Receiver – the player to whom the shuttle is served.

- Second serve – in doubles, the term indicates that one partner has lost the serve, and the other partner is now serving.

- Server – the player putting the shuttle into play.

- Setting – choosing the amount of additional points to play when certain tie scores are reached.

- Short-serve – a serve barely clearing the net and landing just beyond the short service line.

- Shuttlecock/Shuttle – the feathered, plastic or nylon object that players volley back and forth over the net.

- Side Alley – see alley.

- Smash – an overhead stroke hit downward with great velocity and angle.

- "T" – the intersection of the centerline and the short service line.

- Underhand – an upward stroke to hit the shuttle when it has fallen below shoulder level.

- Unsight – illegal position taken by the server's partner so the receiver cannot see the shuttle.

- Up-and-back – an offensive alignment used in doubles. The "up" player is responsible for the forecourt and the "back" player is responsible for both.

Racquetball/Handball Terminology:

- Ace – a serve that completely eludes the receiver.

- Back-wall shot – a shot made from a rebound off the back wall.

- Box – see service box.

- Ceiling shot – a shot that first strikes the ceiling, then the front wall.

- Crotch – the junction of any two playing surfaces, as between the floor and any wall.

- Crotch shot – a ball that simultaneously strikes the front wall and floor (not good).

- Cut throat – a three-man game in which the server plays against the other two players. Each player keeps an individual score.

- Drive shot – a power shot against the front wall rebounding in a fast, low, and straight line.

- Fault – an illegally served ball.

- Handout – retiring the server who fails to serve legally or when the serving team fails to return a ball that is in play.

- Hinder – interference or obstruction of the flight of the ball during play.

- Kill – a ball rebounded off the front wall so close to the floor that it is impossible to return.

- Passing shot – a shot placed out of an opponent's reach on either side.

- Rally – continuous play of the ball by opponents.

- Receiving line – the broken line parallel to the short line on a racquetball court.

- Run-around shot – a ball striking one sidewall, the rear wall, and the other sidewall.

- Safety zone – a five-foot area bounded by the back edge of the short line and receiving line that is only observed during the serve in racquetball.

- Screen – a hinder due to obstruction of the opponent's vision.

- Server – person in the "hand-in" position and eligible to serve.

- Service box – the service zone bounded by the sidewall and a parallel line 18 inches away; denotes where server's partner must stand in doubles during the serve.

- Service court – the area where the ball must land when it is returned from the front wall on the serve.

- Service line – the line that is parallel to and five feet in front of the short line.

- Service zone – the area to which the server must serve the ball.

- Short line – the line on the floor parallel to front wall and equidistant from front and back wall. The serve must go over this line when returning from the front wall.

- Shoot – attempt kill shots.

- Side out – loss of serve.

- Thong – the strap on the bottom handle of the racquetball racquet that is worn around the player's wrist.

- Volley – returning the ball to the front wall before it bounces on the floor.

- Z-ball – defensive shot that strikes the front wall, a sidewall, and then the opposite sidewall.

Tennis Terminology:

- Ace – serving a ball untouched by the opponent's racket.

- Advantage (Ad) – a scoring term. The next point won after the score is "deuce."

- Alley – the 4.5-foot strip on either side of the singles court used to enlarge the court for doubles.

- Approach shot – a shot hit inside the baseline while approaching the net.

- Backcourt – the area between the service line and the baseline.

- Backhand – strokes hit on the left side of a right-handed player.

- Backspin – spin placed on a ball that causes the ball to bounce back toward the hitter.

- Back swing – the beginning of all groundstrokes and service motion requiring a back swing to gather energy for the forward swing.

- Baseline – the end line of a tennis court.

- Break – winning a game in when the opponent serves.

- Center mark – a short mark bisecting the baseline.

- Center service line – the perpendicular line to the net dividing the two service courts in halves.

- Center strap – the strap at the center of the net anchored to the court to facilitate a constant 3-foot height for the net at its center.

- Center stripe – same as the center service line.

- Chip – a short chopping motion of the racket against the back and bottom side of the ball imparting backspin.

- Chop – placing backspin on the ball with a short, high-to-low forward swing.

- Cross-court – a shot hit diagonally from one corner of the court over the net into the opposite corner of the court.

- Cut off the angle – moving forward quickly against an opponent's cross-court shot, allowing the player to hit the ball near the center of the court rather than near the sidelines.

- Deep (depth) – a shot bouncing near the baseline on groundstrokes and near the service line on serves.

- Default – a player who forfeits his/her position in a tournament by not playing a scheduled match.

- Deuce – a term used when the game score is 40-40.

- Dink – a ball hit very softly and relatively high to ensure its safe landing.

- Double fault – two consecutive out-of-bounds serves on the same point resulting in loss of the point.

- Doubles lines – the outside sidelines on a court used only for doubles.

- Down the line – a shot hit near a sideline traveling close to, and parallel to, the same line from which the shot was initially hit.

- Drive – an offensive shot hit with extra force.

- Drop shot – a groundstroke hit so that it drops just over the net with little or no forward bounce.

- Drop volley – a volley hit in such a manner that it drops just over the net with little or no forward bounce.

- Error – a mistake made by a player during competition.

- Flat shot – a ball hit so there is no rotation or spin when traveling through the air.

- Foot fault – illegal foot movement before service, penalized by losing that particular serve. Common foot faults are stepping on or ahead of the baseline before contacting the ball and running along the baseline before serving.

- Forecourt – the area between the net and the service line.

- Forehand – the stroke hit on the right side of a right-handed player.

- Frame – the rim of the racket head plus the handle of the racket.

- Game – scoring term when a player wins 4 points before an opponent while holding a minimum 2-point lead.

- Grip – the portion of the racket that is grasped in the player's hand.

- Groundstroke – any ball hit after it has bounced.

- Half volley – a ball hit inches away from the court's surface after the ball has bounced.

- Hold serve – winning your own serve. If you lose your own serve, your serve has been "broken."

- Let (ball) – a point replayed because of some kind of interference.

- Let serve – a serve that touches the net tape, falls into the proper square, and is played over.

- Linesman – a match official who calls balls "in" or "out."

- Lob – a ball hit with sufficient height to pass over the out-stretched arm of a net player.

- Lob volley – a shot hit high into the air from a volleying position.

- Love – scoring term that means zero points or games.

- Match – a contest between two or four opponents.

- Match point – the point immediately before the final point of a match.

- Midcourt – the area in front of the baseline or behind the service line of the playing court.

- Netball – a ball that hits the net, falling on the same side as the hitter.

- No man's land – a general area within the baseline and proper net position area. When caught in that area, the player must volley or hit ground strokes near his/her feet.

- Offensive lob – a ball hit just above the racket reach of an opposing net player.

- Open face racket – a racket whose face is moving under the ball. A wide-open racket face is parallel to the court surface.

- Overhead – a shot hit from a position higher than the player's head.

- Over-hitting – hitting shots with too much force; over-hitting usually results in errors.

- Pace – the speed of the ball.

- Passing shot – a shot passing beyond the reach of the net player landing inbounds.

- Poach – to cross over into your partner's territory in doubles in an attempt to intercept the ball.

- Racket face – the racket's hitting surface.

- Racket head – the top portion of the racket frame that includes the strings.

- Rally – opponents hitting balls back and forth across the net.

- Receiver – the player about to return the opponent's serve.

- Server – the player initiating play.

- Service line – the line at the end of the service courts parallel to the net.

- Set – a scoring term meaning the first player to win six games with a minimum two-game lead.

- Set point – the point, if won, which will give the player the set.

- Sidespin – a ball hit rotating on a horizontal plane.

- Signals in doubles – signaling your partner that you are going to poach at the net.

- Singles line – the sideline closest to the center mark that runs the entire length of the court.

- Slice – motion of the racket head going around the side of the ball, producing a horizontal spin on ball.

- Tape – the band of cloth or plastic running across the top of the net.

- Telegraphing the play – indicating the direction of one's intended target before hitting the ball.

- Topspin – forward rotation of the ball.

- Touch – the ability to make delicate, soft shots from several positions on the court.

- Twist – a special rotation applied to the ball during the serve causing the ball to jump to the left (of right-handed server).

- Umpire – the official that calls lines.

- Under spin – a counterclockwise spin placed on the ball (i.e. backspin).

- Volley – hitting the ball in the air before it bounces on the court.

Volleyball Terminology:

- Attack – returning the ball across the net in an attempt to put the opponents at a disadvantage.

- Ball handling – executing any passing fundamental.

- Block – intercepting the ball just before or as it crosses the net.

- Bump – see forearm pass.

- Court coverage – a defensive player's court assignment.

- Dig – an emergency pass usually used to defend a hard-driven attack.

- Dink – a soft shot off the fingertips to lob the ball over a block.

- Double foul – infraction of rules by both teams during the same play.

- Drive – an attacking shot contacted in the center that attempts to hit the ball off the blocker's hands.

- Fault – any infraction of the rules.

- Forearm pass – a pass made off the forearms used to play served balls, hard-driven spikes, or any low ball.

- Free ball – a ball returned by the opponent that is easily handled.

- Frontcourt – the playing area where it is legal to block or attack.

- Held ball – a ball that opponents simultaneously contact and momentarily hold above the net.

- Kill – an attack that the opponents cannot return.

- Lob – a soft attack contacted on the back bottom-quarter of the ball causing an upward trajectory.

- Overhand pass – a pass made by contacting the ball above the head with the fingers.

- Overlap – an illegal foot position when the ball is dead, with an adjacent player putting another out of position.

- Play over – replaying the rally because of a held ball or the official prematurely suspending play. The server re-serves with no point awarded.

- Point – a point is scored when the receiving team fails to return the ball to the opponents' court legally.

- Rotation – clockwise rotation of the players upon gaining the ball from the opponents.

- Serve – putting the ball in play over the net by striking it with the hand.

- Set – placing the ball near the net to facilitate attacking.

- Setter – the player assigned to set the ball.

- Side out – side is out when the serving team fails to win a point or plays the ball illegally.

- Spike – a ball hit with top spin and with a strong downward force into the opponents' court.

- Spiker – the player assigned to attack the ball.

- Spike-roll – an attack that first takes an upward trajectory using the spiking action (with or without jumping).

- Topspin (Overspin) – applying forward spin to the ball during the serve, spike, or spike roll.

TEAM PASSING SPORTS – OVERVIEW

Basketball – The fundamental skills of basketball include passing, dribbling, and shooting. As students' skills improve, they may begin to specialize in playing a specific position (point guard, shooting guard, small forward, power forward or center).

Touch/Flag Football – Skills that students will practice include running and passing – tackling is not relevant in touch or flag football situations. As students improve, they may begin to specialize in playing specific positions (e.g. quarterbacks or receivers). They may also become more involved in the study and implementation of strategy.

The main goal of offensive strategy in football is to move closer to the opposing team's end zone, to the point where the ball is close enough to score either a touchdown or a field goal. The aim of defensive strategies is to prevent this same movement towards the end zone by the opposition. Both offensive and defensive strategies make important use of concepts of time management and the possibility of "running out the clock". Formations are central to football strategy, both on offense and on defense, and students should become familiar with simple formations for both.

Lacrosse – Lacrosse players must master the skills of catching and throwing the ball with their sticks and cradling (the motion that allows players to run with the ball in their stick).

Lacrosse strategy has many parallels with other team sports like basketball, soccer, and field hockey. In all of these sports, the team of players has to maneuver to outflank and outsmart their opponents in order to score a goal.

Soccer – Soccer players must master the skills of running, accurate kicking, manipulation of the ball, and footwork that allows the student to maneuver when in motion.

The key to soccer strategy is for students to understand that the goal is to get the ball to the right person's feet – the one who has the most time and space (facing the least pressure) and is in the most advantageous position to score (or make a goal-scoring pass). Broadly, offensive strategy will spread the team out, to allow for coverage of more of the field. Defensive strategy will have the team compress to a compact unit that is able to cover the goal effectively.

Team Handball – Skills that students will learn in a handball class will include catching and accurately throwing the ball, taking steps while bouncing the ball (similar to basketball's dribble), and quick analysis of the playing situation to ascertain who the best target is for a pass.

Strategy in handball centers around staying one step ahead of the opposing team, keeping them guessing, and having multiple contingencies for given situations so that game play doesn't become predictable (and easier to counter). Specific tactics can include types of shots that are harder for the opponent to hit and shots that will put the ball out of play (when it is advantageous to do so).

Ultimate Frisbee – Skills that students must acquire to play ultimate Frisbee proficiently include catching the Frisbee, accurately throwing the Frisbee, and running. Instructors should also emphasize strategic thinking, as there is limited time to select a destination for and execute a throw.

The goal of offensive strategy in ultimate Frisbee is to create open lanes in the field that are free of defenders. Common offensive strategies include the 'vertical stack' and 'horizontal stack' (similar to a spread offense in football). Defensive strategy aims to gain control of the Frisbee and deflect passes made by the opposing team. A basic defensive principle is the 'force', which calls for the defense to cut off the handler's access to half of the field, thereby forcing the offensive player to throw the Frisbee to the other side of the field.

TERMINOLOGY OF VARIOUS TEAM PASSING SPORTS

Basketball Terminology:

- Backcourt players (Guards) – players who set up a team's offensive pattern and bring the ball up the court.

- Backdoor – an offensive maneuver in which a player cuts toward the baseline to the basket, behind the defenders, and receives a ball for a field goal attempt.

- Baseline – the end line of the court.

- Blocking/Boxing out – a term used when a player positions himself under the backboard to prevent an opposing player from achieving a good rebounding position.

- Charging – personal contact by a player with the ball against the body of a defensive opponent.

- Corner players (Forwards) – tall players that make up the sides of the offensive set-up who are responsible for the rebounding and shooting phases of the team's offense.

- Cut – a quick, offensive move by a player attempting to get free for a pass.

- Denial defense – aggressive individual defense to keep an offensive player from receiving a pass.

- Double foul – two opponents committing personal fouls against each other simultaneously.

- Dribble – ball movement by a player in control who throws or taps the ball in the air or onto the floor and then touches it. The dribble ends when the dribbler touches the ball with both hands concurrently, loses control, or permits it to come to rest while in contact with it.

- Drive – an aggressive move by a player with the ball toward the basket.

- Fake (Feint) – using a deceptive move with the ball pulling the defensive player out of position.

- Fast break – quickly moving the ball down court to score before the defense has a chance to set up.

- Field goal – a basket scored from the field.

- Freelance – no structure or set plays in the offense.

- Free throw – the right given a player to score one or two points by unhindered shots for a goal from within the free throw circle and behind the free throw line.

- Give-and-go – a maneuver when the offensive player passes to a teammate and then immediately cuts in toward the basket for a return pass.

- Held ball – occurs when two opponents have one or both hands firmly on the ball and neither can gain possession without undue roughness.

- Inside player (Center, Post, Pivot) – this player is usually the tallest team player who is situated near the basket, around the three-second lane area, and is responsible for rebounding and close-range shooting.

- Jump ball – a method of putting the ball into play by tossing it up between two opponents in the center circle to start the game or any overtime periods.

- Outlet pass – a term used that designates a direct pass from a rebounder to a teammate (the main objective is starting a fast break).

- Overtime period – an additional period of playing time when the score is tied at the end of the regulation game.

- Personal foul – a player foul that involves contact with an opponent while the ball is alive or after the ball is in possession of a player for a throw-in.

- Pick – a special type of screen where a player stands so the defensive player slides to make contact to free an offensive teammate for a shot or drive.

- Pivot – occurs when a player who is holding the ball steps once or more than once in any direction with the same foot while the other foot, called the pivot foot, remains at its point of contact with the floor. Also, another term for the inside player.

- Posting up – a player cutting to the three-second lane area, pausing, and anticipating a pass.

- Rebound – when the ball bounces off the backboard or basket.

- Restraining circles – three circles with a six-foot radius. One is located in the center of the court, and the others are located at each of the free-throw lines.

- Running time – not stopping the clock for fouls or violations.

- Screen – an offensive maneuver positioning a player between the defender and a teammate to free the teammate for an uncontested shot.

- Switching – defensive guards reversing their guarding assignments.

- Technical foul – a non-contact foul by a player, team, or coach for unsportsmanlike behavior or failing to abide by rules regarding submission of lineups, uniform numbering, and substitution procedures.

- Telegraphing a pass – a look or signal to indicate where the ball is going to be passed.

- Throw-in – a method of putting the ball in play from out-of-bounds.

- Traveling – illegal movement, in any direction, of a player in possession of the ball within bounds. Moving with the ball without dribbling.

- Violation – an infraction of the rules resulting in a throw-in from out-of-bounds.

Soccer Terminology:

- Center – passing from the outside of the field near the sideline into the center.

- Charge – illegal or legal body contact between opponents.

- Chip – lofting the ball into the air using the instep kick technique; contacting the ball very low causing it to loft quickly with backspin.

- Clear – attempting to move the ball out of danger by playing the ball a great distance.

- Corner kick – a direct free kick from the corner arc awarded to the attacking player when the defending team last played the ball over their own end line.

- Cross – a pass from the outside of the field near the end line to a position in front of the goal.

- Dead ball situation – the organized restarting of the game after stopping play.

- Direct free kick – a free kick whereby the kicker may score immediately from that initial contact.

- Dribble – the technique of a player self-propelling the ball with the foot in order to maintain control of the ball while moving from one spot to another.

- Drop ball – the method used to restart the game after temporary suspension of play when the ball is still in play.

- Goal area – the rectangular area in front of the goal where the ball is placed for a goal kick.

- Half volley – contacting the ball just as it hits the ground after being airborne.

- Head – playing the ball with the head.

- Indirect free kick – a free kick from which a player, other than the kicker, must contact the ball before a goal can be scored.

- Kickoff – the free kick starting play at the beginning of the game, after each period, or after a score.

- Obstruction – illegally using the body to shield an opponent from reaching the ball.

- One-touch – immediately passing or shooting a received ball without stopping it.

- Penalty area – the large rectangular area in front of the goal where the goalkeeper may use the hands to play the ball.

- Penalty kick – a direct free kick awarded in the penalty area against the defending team for a Direct Free Kick foul.

- Settle – taking a ball out of the air and settling it on the ground so that it is rolling and no longer bouncing.

- Square pass – a pass directed toward the side of a player.

- Tackle – a technique to take the ball away from the opponents.

- Through pass – a pass penetrating between and past the defenders.

- Throw-in – the technique to restart the game when the ball goes out of play over the sideline.

- Touchline – the side line of the field.

- Trap – the technique used for receiving the ball and bringing it under control.

- Two-touch- receiving – trapping and immediately re-passing the ball.

SAFETY PRACTICES AND EQUIPMENT – TEAM PASSING SPORTS

Important safety considerations for team passing sports include proper maintenance of facilities and playing fields, use of protective equipment, and proper enforcement of the rules of play. Enforcement of rules is particularly important to prevent participants from injuring other participants either intentionally or unintentionally through reckless play.

The following is a list of sport-specific equipment for team passing sports:

- Basketball – basketballs, goals, appropriate shoes
- Touch or Flag Football – footballs, flags and flag belts, cones to mark boundaries and end zones
- Lacrosse – lacrosse sticks and balls, protective pads, goals (nets)
- Soccer – soccer balls, goals, field markers, protective shin guards
- Team Handball – handballs and goals
- Ultimate Frisbee – Frisbees and an open playing field

RULES OF PLAY OF VARIOUS GAME AND SPORT SITUATIONS

ARCHERY:

- Arrows that bounce off the target or go through the target count as 7 points.

- Arrows landing on lines between two rings receive the higher score of the two rings.

- Arrows hitting the petticoat receive no score.

BADMINTON:

- Intentionally balking opponent or making preliminary feints results in a fault (side in = loss of serve; side out = point awarded to side in).

- When a shuttlecock falls on a line, it is in play (i.e. a fair play).

- If the striking team hits shuttlecock before it crosses net it is a fault.

- Touching the net when the shuttlecock is in play is a fault.

- The same player hitting the shuttlecock twice is a fault.

- The shuttlecock going through the net is a fault.

BOWLING:

- No score for a pin knocked down by a pinsetter (human or mechanical).

- There is no score for the pins when any part of the foot, hand, or arm extends or crosses over the foul line (even after ball leaves the hand) or if any part of the body contacts division boards, walls, or uprights that are beyond the foul line.

- There is no count for pins displaced or knocked down by a ball leaving the lane before it reaches the pins.

- There is no count when balls rebound from the rear cushion.

RACQUETBALL/HANDBALL:

- A server stepping outside service area when serving faults.

- The server is out (relinquishes serve) if he/she steps outside of serving zone twice in succession while serving.

- Server is out if he/she fails to hit the ball rebounding off the floor during the serve.

- The opponent must have a chance to take a position or the referee must call for play before the server can serve the ball.

- The server re-serves the ball if the receiver is not behind the short line when the ball is served.

- A served ball that hits the front line and does not land back of the short line is "short"; therefore, it is a fault. The ball is also short when it hits the front wall and two sidewalls before it lands on the floor back of the short line.

- A serve is a fault when the ball touches the ceiling from rebounding off the front wall.

- A fault occurs when any part of the foot steps over the outer edges of the service or the short line while serving.

- A hinder (dead ball) occurs when a returned ball hits an opponent on its way to the front wall - even if the ball continues to the front wall.

- A hinder is any intentional or unintentional interference of an opponent's opportunity to return the ball.

TENNIS:

A player loses a point when:

- The ball bounces twice on her side of the net.

- The player returns the ball to any place outside of designated areas.

- The player stops or touches the ball in the air before it lands out-of-bounds.

- The player intentionally strikes the ball twice with the racket.

- The ball strikes any part of a player or racket after initial attempt to hit the ball.

- A player reaches over the net to hit the ball.

- A player throws his racket at the ball.

- The ball strikes any permanent fixture that is out-of-bounds (other than the net).
    - a ball touching the net and landing inside the boundary lines is in play (except on the serve, where a ball contacting the net results in a "let" – replay of the point)

- A player fails, on two consecutive attempts, to serve the ball into the designated area (i.e. double fault).

TRACK AND FIELD:

The following are common track and field events:

- Sprint Races – 100, 200, 400 meter dash; 110, 400 meter hurdles
- Distance Races – one-mile, 5000 and 10000 meter foot races
- Jumping Events – high jump, long jump, broad jump, triple jump, pole vault
- Relay Races – team sprint or distance foot races
- Throwing Events – hammer, discus, javelin, shot put

Rules of track and field events:
- In all sprint races, runners must stay in their lane on the track and the first person to cross the finish line wins.
    - depending on local rules, one or two "false starts" – running before the start signal – results in disqualification
- In all jumping events, participants must take off on or before a designated "foul line" and the person with the longest jump wins.
    - "foul" jumps do not receive a score
- In all relay races, teams must pass a baton within a designated transition area and the first team to cross the finish line with the baton wins.
    - failed exchanges result in disqualification
- In all throwing events, participants must release the object within a specified area and the person with the longest throw wins.
    - releasing the object outside the designated area is a "foul" and foul throws do not receive a measurement

BASKETBALL:

- A player touching the floor on or outside the boundary line is out-of-bounds.

- The ball is out of bounds if it touches anything (a player, the floor, an object, or any person) that is on or outside the boundary line.

- An offensive player remaining in the three-second zone of the free-throw lane for more than three seconds is a violation.

- A ball firmly held by two opposing players results in a jump ball.

- A throw-in is awarded to the opposing team of the last player touching a ball that goes out-of-bounds.

SOCCER:

The following are direct free-kick offenses:

- Hand or arm contact with the ball
- Using hands to hold an opponent
- Pushing an opponent
- Striking/kicking/tripping or attempting to strike/kick/trip an opponent
- Goalie using the ball to strike an opponent
- Jumping at or charging an opponent
- Kneeing an opponent
- Any contact fouls

The following are indirect free-kick offenses:

- Same player playing the ball twice at the kickoff, on a throw-in, on a goal kick, on a free kick, or on a corner kick.
- The goalie delaying the game by holding the ball or carrying the ball more than four steps.
- Failure to notify the referee of substitutions/re-substitutions and that player then handling the ball in the penalty area.
- Any person that is not a player entering playing field without a referee's permission.
- Unsportsmanlike actions or words in reference to a referee's decision.
- Dangerously lowering the head or raising the foot too high to make a play.
- A player resuming play after being ordered off the field.
- Offsides – an offensive player must have two defenders between him and the goal when a teammate passes the ball to him or else he is offsides.
- Attempting to kick the ball when the goalkeeper has possession or interference with the goalkeeper to hinder him/her from releasing the ball.
- Illegal charging.

- Leaving the playing field without referee's permission while the ball is in play.

SOFTBALL:

- Each team plays nine players in the field (sometimes 10 for slow pitch).

- Field positions are one pitcher, one catcher, four infielders, and three outfielders (four outfielders in ten player formats).

- The four bases are 60 feet apart.

- Any ball hit outside of the first or third base line is a foul ball (i.e. runners cannot advance and the pitch counts as a strike against the batter)

- If a batter receives three strikes (i.e. failed attempts at hitting the ball) in a single at bat he/she strikes out.

- The pitcher must start with both feet on the pitcher's rubber and can only take one step forward when delivering the underhand pitch.

- A base runner is out if:
    - A. The opposition tags him with the ball before he reaches a base.
    - B. The ball reaches first base before he does.
    - C. He runs outside of the base path to avoid a tag.
    - D. A batted ball strikes him in fair territory.

- A team must maintain the same batting order throughout the game.

- Runners cannot lead off and base stealing is illegal.

- Runners may overrun first base, but can be tagged out if off any other base.

VOLLEYBALL:

The following infractions by the receiving team result in a point awarded to the serving side and an infraction by serving team results in side-out:

- Illegal serves or serving out of turn.

- Illegal returns or catching or holding the ball.

- Dribbling or a player touching the ball twice in succession.

- Contact with the net (two opposing players making contact with the net at the same time results in a replay of the point).

- Touching the ball after it has been played three times without passing over the net.

- A player's foot completely touching the floor over the centerline.

- Reaching under the net and touching a player or the ball while the ball is in play.

- The players changing positions prior to the serve.

SAMPLE OFFICIATING SITUATIONS

NOTE: Since rules change yearly, acquiring new rulebooks every year is necessary for proper officiating.

Basketball situation: Actions of the spectators interfere with the progression of the game.

Ruling: An official may call a foul on the team whose supporters are interfering with the game.

Basketball situation: A1 is attempting a field goal and B1 fouls him. A1 continues with the field goal attempt and, before releasing the ball, crashes into B2 who has a legal position on the floor. A1 successfully completes the field goal.

Ruling: The ball was immediately dead when A1 fouled B2; therefore, field goal does not count. However, since B1 fouled A1 while A1 attempted the field goal, A1 receives two free throws.

Basketball situation: The official in the frontcourt runs into a pass thrown from the backcourt by A1 and goes out-of-bounds.

Ruling: Throw-in is awarded to B. The official is part of the court.

Basketball Situation: A1 catches the ball in mid-air and lands with the right foot first and then the left foot. A1 pivots on the left foot.

Ruling: A violation has occurred because A1 can only pivot on the foot that first lands on the floor, which was the right foot.

Soccer situation: The ball is alive when a substitute enters the playing field.

Ruling: A non-player foul. Referee can either penalize at location of the next dead ball or at the place of entry (usually when the team offended is at an advantage).

Soccer situation: B1 charges A1's goalie in A1's penalty area.

Ruling: Team A is awarded a direct free kick at the spot of foul. A flagrant charge awards team A a penalty-kick at the other end of the field, and B1 is disqualified.

Soccer situation: The goalie is out of position when a back on team B heads the ball out and falls into the net. A2 gets the ball, passes it to A1, and has only the goalie to beat.

Ruling: A1 is not offside because the B back left the field during legal play.

Volleyball situation: Team A's second volley hits an obstruction directly over the net, returns to A's playing area, and team A plays it again.

Ruling: Fair play and the next play is team A's third play.

Volleyball situation: The serving team has three front line players standing close together in front of the server at the spiking line.

Ruling: Illegal alignment is called for intentional screening.

Volleyball situation: RB and CB on the receiving team are overlapping when the server strikes the serve, and the serve lands out-of-bounds.

Ruling: Serving team is awarded a point because of receiving team's illegal alignment.

Volleyball situation: LB on team B saves a spiked ball and it deflects off his/her shoulder.

Ruling: A legal hit.

Skill 5.2 Apply knowledge of developmental progressions for sports activities.

SEE ALSO Domain 5, Skill 5.1 (previous skill)

KNOWLEDGE OF ACTIVITIES FOR BODY MANAGEMENT SKILL DEVELOPMENT

Sequential development and activities for locomotor skills acquisition

Sequential Development = crawl, creep, walk, run, jump, hop, gallop, slide, leap, skip, step-hop.

- **Activities to develop walking skills** include walking slower and faster in place; walking forward, backward, and sideways with slower and faster paces in straight, curving, and zigzag pathways with various lengths of steps; pausing between steps; and changing the height of the body.

- **Activities to develop running skills** include having students pretend they are playing basketball, trying to score a touchdown, trying to catch a bus, finishing a lengthy race, or running on a hot surface.

- **Activities to develop jumping skills** include alternating jumping with feet together and feet apart, taking off and landing on the balls of the feet, clicking the heels together while airborne, and landing with a foot forward and a foot backward.

- **Activities to develop galloping skills** include having students play a game of Fox and Hound, with the lead foot representing the fox and the back foot the hound trying to catch the fox (alternate the lead foot).

- **Activities to develop sliding skills** include having students hold hands in a circle and sliding in one direction, then sliding in the other direction.

- **Activities to develop hopping skills** include having students hop all the way around a hoop and hopping in and out of a hoop reversing direction. Students can also place ropes in straight lines and hop side-to-side over the rope from one end to the other and change (reverse) the direction.

- **Activities to develop skipping skills** include having students combine walking and hopping activities leading up to skipping.

- **Activities to develop step-hopping skills** include having students practice stepping and hopping activities while clapping hands to an uneven beat.

Sequential development and activities for nonlocomotor skill acquisition

Sequential Development = stretch, bend, sit, shake, turn, rock and sway, swing, twist, dodge, and fall.

- **Activities to develop stretching** include lying on the back and stomach and stretching as far as possible; stretching as though one is reaching for a star, picking fruit off a tree, climbing a ladder, shooting a basketball, or placing an item on a high self; waking and yawning.

- **Activities to develop bending** include touching knees and toes then straightening the entire body and straightening the body halfway; bending as though picking up a coin, tying shoes, picking flowers/vegetables, and petting animals of different sizes.

- **Activities to develop sitting** include practicing sitting from standing, kneeling, and lying positions without the use of hands.

- **Activities to develop falling skills** include first collapsing in one's own space and then pretending to fall like bowling pins, raindrops, snowflakes, a rag doll, or Humpty Dumpty.

Sequential development and activities for manipulative skill acquisition

Sequential Development = striking, throwing, kicking, ball rolling, volleying, bouncing, catching, and trapping.

- **Activities to develop striking** begin with the striking of stationary objects by a participant in a stationary position. Next, the person remains still while trying to strike a moving object. Then, both the object and the participant are in motion as the participant attempts to strike the moving object.

- **Activities to develop throwing** include throwing yarn/foam balls against a wall, then at a big target, and finally at targets decreasing in size.

- **Activities to develop kicking** include alternating feet to kick balloons/beach balls, then kicking them under and over ropes. Change the type of ball as proficiency develops.

- **Activities to develop ball rolling** include rolling different size balls to a wall, then to targets decreasing in size.

- **Activities to develop volleying** include using a large balloon and, first, hitting it with both hands, then one hand (alternating hands), and then using different parts of the body. Change the object as students progress (balloon, to beach ball, to foam ball, etc.)

- **Activities to develop bouncing** include starting with large balls and, first, using both hands to bounce and then using one hand (alternate hands).

- **Activities to develop catching** include using various objects (balloons, beanbags, balls, etc.) to catch and, first, catching the object the participant has thrown him/herself, then catching objects someone else threw, and finally increasing the distance between the catcher and the thrower.

- **Activities to develop trapping** include trapping slow and fast rolling balls; trapping balls (or other objects such as beanbags) that are lightly thrown at waist, chest, and stomach levels; trapping different size balls.

Skill 5.3 Demonstrate an understanding of principles of game strategies.

APPLY APPROPRIATE STRATEGIES TO GAME AND SPORT SITUATIONS

Basketball Strategies:

Use a Zone Defense

- To prevent drive-ins for easy lay-up shots.
- When playing area is small.
- When team is in foul trouble.
- To keep an excellent rebounder near opponent's basket.
- When opponents' outside shooting is weak.
- When opponents have an advantage in height.
- When opponents have an exceptional offensive player, or when the best defenders cannot handle one-on-one defense.

Offensive Strategies Against Zone Defense

- Using quick, sharp passing to penetrate zone forcing opposing player out of assigned position.
- Overloading and mismatching.

Offensive Strategies for One-On-One Defense

- Using the "pick-and-roll" and the "give-and-go" to screen defensive players to open up offensive players for shot attempts.

- Teams may use free-lancing (spontaneous one-one-one offense), but more commonly they use "sets" of plays.

Soccer Strategies:

- **Heading** – using the head to pass, to shoot, or to clear the ball.
- **Tackling** – objective is to take possession of the ball from an opponent. Successful play requires knowledgeable utilization of space.

Badminton Strategies:

Strategies for Return of Service

- Returning serves with shots that are straight ahead.
- Returning service so that opponent must move out of his/her starting position.
- Returning long serves with an overhead clear or drop shot to near corner.
- Returning short serves with underhand clear or a net drop to near corner.

Strategies for Serving

- Serving long to the backcourt near centerline.
- Serving short when opponent is standing too deep in his/her receiving court to return the serve, or using a short serve to eliminate a smash return if opponent has a powerful smash from the backcourt.

Handball or Racquetball Strategies:

- Identifying opponent's strengths and weaknesses.
- Making opponent use less dominant hand or backhand shots if they are weaker.
- Frequently alternating fastballs and lobs to change the pace (changing the pace is particularly effective for serving).
- Maintaining position near middle of court (the well) that is close enough to play low balls and corner shots.
- Placing shots that keep opponent's position at a disadvantage to return cross-court and angle shots.

- Using high lob shots that go overhead but do not hit the back wall with enough force to rebound to drive an opponent out of position when he/she persistently plays close to the front wall.

Tennis Strategies:

- Lobbing – using a high, lob shot for defense giving the player more time to get back into position.

- Identifying opponent's weaknesses, attacking them, and recognizing and protecting one's own weaknesses.

- Outrunning and out-thinking an opponent.

- Using change of pace, lobs, spins, approaching the net, and deception at the correct time.

- Hitting cross-court (from corner to corner of the court) for maximum safety and opportunity to regain position.

- Directing the ball where the opponent is not.

Volleyball Strategies:

- Using forearm passes (bumps, digs, or passes) to play balls below the waist, to play hard driven balls, to pass the serve, and to contact balls distant from a player.

Archery strategies for correcting errors in aiming and releasing:

- Shifting position.

- Relaxing both the arms and shoulders at the moment of release.

- Reaching point of aim before releasing string.

- Pointing aim to the right or left of direct line between the archer and the target's center.

- Aiming with the left eye.

- Sighting with both eyes.

- Using the proper arrow.

Bowling for spares strategies:

- Identifying the key pin and determining where to hit it to pick up remaining pins.

- Using the three basic alignments: center position for center pins, left position for left pins, and right position for right pins.

- Rolling the spare ball in the same manner as rolled for the first ball of frame.

- Concentrating harder for spare ball because of the reduced opportunity for pin action and margin of error.

TECHNIQUES TO ENHANCE SKILL PERFORMANCE AND STRATEGY

Playing complex games requires the combination of skills, the use of skills in more complex ways, and relation to others in both offensive and defensive settings. Sequentially progressive activities allow students to acquire the psychomotor, cognitive, and affective skills necessary for participation in complex games. There are four stages of complex skill development.

Stage One concerns **controlling an object.** For striking or throwing objects, students can consistently practice sending objects to a specified location, developing control of the force that accomplishes the objective. For catching or collecting, students can practice control by securing possession of an object from any direction, level, or speed. For carrying and propelling, students can practice maintaining control of an object by moving in different directions and at different paces. Developing control begins with the completion of easily attainable objectives and progresses gradually to more difficult objectives involving movement and different directions, levels, and force.

Stage Two also concerns controlling an object, however, combining skills increases difficulty. Instructors should stress rules to constrain the execution of skills. Drills such as passing and dribbling belong in stage two.

Stage Three focuses on **offense and defense**, utilizing correct skill performance. Students should now be able to control objects; therefore, the focus shifts to obtaining and maintaining possession, as well as offensive and defensive strategies in the midst of opponents. Net activities and keep-away games help develop this stage. In addition, instructors can add more offensive and defensive players, boundaries, scorekeeping, and conduct rules. Students develop by adjusting their responses with each element introduced to the activity.

Stage Four involves **complex activity.** Students execute the complete activity and modified activities that allow participation by all students. Continuous play is important; thus, the instructor may have to modify rules or a part of the activity to keep the flow of the game constant (e.g. eliminating free throws/kicks, substituting volleyball serve with a throw, initiating play out-of-bounds).

Skill 5.4 Demonstrate knowledge of safety, etiquette, fair play, and fair competition.

SEE ALSO Domain 5, Skill 5.1

APPROPRIATE BEHAVIOR IN PHYSICAL EDUCATION ACTIVITIES

Appropriate Student Etiquette/Behaviors include: following the rules and accepting the consequences of unfair action, good sportsmanship, respecting the rights of other students, reporting own accidents and mishaps, not engaging in inappropriate behavior under peer pressure encouragement, cooperation, paying attention to instructions and demonstrations, moving to assigned places and remaining in own space, complying with directions, practicing as instructed to do so, properly using equipment, and not interfering with the practice of others.

Appropriate Content Etiquette/Behaviors include the teacher describing the performance of tasks and students engaging in the task, the teacher assisting students with task performance, and the teacher modifying and developing tasks.

Appropriate Management Etiquette/Behaviors include the teacher directing the management of equipment, students, and space prior to practicing tasks; students getting equipment and partners; the teacher requesting that students stop "fooling around."

COOPERATIVE AND COMPETITIVE GAMES

Cooperative games are a class of games that promote teamwork and social interaction. The emphasis is on activity, fitness, skill development, and cooperation, rather than competition. There are many cooperative games available to the physical education instructor that help develop various coordination skills and teamwork. Examples of cooperative games include throwing and catching, freeze tag, and parachute.

Competitive games are a class of games that emphasize score, winning, and beating an opponent. Physical education instructors should integrate competitive games into the curriculum to generate student interest and teach concepts of fair play and sportsmanship. Competitive games are most suitable for students that are more mature and possess more developed skills. All of the traditional sporting events are competitive games.

Skill 5.5 **Apply knowledge of how to promote critical-thinking, decision-making, problem solving, collaboration, communication, leadership, conflict resolution, and teamwork skills through participation in sports and games.**

SEE ALSO Domain 4, Skill 2.1 and Domain 1, Skill 6.1

Physical activities usually involve the utilization of motor skills in harmony with physical, emotional, psychological, psychomotor, and mental skills. Sports activities are a combination of movements and rules that often lead to healthy physical development in a child. In turn, the child is more likely to become stronger and fitter, making various other tasks in life easier. These types of activities lead to other qualities such as sportsmanship, mutual respect, and cooperation. Children also develop intellectually during the course of a play or motor skills development. For example, rock climbing and other adventure activities require mental forethought and planning. Participation in such activities promotes the development of critical-thinking, problem solving, and decision making skills.

Further, regard for others and learning to work cooperatively with peers are necessary skills for success in team sports. In addition, participation in sports provides experience in dealing with interpersonal conflict (e.g. between teammates or competitors) and helps develop leadership skills. Children also develop respect for rules, acquire motor skills, and gain the ability to enjoy physical activity early in life, or as soon as they engage in organized or free play.

CRITICAL-THINKING

Physical education instructors can foster critical-thinking and evaluative skills in the context of physical education and health-related activities by making children active partners in the entire learning and training process. If instructors provide students with an understanding of the mechanisms (e.g. cardiorespiratory, muscular, circulatory) underlying their training (in addition to the knowledge they are given about specific training exercises), students can get more involved and think more critically about their training routines and how they could adapt them to better suit their needs.

Instructors should encourage students to employ self-assessment and self-monitoring techniques and skills. For example, they could keep a journal tracking their personal achievements – cardiorespiratory (measured in resting heart-rate, active heart-rate, intensity, and duration of exercise), muscular development (measured by their ability to perform callisthenic exercises).

Instructors should also encourage students to explore and increase their understanding (with educator assistance) of the way that the underlying bodily systems work in relation to other disciplines. For example, students can learn about the chemistry involved in the gas and energy exchanges happening between the cardiorespiratory and circulatory system, they can learn about the biology of the digestive system and the effects of different types of nutrition on the body, and they can learn about the physics involved in energy expenditure by the muscular system.

LEADERSHIP AND TEAMWORK

By participating in physical activities, students develop various aspects of the self that are easily applicable to other settings (e.g., the workplace). Communication is one skill that improves enormously through participation in sports and games. Students will come to understand that skillful communication can contribute to a better all-around outcome, whether it be winning the game or successfully completing a team project. They will see that effective communication helps to develop and maintain healthy personal relationships, organize and convey information, and reduce or avoid conflict.

Physical activities also teach students how to set personal goals. At first, one can set a physical goal such as running one mile in eight minutes. After accomplishing that specific feat, the student will feel capable and will be more willing to set greater goals in various fields within his life.

Finally, physical activities teach perseverance, the importance of following directions, leadership, and teamwork. Recovering from competitive loses and withstanding personal and team setbacks help develop perseverance. All games and sports have rules that participants must follow in order to participate. Leadership and teamwork are both integral parts of team sports. In the team sport setting, participants learn how to work together and lead others to achieve a common goal. These skills are invaluable in real life and the workplace.

Teaching methods that facilitate cognitive learning include:

1. **Problem Solving** - The instructor presents the initial task and students come to an acceptable solution in unique and divergent ways,

2. **Conceptual Theory** - The instructor's focus is on acquisition of knowledge,

3. **Guided Inquiry** - careful stages of instructions strategically guide students through a sequence of experiences, helping them reach their goals.

Skill 5.6 **Demonstrate knowledge of the application of motor learning principles (e.g. transfer, game-like conditions) in instruction for sports and games.**

The development of motor skills in children is a sequential process. We can classify motor skill competency into stages of development by observing children practicing physical skills. The sequence of development begins with simple reflexes and progresses to the learning of postural elements, locomotor skills, and, finally, fine motor skills. The stages of development consider both innate and learned behaviors.

STAGES OF MOTOR LEARNING

Stage 1 – Children progress from simple reflexes to basic movements such as sitting, crawling, creeping, standing, and walking.

Stage 2 – Children learn more complex motor patterns including running, climbing, jumping, balancing, catching, and throwing.

Stage 3 – During late childhood, children learn more specific movement skills. In addition, the basic motor patterns learned in stage 2 become more fluid and automatic.

Stage 4 – During adolescence, children continue to develop general and specific motor skills and master specialized movements. At this point, factors including practice, motivation, and talent begin to affect the level of further development.

COMBINING AND INTEGRATING SKILLS

Locomotor skills are movements that take an individual from one place to another. Walking and running are the simplest examples of locomotor skills. Skipping, jumping, leaping, hopping, and sliding are other locomotor skills that physical educators teach their students.

Trainers adopt various strategies to incorporate the locomotor, nonlocomotor, and object control skills into their workout schedule. These skills are very effective in making students stronger and healthier.

Initially, instructors try to combine those locomotor skills into their training schedule in an easy-to-follow manner. Combining running and sliding or running and jumping will play a huge part in making children understand the fundamentals of locomotor skills.

Once they become familiar with the procedure, physical educators can show students how to balance and transfer weight through the use various locomotor skills. However, the teacher should demonstrate how to control locomotor movements at proper speeds and forces. Shot put, tumbling, and give-and-go are some examples of how to teach students the nuances of locomotor skills.

We can apply the same strategies to nonlocomotor skill instruction. First, the students should learn the basics of every skill from simple nonlocomotive movements such as 360-degree turns and lifting weights, to complex movements like tug-of-war and scissors kicks. It is important for the instructor to maintain a smooth transition. This makes comprehension as unproblematic as possible. Locomotor and nonlocomotor skills make children agile and physically fit. It is the job of a physical educator to make learning and practicing the skills more enjoyable and entertaining.

APPLICATION TO SPORTS AND GAMES

All sports require the application of motor skills in complex forms. For example, the motor skills required to play tennis include running, jumping, striking, and volleying. In addition, tennis players must combine these skills. For example, a player often has to strike the ball while running or jumping. To play any sport at a high level, athletes must master many motor skills and develop the ability to combine those skills to master sport-specific movements.

COMPETENCY 6.0   OUTDOOR EDUCATION

Skill 6.1   Demonstrate knowledge of techniques, skills, and safety issues for outdoor education activities.

OUTDOOR EDUCATION

Techniques and skills include:

Walking and Hiking – Instructors can take students on walking/hiking trips through nature reserves and national parks. Such trips can incorporate team-building activities and nature education.

Sail Training – Students taught to sail should display competence in the maintenance and piloting of a boat, including cooperative activities necessary to a successful sailing endeavor (e.g. working together to get the boat into and out of the water, paddling in rhythm, turning the boat, etc.). Prior to the start of sail training, students should understand all safety procedures and acceptable forms of behavior on a boat (e.g. only standing when necessary, no pushing, following instructions, wearing a life jacket, etc.). Students must also demonstrate swimming competence (i.e. ability to tread water, swim a distance continuously, and put on a life jacket while in the water).

Bicycling – In bicycling classes, students should learn proper bicycling form and how to gauge which gear is most appropriate for their current speed and level of inclination. Students should also become familiar with the proper way to maintain and care for their bicycles.

Bicycling strategy is similar to track events – learning to gauge the appropriate levels of energy expenditure relative to the length of the track and the fitness of the cyclist.

Safety practices while bicycling include seriousness in practice (no horseplay, which can result in injury) and attentiveness to the track so that students can avoid potentially dangerous bumps or cracks. Instructors should remind students not to race with each other, but rather to focus on their own physical activity.

Equipment required for bicycling with students includes proper gear (which includes clothing without loose appendages that can catch in bicycle gears), water for longer trips, and, of course, the bicycles themselves.

Cross-country skiing – Students in cross-country skiing classes will learn the proper form for cross-country skiing (e.g. herringbone, diagonal stride, double pole) and will greatly improve their fitness (as cross-country skiing is a very taxing activity on a very wide range of muscle groups).

Like most endurance activities, cross-country skiing strategy involves regulating the levels of energy expenditure relative to the length of the course and the fitness level of the athlete.

Safety practices in cross-country skiing include ensuring the availability of first aid and instructor attentiveness to the students (as it is easier to 'lose track' of a student who is having trouble). Instructors should also instruct students not to wander away from the group – a good solution is the implementation of a buddy system.

Equipment required for cross-country skiing trips includes appropriate dress (make sure students dress warmly), cross-country skis, and poles.

Canoeing – Students in canoeing classes will learn the various forms of paddling strokes, how to manage their weight, and how to work as a team to maneuver a canoe properly.

Strategies for effective canoeing include the clear delineation of members of a rowing team and the role that each individual serves. The 'captain' coordinates the efforts of the rowers on the canoe and should become familiar with the course and destination.

Safety practices for canoeing call for the instructor to ensure that the students are all able to swim and equipped with proper flotation equipment (e.g. lifejackets). First aid should be available and the instructor should see to it that he remains close enough to students in different canoes to be able to hear them and reach them if needed.

Equipment required for canoeing classes includes canoes, canoeing paddles, and proper flotation equipment. Instructors should advise students to have a change of clothes available in the event that they get wet.

Orienteering – Skills that students will acquire during orienteering activities include the ability to read a map, critical thinking stemming from practice identifying locations, navigation ability, and strategic thinking for selection of efficient movement patterns between several points.

Strategies for orienteering include ascertaining early the destination points and mapping an efficient course to pass through all of them.

Safety practices include ensuring the availability and accessibility of first aid, properly instructing the students in emergency procedures (e.g. blow the whistle and remain where you are), and selecting an area small enough so the instructor can hear the whistle from any position.

Equipment required for orienteering with students includes proper outdoor clothing and a whistle for use in emergency situations. Students will also need a map and possibly a compass.

Fishing – Students studying fishing will learn the correct technique for casting a line and will learn to identify spots where fish are most likely to congregate. Fishing also teaches patience to students.

Strategies for effective fishing with groups of students include deploying students in such a way that one will not interfere with another's fishing activities. Students should also learn about the habits of the fish that they are after, to allow them to tailor their approaches accordingly.

Safety practices for fishing call for instructors to remind students that their equipment does not consist of toys and they should not play with it. Students should definitely handle fishing rods and hooks carefully around other students.

Equipment required for fishing includes fishing rods, hooks, bait, gear (e.g. boots), and a bucket or other receptacle for the fish.

Inline skating – Skills that students in inline skating class will acquire include skating techniques (e.g. braking and stopping, skating backwards, skating downhill) and improved balance. Students should also learn to care for their skating equipment.

Strategies in inline skating focus on maintaining proper form during the activity.

Safety practices in inline skating include requiring students to wear appropriate protective gear and ensuring that first aid is available. Instructors should instruct students not to attempt stunts, especially without supervision.

Equipment required for inline skating includes skates and appropriate protective gear (e.g. helmets, kneepads, elbow pads).

Rope Challenge Courses – A good activity for team-building purposes. Challenges include personal physical challenges (climbing various structures), or group activities (e.g. requiring students to work together to coordinate the crossing of a course). Safety requirements include helmets, harnesses, spotters, trained supervisors, and strict adherence to all safety procedures and educator instructions.

Rock climbing – Students studying rock climbing will gain proficiency in climbing techniques (including body positioning and learning to find proper toeholds and handholds in the rock face) belaying, and managing the climbing and harness equipment.

Strategies in rock climbing require the climber to remain aware not only of the current 'next step' of the climbing process, but to also remain aware of the entire rock face, and to plan on a course that she can follow through to completion (so as to prevent climbing to a dead-end area).

Safety practices include explaining all safety practices so students understand, ensuring that students wear all safety gear (protective gear and harnesses) properly, and that all students have spotters monitoring their activities.

Equipment required for rock climbing activities includes proper attire, suitable footwear, protective equipment, and harnessing equipment.

Alpine skiing (downhill skiing) – The skills that students of alpine skiing will gain center on learning to control the direction and speed of their descent; novices will begin by learning the "snow plough" technique to turn, and will learn to point their skis inward to stop. More advanced technique will center on "carving", which allows the skis to turn without skidding or slowing down.

Alpine skiing strategy calls for awareness of the practitioner's current level of skill and avoiding over-reaching (i.e. attempting courses that are too advanced and thus dangerous). Instructors should teach students to be aware of the course ahead of them, allowing them to better plan their movements.

Safety practices in alpine skiing include proper inspection of the equipment to ensure that everything is in order and instructing the students in appropriate safety procedures. Most importantly, instructors should not allow students to attempt courses that are beyond their current skill levels.

Equipment required for alpine skiing includes appropriate dress that is adequately warm (hats, gloves, and goggles), skis, and poles.

Camping – Camping imparts a wide range of skills, from tent pitching to fire building to outdoor cooking.

Successful camping strategy focuses on planning and preparing the students (mentally, physically, and in terms of their equipment) for the camping experience.

Safety practices for camping include packing a first aid kit and emergency supplies (e.g. a map, compass, whistle), checking the weather before departure, avoiding areas of natural hazards, and putting out fires appropriately. Instructors should teach students to identify and avoid poisonous plants.

Camping equipment includes a tent, lean-to, or other shelter device, a sleeping bag and sleeping pad (or air mattress), a portable stove (where campfires are impractical or not allowed), a lantern or flashlight, a hatchet, axe or saw, ropes, and tarps.

SAFETY

Related safety education should emphasize the importance of planning and research. Students should consider in advance what the potential dangers of an activity might be and to prepare plans accordingly (students and instructors should also examine weather forecasts). Of course, educator supervision is required. First-aid equipment and properly trained educators must be present for outdoor education activities. Students should use proper safety gear when appropriate (e.g. helmets, harnesses, etc.). Parental consent is generally required for outdoor education activities.

Skill 6.2 Identify long-term psychological, physiological, and lifestyle benefits of participation in outdoor education activities.

We can divide the benefits of lifelong participation in aesthetic activities, personal performance activities, and outdoor and adventure activities into physical and psychological dimensions (which, of course, have a reciprocal relationship).

On a physical level, personal performance activities contribute to the health and physical fitness of the participating individual. Physical benefits include increased cardiorespiratory fitness, improved circulation, and an increase in muscle tone.

On a psychological level, these activities contribute to the individual's sense of accomplishment and ability to deal with adversity (which is a part of any personal performance activity). When participants become more involved in their personal performance activity of choice, it can contribute to their sense of positive personal identity.

Strategies for promoting enjoyment and participation in personal performance activities throughout life are centered on matching the right activity to the interests, lifestyle, availability, and physical capabilities of the individual. Individuals must enjoy personal performance activities to devote their time on a regular basis, and the time required has to fit into the lifestyle and schedule of the person in question. It is also important to consider the physical condition of the individual. The activity in question must be compatible with their capabilities and they should work their way into the activity gradually.

Physiological benefits of physical activity include:

    SEE Domain 3, Skill 4.2

Psychological benefits of physical activity include:

- relief of stress

- improved mental health via better physical health

- reduced mental tension (relieves depression, improves sleeping patterns)
- better resistance to fatigue
- better quality of life
- more enjoyment of leisure
- better capability to handle some stressors
- opportunity for successful experiences
- better self-concept
- better ability to recognize and accept limitations
- improved appearance and sense of well-being
- better ability to meet challenges
- better sense of accomplishments

Sociological benefits of physical activity include:

- the opportunity to spend time with family and friends and make new friends
- the opportunity to be part of a team
- the opportunity to participate in competitive experiences
- the opportunity to experience the thrill of victory

TEACHER CERTIFICATION STUDY GUIDE

COMPETENCY 7.0   NON-TRADITIONAL AND COOPERATIVE ACTIVITIES

Skill 7.1   Identify examples of nontraditional, global, and cooperative games and activities (e.g. Pickle ball, bocce ball, team juggling).

Examples of nontraditional, global and cooperative games and activities include:

- **Pickle-Ball** – When playing Pickle-Ball the server must hit the serve underhand and each team must play the first shot off the bounce. After the ball bounces once on each side, both teams can either volley the ball in the air or play it off the bounce. No volleying is permitted within the seven foot non-volley zone. The first team to win eleven points (with a two point margin) is the winner. Players lose points by hitting the ball out of bounds, hitting the net, volleying the ball from the non-volley zone, or volleying the ball before it has bounced on both sides of the net.

- **Bocce ball** – Requires a flat, level playing surface (packed dirt, gravel or grass is ideal). Students divide into two teams of one, two, or four players each. Each team gets four balls, divided equally among the players. A player from the starting team stands behind the foul line (10 feet from the throwing end of the court) and throws the small ball ("pallina") toward the opposite end of the playing surface. The player then throws one of the larger balls ("boccia"), trying to get it as close to the pallina as possible without touching it. Players from the opposing team take turns throwing their balls until one of the balls stops closer to the pallina than the starting player's ball. If they fail to do so, the starting team tries to outdo its first attempt. Teams continue to take turns in this manner until they have thrown all of the balls. The team with closest ball gets a point. This game emphasizes throwing skills (coordination, gross and fine motor skills).

- **Unicycling** – Good activity for training coordination, gross motor skills, and balance. Safety considerations include practicing on a padded surface if possible (gym mats or grass), and wearing safety gear (helmets, elbow and knee pads). As with most activities, horseplay is prohibited and nobody should interfere with a practicing unicyclist – the practice area should be kept free of obstruction and the unicyclist has the "right-of-way." Unicyclists should have a spotter at all times.

- **Juggling and Team Juggling** – Develops psychomotor skills (timing, hand-eye coordination, throwing and catching – both gross and fine motor skills); cognitive skills (recognizing rise and fall patterns of the juggled objects, comprehending cyclic rhythm); affective skills (goal setting, tracking improvement, perseverance and delay of gratification); and teamwork in the case of Team Juggling.

Skill 7.2 **Apply knowledge of how to promote critical-thinking, decision making, problem solving, collaboration, cooperation, leadership, and communication through participation in nontraditional and cooperative activities.**

SEE ALSO Domain 4, Skill 2.1; Domain 1, Skill 6.1; and Domain 5, Skill 5.5

Nontraditional and cooperative activities, like all physical activities, promote personal development. For example, bocce involves critical-thinking, planning, and decision making. Team juggling requires a great amount of cooperation, communication, collaboration, and leadership.

TEACHER CERTIFICATION STUDY GUIDE

COMPETENCY 8.0 COMBATIVE ACTIVITIES

Skill 8.1 Demonstrate knowledge of one or more basic combative activities (e.g. fencing, wrestling, self-defense) and related safety issues.

COMBATIVE ACTIVITIES

Basic knowledge of wrestling includes knowledge of basic techniques (familiarity with pins, reversals, and positioning transitions), drills for practicing technique (e.g. students can drill shooting and sprawling, drill reversals from pinned positions, etc.), and terminology (naming the techniques, e.g. shoot, sprawl, half nelson, full nelson, etc.).

Basic knowledge of self-defense includes familiarity with basic striking techniques (punches and kicks), blocks and evasions, knowledge of major vital points on the body (eyes, nose, ears, jaw, throat, solar plexus, groin, knees, instep), knowledge of basic escape techniques (from chokes, grabs and bear-hugs) and some situational training (to prevent 'freezing' in a real-life encounter). Martial arts (e.g. judo, karate) are common forms of self-defense that physical education instructors can teach to students.

In-class focus should be placed on strategies for conflict recognition (based on developing an understanding of threat factors, like individuals in a hostile frame of mind), avoidance (physically avoiding potentially dangerous situations), and diffusion (overview of the psychology of confrontations, evaluation of the motivations behind a hostile encounter, understanding of the way body language and eye contact can impact the situation).

Related safety issues include stressing the potential harm that can result from the techniques being practiced (stressing specific damage potential to musculoskeletal systems), emphasizing students' responsibility for the well-being of their training partners, maintaining discipline throughout the class (ensuring students remain focused on their training activities and alert to the educator's instructions), and ensuring that students are aware and observant of the limits to force that they may apply (no-striking zones, like above the neck and below the belt; limits on striking force, like semi-contact or no-contact sparring; familiarity with the concept of a tap-out indicating submission). Students should perform warm-up, cool-down, and stretching as with any physical training program.

Fencing – Fencing practice will impart to students proficiency in proper fencing form, techniques (for example parries and strikes), and an awareness of open target areas on their opponents. Students will also acquire efficient movement skills.

Fencing strategy focuses on minimizing the number and size of vulnerable target areas on the body, while maneuvering (with the feet, body, and foil) to maximize the vulnerability of opponent target areas in order to score a point.
Safety practices include proper attention to full protective gear, proper form, and careful monitoring of students in practice. Instructors should remind students frequently that they should not take frustrations out on training partners.

Equipment required for fencing practice includes the full gamut of protective gear (suit and helmet), appropriate footwear, and, of course, the fencing foil or saber. Higher technology suits that record points are also available, but are not required.

TEACHER CERTIFICATION STUDY GUIDE

COMPETENCY 9.0 FITNESS ACTIVITIES

Skill 9.1 Demonstrate an understanding of fitness activities such as aerobic conditioning, resistance and weight training, and stretching that increase cardiovascular efficiency, muscular strength and endurance, and flexibility.

FITNESS PRINCIPLES

1. Cardio-respiratory Fitness:

Overloading for cardio-respiratory fitness:

- **Frequency** = minimum of 3 days/week
- **Intensity** = exercising in target heart-rate zone
- **Time** = minimum of 15 minutes rate

Progression for cardiovascular fitness:

- begin at a frequency of 3 days/week and work up to no more than 6 days/week
- begin at an intensity near THR threshold and work up to 80% of THR
- begin at 15 minutes and work up to 60 minutes

Specificity for cardiovascular fitness:

- To develop cardiovascular fitness, you must perform aerobic (with oxygen) activities for at least fifteen minutes without developing an oxygen debt. Aerobic activities include, but are not limited to brisk walking, jogging, bicycling, and swimming.

2. Muscle Strength:

Overloading for muscle strength:

- **Frequency** = every other day
- **Intensity** = 60% to 90% of assessed muscle strength
- **Time** = 3 sets of 3 - 8 reps (high resistance with a low number of repetitions)

PHYSICAL EDUCATION

Progression for muscle strength:

- begin 3 days/week and work up to every other day
- begin near 60% of determined muscle strength and work up to no more than 90% of muscle strength
- begin with 1 set with 3 reps and work up to 3 sets with 8 reps

Specificity for muscle strength:

- to increase muscle strength for a specific part(s) of the body, you must target that/those part(s) of the body

3. Muscle endurance:

Overloading for muscle endurance:

- **Frequency** = every other day
- **Intensity** = 30% to 60% of assessed muscle strength
- **Time** = 3 sets of 12 - 20 reps (low resistance with a high number of repetitions)

Progression for muscle endurance:

- begin 3 days/week and work up to every other day
- begin at 20% to 30% of muscle strength and work up to no more than 60% of muscle strength
- begin with 1 set with 12 reps and work up to 3 sets with 20 reps

Specificity for muscle endurance:

- same as muscle strength

4. Flexibility:

Overloading for flexibility:

- **Frequency**: 3 to 7 days/week
- **Intensity**: stretch muscle beyond its normal length
- **Time**: 3 sets of 3 reps holding stretch 15 to 60 seconds

Progression for flexibility:

- begin 3 days/week and work up to every day

- begin stretching with slow movement as far as possible without pain, holding at the end of the range of motion (ROM) and work up to stretching no more than 10% beyond the normal ROM

- begin with 1 set with 1 rep, holding stretches 15 seconds, and work up to 3 sets with 3 reps, holding stretches for 60 seconds

Specificity for flexibility:

- ROM is joint specific

5. Body composition:

Overloading to improve body composition:

- **Frequency**: daily aerobic exercise

- **Intensity**: low

- **Time**: approximately one hour

Progression to improve body composition:

- begin daily

- begin a low aerobic intensity and work up to a longer duration (see cardio-respiratory progression)

- begin low-intensity aerobic exercise for 30 minutes and work up to 60 minutes

Specificity to improve body composition:

increase aerobic exercise and decrease caloric intake
The practice of progressive resistance is an integral part of individual physical development and training programs. As with all other forms of exercise, participants should always follow certain principles and safety practices when performing progressive-resistance exercises.

As a safety precaution, instructors should formulate a health or medical questionnaire for students to complete. This can serve as a screening tool before enrolling a student into a progressive-resistance program. When beginning a weight-training program, novices should not attempt to lift too much weight.

Other principles and guidelines that participants should follow include:
- Warm-up prior to performing resistance exercises
- Gradually increase the number of repetitions for each exercise
- Exercise at least two days and receive adequate rest to achieve proper muscle development
- Perform exercises in a controlled manner
- Perform each exercise through a functional range of motion
- Work in conjunction with instructors who provide adequate feedback and guidance

Apart from the aforementioned principles, other basic principles of progressive resistance training include careful monitoring of types of lifts, intensity, volume, and variety of lifts, and taking adequate rest for recovery.

The equipment used for progressive resistance training or exercise include fit strips, dumbbells or barbells, and weight machines. Circuit training involves engaging in a variety of fitness exercises to achieve a full-body workout.

Partner-Resistance Exercises

For partner-resistance exercises, instructors should instruct students to pair-up with classmates of comparable size and strength, to ensure that the activity is productive and both training partners can apply sufficient resistance. Safety procedures for partner-resistance activities include properly demonstrating the required activity and clarifying to students that excessive competitiveness (to the extent of risking damage to another student) is not acceptable. In partner-resistance activities, the paired students serve as spotters for each other.

Weight Training

Weight training involves the use of weights (e.g. barbells or dumbbells) to create resistance to physical motion of body parts. In the case of weight training, properly demonstrating the required activity is fundamental, as the physical weights can present a heightened possibility for injuries. Instructors should instruct students to err on the side of less weight when unsure how much to use. A spotter should monitor students at all times. For students to make educated decisions about weight training (always under supervision), they must understand the risks and benefits of weight training for personal muscular strength and endurance development.

Circuit Training

Athletes use circuit training to increase the efficiency and intensity of a training routine by alternating exercises that target different muscle groups instead of alternating exercises with rest-periods. This form of workout promotes muscular endurance development, but is more taxing on the students. Only those students who already exercising regularly and have proven their ability to remain disciplined and follow directions should attempt circuit training.

Proper Technique

Instructors should stress proper exercise technique at all times, especially with beginners to prevent development of bad habits. Whether it is weightlifting, running, or stretching, participants should not force any body part beyond the normal range of motion. Pain is a good indicator of overextension. Living by the phrase, "No pain, no gain", is potentially dangerous. Participants should use slow and controlled movements. In addition, participants must engage in a proper warm-up and cool-down before and after exercise. When lifting weights, lifters should always have a partner. A spotter can help correct the lifter's technique and help lift the weight to safety if the lifter is unable to do so. A partner can also offer encouragement and motivation. Flexibility is an often overlooked, yet important, part of exercise that can play a key role in injury prevention. Participants should perform stretching exercises after each workout session.

RESISTANCE TRAINING – SAFETY AND EFFECTIVENESS

Possessing the strength and ability to overcome any resistance in one single effort or in repeated efforts over a period of time is muscular strength and endurance. It represents the ability to complete a heavy task in a single effort. Muscular strength and endurance not only helps in keeping body ailments in check, but also in enabling better performance in any sporting event.

Most fitness experts regard calisthenics as the best form of exercises in order to increase muscular development and strength. Although calisthenics are good beginning exercises, later on participants should complement them with progressive resistance training so that there will be an increase in bone mass and connective tissue strength. Such a combination would also help in minimizing any damages or injuries that are apt to occur at the beginning or initial training stages.

Besides calisthenics and progressive resistance training, aerobics can also help in maintaining muscular strength and endurance.

Muscular strength is the maximum amount of force that one can generate in an isolated movement. Muscular endurance is the ability of the muscles to perform a submaximal task repeatedly or to maintain a submaximal muscle contraction for extended periods of time. Body-support activities (e.g. push-ups and sit-ups) and callisthenic activities (e.g. rope jumping) are good exercises for young students or beginners of all ages. Such exercises use multiple muscle groups and have minimal risk of injury. At more advanced levels of development and for those students interested in developing higher levels of strength and muscle mass, weight lifting is the optimal activity.

To improve muscular strength and endurance a student can:

- Train with free weights
- Perform exercised that use an individual's body weight for resistance (e.g., push-ups, sit-ups, dips, etc.)
- Do strength training exercises two times per week that incorporate all major muscle groups

EXERCISES THAT BENEFIT THE MAJOR MUSCLE GROUPS OF THE BODY

Some of the major muscle groups of the body important to physical fitness are the traps, delts, pecs, lats, obliques, abs, biceps, quadriceps, hamstrings, adductors, triceps, biceps, and gluts.

Dumbbell Shoulder Shrug
(Trapezius)

Seated Bent-Over Rear Deltoid Raise
(Rear Deltoids)

Seated Side Lateral Raise
(Front and Outer Deltoids)

Lying Low-Pulley One-Arm Chest
(Lateral Pectorals)

Flat Dumbbell Press
(Pectorals)

Medium-Grip Front-to-Rear Lat Pull Down
(Lats)

Straight-Arm Close-Grip Lat Pull Down
(Lats)

Dumbbell Side Bend
(Obliques)

Seated Barbell Twist
(Obliques)

Leg Pull-In
(Lower Abdominals)

Jackknife Sit-Up
(Upper and Lower Abdominals)

Standing Alternated Dumbbell Curl
(Biceps)

Standing Medium-Grip Barbell Curl
(Biceps)

Standing Close-Grip Easy-Curl-Bar Triceps Curl
(Triceps)

Standing Bent-Over One-Arm-Dumbbell Triceps Extension
(Triceps)

Flat-Footed Medium-Stance Barbell Half-Squat
(Thighs)

Freehand Front Lunge
(Thighs and Hamstrings)

Thigh Curl on Leg Extension Machine
(Hamstrings)

One-at-a-Time Thigh Curl on Leg Extension Machine
(Hamstings)

TEACHER CERTIFICATION STUDY GUIDE

Hip Abduction
(Hips)

Hip Adduction
(Inner Thigh)

Standing Toe Raise on Wall Calf Machine
(Main Calf Muscles)

Standing Barbell Toe Raise
(Main Calf Muscles)

Hip Extension
(Hips and Thighs)

Hip Flexion
(Hip Flexors)

FLEXIBILITY – ACTIVITIES

Flexibility, a form of physical training, encompasses a wide range of activities. With a range of advantages for children, youths, and especially older people (i.e., those with joint problems), flexibility has become an important part of every physical training program.

While starting any exercise program, the best way to begin is by stretching or flexing muscles as a warm up. This will allow the body to adapt to exercise. Flexibility activities are necessary for any physical training or exercising program as they help prevent against injuries.

Activities that can improve flexibility include stretching, bending, doing yoga, dancing, martial arts, and even other muscle work that is gentle and not strenuous at all. The different classifications of stretching and flexibility exercises include proprioceptive neuromuscular facilitation (PNF), static, dynamic, and partner resistance.

Static and dynamic stretching are the two most traditional classifications of flexibility training. Static stretching involves holding a position. In other words, the participant stretches to the farthest point possible and holds for several seconds. Dynamic stretching, on the other hand, involves slow, steady movements through a range of motion. Examples of dynamic stretches include arm and leg swings. Both static and dynamic stretching is suitable to individuals of all developmental levels. Static stretching is effective for improving range of flexibility. A warm up is necessary prior to static stretching to reduce the risk of injury. Dynamic stretching is an excellent warm up in itself because it involves slow, gradual movements.

Proprioceptive neuromuscular facilitation (PNF) is a more advanced form of flexibility training that combines traditional stretching with muscle contraction. Particularly effective for rehabilitation, PNF can also target specific muscle groups and increase muscular strength. PNF is best suited for individuals training at higher levels of fitness. PNF is not suitable for children or any persons whose bones are still growing.

Finally, in partner resistance stretching a partner applies resistance to a specific body part to stretch the targeted muscle actively. This is a more advanced technique that is a key component of PNF. Partner resistance stretching is best suited for more advanced athletes and caution is necessary to avoid injury. Because the partner cannot feel the stretch, he or she must communicate with the participant to prevent overextension.

FLEXIBILITY – SAFETY AND EFFECTIVENESS

Flexibility training is perhaps the most undervalued component of conditioning. Dynamic flexibility is the ability to perform dynamic movements within the full range of motion of the specified joint. Static active flexibility refers to the ability to stretch an antagonist muscle using only the tension in the antagonist muscle. Static-passive flexibility is the ability to hold a stretch using body weight or some other external force.

Dynamic stretching is generally very safe and very effective for warming up muscle groups and moderately improving flexibility. When performing dynamic stretches, participants must be careful to avoid sudden, jerky movements.

Static stretching is also safe, if the participant warms up the muscles prior to stretching. Because cold muscles are less elastic, static stretching without adequate warm up can lead to injury. Static stretching is very effective in increasing muscle flexibility.

Isometric, PNF, and ballistic stretching are more advanced techniques that require extreme caution and supervision. Most physical trainers believe ballistic stretching, bouncing into stretches, is ineffective and dangerous. Most trainers do not recommend ballistic stretching. PNF and isometric stretching are effective in certain situations such as rehabilitation and advanced training, but require close supervision.

FLEXIBILITY TRAINING – SAFETY

Safety and proper form are important considerations when engaging in flexibility exercises. The following is a list of rules that participants should follow when performing stretches:

- Always warm up before stretching: perform light to moderate cardiovascular activity prior to stretching to increase muscle elasticity – stretching while "cold" can cause injury because the muscles are tight and less elastic

- Stop if you feel pain: stretching should not cause acute pain, mild discomfort or a mild pulling sensation is acceptable

- Move into each stretch slowly and steadily – don't bounce

- Avoid "locking" joints by completely straightening them during stretches – always allow a small amount of bend when stretching

- Relax the shoulders, hands, and feet while stretching

- Maintain proper posture

PRINCIPLES AND ACTIVITIES FOR DEVELOPING AEROBIC ENDURANCE

The term aerobic refers to conditioning or exercise that requires the use of oxygen to derive energy. Aerobic conditioning is essential for fat loss, energy production, and effective functioning of the cardiovascular system. Aerobic exercise is difficult to perform for many people and participants must follow certain principles and activities in order to develop aerobic endurance.

Slow twitch muscle tissue, fueled by oxygen, powers aerobic activities. For the body to sustain aerobic activity for an extended period of time, the heart must pump oxygen-rich blood to the muscles of the body. When the heart tires due to insufficient cardiorespiratory fitness, the quantities of oxygen delivered to the muscles decreases to levels that cannot sustain the activity.

Other physiological processes involved in aerobic endurance include the respiratory system (which must take sufficient air into the body and efficiently supply oxygen to the blood), the blood itself (which must efficiently carry oxygen), the circulatory system (that takes blood to the muscles and then returns it to the heart), and the muscles themselves (which must efficiently extract oxygen from the blood).

Tips that aid in developing and building aerobic endurance include working out for extended periods at the target heart rate, slowly increasing aerobic exercises, exercising for three or four times per week, and taking adequate rest to help the body recover.

Exercising in the target heart rate zone for 30-45 minute periods is the most important principle in the development of aerobic endurance. Submaximal intensity activities, such as walking and slow jogging, are effective aerobic activities that improve aerobic endurance without unnecessary strain on the body.

Aerobics are a fundamental component of every physical education or training program. Aerobic activities are necessary for all because they are central to weight reduction, cardiovascular fitness, muscular strength development, and performance in all sports events.

Appropriate aerobic activities for various developmental levels vary from low and moderate intensity exercises to high intensity ones. Low and moderate intensity activities include doing household work, walking, playing with children, and working on the lawn. High-intensity aerobic activities include jogging, cycling, participating in sports like ice or roller-skating, downhill skiing, and swimming. Treadmills and other equipment help create strenuous aerobic exercises.

Instructors and students must take care while undertaking such high-intensity aerobic exercises, because they can be highly strenuous and taxing on muscles, especially during the initial stages. At this beginning stage, the exercise intensity must be low. With passage of time and development towards higher stages, the student can increase the level and intensity of aerobic exercises.

Whether the goal is to develop the body's ability to undergo high levels of muscular activity or just to remain fit, there are aerobic activities suited to every developmental stage and for every person.

CARDIOVASCULAR ACTIVITIES

Walking is a good generic cardiorespiratory activity for promoting basic fitness. Instructors can incorporate it into a variety of class settings (not only physical education instructors – for example, a Biology class might include a field trip to a natural setting that would involve a great deal of walking). Walking is appropriate for practically all age groups, but can only serve as noteworthy exercise for students who lead a fairly sedentary lifestyle (athletic students who train regularly or participate in some sport will not benefit greatly from walking).

Jogging or **Running** is a classic cardiorespiratory activity in which instructors can adjust the difficulty level by modifying the running speed or the incline of the track. It is important to stress proper footwear and gradual increase of intensity so as to prevent overuse injuries (e.g. stress fractures or shin splints).

Bicycling is another good cardiorespiratory activity that is appropriate for most age groups. Obviously, knowing how to ride a bicycle is a prerequisite, and it is important to follow safety procedures (e.g. ensuring that students wear helmets). An additional benefit of bicycle riding is that it places less strain on the knee joints than walking or running.

Swimming is an excellent cardiorespiratory activity that has the added benefit of working more of the body's muscles, more evenly than most other exercises, without excessive resistance to any one part of the body that could result in an overuse injury. To use swimming as an educational cardiorespiratory activity, there must be qualified lifeguards present, and all students must have passed basic tests of swimming ability.

There are many alternatives for cardiorespiratory activities, like **inline skating** and **cross-country skiing**. More importantly, instructors should modify the above exercises to match the developmental needs of the students – for example, younger students should receive most of their exercise in the form of games. An instructor could incorporate running in the form of a game of tag, soccer, or a relay race.

DOMAIN 6. ASSESSMENT AND EVALUATION PRINCIPLES

COMPETENCY 1.0 EVALUATION METHODS IN PHYSICAL EDUCATION

Skill 1.1 Demonstrate knowledge of evaluation methods used for the various domains of learning in physical education (e.g. physical, psychomotor, cognitive, social, affective).

SEE ALSO Domain 2, Skill 4.2 and Domain 3, Skill 4.1

There are many methods of assessment available to the physical education instructor. Standardized tests are traditional assessment tools that have limited effectiveness in physical education. Because students differ greatly in natural ability and fitness, measurement against personal standards is more useful than measurement against generic standards. Some of the tools for personal assessment include observational checklists, portfolios, journals, peer assessments, and rating scales.

ASSESSMENT IN THE AFFECTIVE DOMAIN

The affective domain includes interests, appreciations, attitudes, values, and adjustments inherent in the acquisition of physical activities. To measure in the affective domain, the teacher can observe the student and keep a record of those observations. Alternatively, the instructor can use opinion polls or surveys. To measure the social progress of an individual, use a sociogram. It plots the associations an individual student has with his peers.

The following is a list of appropriate tools for the assessment of affective development.

SOCIAL MEASURES (behavior, leadership, acceptance, and personality/character):

- **Harrocks Prosocial Behavior Inventory** (HPBBI) – measures prosocial play behavior of 5th and 6th graders in recreational play.

- **Adams Prosocial Inventory** – measures high school students' prosocial behaviors in physical education classes.

- **Nelson Leadership Questionnaire** – determines leaders as perceived by instructors, coaches, classmates, and teammates.

- **Cowell Personal Distance Scale** – measures congruity of a student within a group and his/her yearly development.

- **Blanchard Behavior Rating Scale** – measures student personality and character.

ATTITUDE MEASURES (predisposition to certain actions):

- **McKethan Student Attitude Inventory-Instructional Processes in Secondary Physical Education** (SAI-IPSPE) – measures attitudes of students toward instructional processes (e.g. teacher's verbal behavior, nature of activities, patterns of class organization, and regulations and policies in conceptual physical education environment).

- **Toulmin Elementary Physical Education Attitude Scale** (TEPEAS) – measures attitudes of the physical education program of elementary school students.

- **Feelings About Physical Activity** – measures commitment to activity.

- **Children's Attitudes Toward Physical Activity -Revised** (CATPA) – measures significance students place on physical activity.

- **Willis Sports Attitudes Inventory - Form C** - measures motives of competition in sports (achievement, power, success, avoiding failure).

- **Sport Orientation Questionnaire - Form B** - measures behaviors of achievement and competition during exercising and sports.

- **McMahan Sportsmanship Questionnaire** – measures high school students' attitudes toward sportsmanship.

- **Physical Estimation and Attraction Scale** – measures motivation and interest.

SELF-CONCEPT MEASURES (self-perception):

- **Cratly Adaptation of Piers-Harris Self-Concept and Scale** – measures/estimates students' own feelings about their appearance and skill performance abilities.

- **Merkley Measure of Actual Physical Self** – measures perception of physical self relating to exercise and activity.

- **Nelson-Allen Movement Satisfaction** – measures satisfaction of movement.

- **Tanner Movement Satisfaction Scale** – measures students' own level of satisfaction/dissatisfaction with their own movement.

STRESS AND ANXIETY:

- **Stress Inventory** (Miller and Allen) – measures level of stress according to stress indicators.

- **Sport Competition Anxiety Tests** – measures anxiety toward competition via one's perception of the competition as threatening or non-threatening.

ASSESSMENT IN THE COGNITIVE DOMAIN

1. **Standardized Tests** – scientifically constructed test with established validity and reliability.

2. **Teacher-made Tests** – developed personally by the teacher.

3. **Essay Tests/Written Assignments** – tests the ability to organize information presented logically in written paragraphs.

4. **Objective Tests** – true/false, multiple choice, matching, diagrams, completion, or short written response.

5. **Norm-Referenced Tests** – compares individual's score to the scores of others.

6. **Criterion-Referenced Tests** – Interpreting a score by comparing it to a predetermined standard.

ASSESSMENT IN THE PHYSICAL AND PSYCHOMOTOR DOMAINS

Evaluations determine the value of a particular activity. Instructors should integrate the continuous process of evaluation into the teaching-learning experience. The goal of an evaluation should not be limited to the school setting and the students' experiences. Rather, we should also think of it in terms of a community's progress. Measurements for evaluation provide other valuable services that instructors can use to classify students, determine students' status for grading, and aid in the diagnosis of students' weaknesses in relation to fitness skill development.

A renowned guide for educators includes the following three principles:

- Students should accept evaluations as an integral part of the teaching process.
- Instructors should use evaluations to assist students in achieving terminal competencies (psychomotor, cognitive, and affective).
- Instructors should base evaluations on the status of the individual student.

The Office of Instructional Services enumerates achievement standards for children in elementary school. An individualized, well-executed physical education program should enable a student to:

- Walk 500 yards without stopping.
- Run 30 yards dash in six seconds or less.
- Jump a standing broad jump a distance of approximately their height plus three inches.
- Bounce a ball to 2/4 or 4/4 music count.

Portfolio assessments are evaluations of the learning that happens in a natural setting. They can capitalize on student work, enhance both teacher and student involvement in evaluation, and satisfy the accountability needed to prompt school reform. Portfolio assessment includes active diaries, attitude inventories, entry-level skill test, and teacher/peer rating forms.

Interactive health CD-ROMs allow students and instructors to enter personal fitness data and evaluation results and receive immediate feedback and suggestions for improvement.

CARDIORESPIRATORY FITNESS MEASUREMENT

We can measure cardiorespiratory fitness in a number of ways. The simplest way is for the students to check their resting heart rate. To do this, the students should:

- Find their pulse in any point of the body where an artery is close to the surface (e.g., wrist [radial artery], neck [Carotid artery], or the elbow [brachial artery]).

- Count how many heartbeats they feel in one minute's time.

We usually express resting heart rate in "beats per minute" (bpm). For males, the norm is about 70 bpm. For women, the norm is about 75 bpm. This rate varies between people and the reference range is normally between 60 bpm and 100 bpm. It is important to note that resting heart rates can be significantly lower in athletes, and significantly higher in the obese.

Another way to measure cardiorespiratory fitness is by having students determine their Target Heart Rate (THR). The Target Heart Rate, or Training Heart Rate, is a desired range of heart rate reached during aerobic exercise, which allows a student's heart and lungs to receive the most benefit from a workout. There are three methods used to measure a student's THR discussed in SKILL 3.2. Students should check their heart rates frequently during activity to ensure they train within their THR zones.

Finally, another useful technique for self-assessment, which instructors can combine with the pulse-rate monitoring mentioned above, is to instruct the students to keep a training log. The indicators tracked in the log may be very concrete (e.g. heart rate during exertion, duration of exertion, or resting heart rate and blood pressure), or more subjective (e.g. how students feel during and after their workouts). Instructors should also encourage older students to devise their own training benchmarks based on their knowledge of cardiorespiratory fitness training processes and their personal fitness goals.

COMPETENCY 2.0 TECHNIQUES OF TEST CONSTRUCTION, EVALUATION, AND ADMINISTRATION

Skill 2.1 Demonstrate knowledge of basic strategies of test construction, evaluation, and administration for traditional, holistic, and authentic assessments such as developing and using criteria to assess attainment of goals and objectives.

SEE ALSO Domain 2, Skill 4.2

TECHNIQUES FOR SELECTING, CONSTRUCTING, ADAPTING, AND IMPLEMENTING FORMAL AND INFORMAL ASSESSMENTS

Physical educators should construct assessments that evaluate all three domains of physical education: psychomotor, cognitive, and affective. Teachers should divide assessments in the psychomotor domain into two groups: skill-related fitness and sport-specific skills. The physical education teacher can objectively measure skill-related fitness utilizing assessments specifically designed to evaluate each component. Speed, agility, coordination, balance, and reaction time are the components of skill-related fitness. Teachers may choose to use standardized tests developed to assess each of these components. Most of these tests also include normative data. Similarly, many standardized tests are also available as an objective assessment of sport-specific skills. Many of these tests also include normative data.

Teachers should thoroughly evaluate an assessment before choosing to utilize it, as some of the existing tests are quite complicated and burdensome to implement. If a teacher chooses not to use an existing assessment, adaptation of an existing assessment is always an option. To adapt an existing assessment, the physical educator can evaluate the assessment and determine which components of the assessment are reasonable to implement and provide a valid assessment of the specified skill. The teacher would delete the remaining components from the assessment prior to implementation. In addition to the option of deleting segments of the existing assessment, the teacher might choose to make general modifications to the overall assessment. The physical educator can measure both skill-related fitness and sport-specific skills subjectively through informal assessments. Examples of informal assessments include student interviews, student self-evaluation, and checklists.

In addition to psychomotor skills, the physical educator also assesses development of the cognitive domain. Evaluation of the cognitive domain includes formal written assessments. When constructing a written assessment, the physical educator should design the assessment at an age appropriate level, include all written instructions on the test, and arrange similarly formatted questions together. Sample types of written test questions include matching, multiple choice, true-false, fill-in-the-blank, short answer, and essay. When possible, the physical educator should administer written assessments in a classroom setting, rather than on the gymnasium floor. Assessment of both the psychomotor and cognitive domains will occur at the end of each unit of instruction.

Finally, the physical educator should assess development in the affective domain. Informal assessment of the affective domain might include checklists similar to the informal checklists utilized to assess development in the psychomotor domain. Utilizing these affective checklists clarifies behavioral expectations. Additionally, standardized attitude scales are also available to physical educators. Instructors should measure development in the affective domain at various intervals throughout the school year.

Skill 2.2 Apply knowledge of test characteristics such as validity, reliability, and objectivity.

A valid measure is one that measures what it is supposed to measure. Validity refers to getting results that accurately reflect the concept measured. Rulers, thermometers, measures of weight, and many other instruments used to measure the physical world have demonstrable validity. Validity implies reliability, which means consistency. A valid measure must be reliable, but a reliable measure need not be valid. Reliability deals with the quality of measurement. In other words, reliability is the "consistency" or "repeatability" of measurements. Objectivity is impartiality. In testing, objectivity is a matter of determining the accuracy of measures by examining consistency across multiple observations that typically involve the use of rating scales. In dance, one can use a performance testing measurement, wherein we are testing the culmination of the elements of dance, including musicality, flexibility, strength, and coordination at a performance. However, our validity test might be difficult to assess. Though we would check for the earlier-mentioned elements of dance, what we could be measuring is our degree of enjoyment and pleasure. Reliability described as consistency or repeatability is questionable in this case because the performer cannot recreate the performance exactly. We may be able to use validity and reliability tests in some technical areas, but the true test is subjective.

Skill 2.3 **Apply knowledge of assessment strategies and instruments, including technology, that are appropriate for individuals with diverse backgrounds, special needs, and disabilities.**

SEE ALSO Domain 6, Skill 1.1

The trend in physical education assessment is to move increasingly away from norm- and criterion-referenced evaluations (i.e. measuring a student's achievements against the achievements of a normative group or against criteria that are arbitrarily set by either the educator or the governing educational body), and towards performance-based, or "authentic" evaluations. This creates difficulty for physical educators because it eliminates preset reference points.

The advantage of performance-based evaluations is they are equally fair to individuals with diverse backgrounds, special needs, and disabilities. In all cases, the instructor evaluates students based on their personal performance.

Portfolio construction is one way of assessing the performance of a student. The student chooses the achievements to add to the portfolio. This creates a tool that assesses current abilities and serves as a benchmark against which the instructor can measure future performance (thus evaluating progress over time, and not just a localized achievement).

Student self-assessment is often an important part of portfolios. The instructor should ask children questions like, "Where am I now? Where am I trying to go? What am I trying to achieve? How can I get from here to there?" This type of questioning involves the child more deeply in the learning process.

STUDENT AND PROGRAM EVALUATIONS IN PHYSICAL EDUCATION

The **Cheffers Adaptation of the Flanders Interaction Analysis System** (CAFAIS) and the **Academic Learning Time in Physical Education** (ALT-PE) are *Systematic Analyses* that detect continuous and discrete behaviors, actions and interactions, and teaching characteristics. Relating the goals of a systematic analysis to the data obtained during the instructional process can indicate which of the following instructional strategies need changing:

- The ability of the teacher to question and the time engaged in questioning

- The cognitive response of students

- The time spent on task instruction (rate per minute)

- The number of times task instruction takes place (rate of occurrence)

Instructors can use the following **Systematic Observational Evaluations** to identify necessary changes in events, in duration, in groups, and in self-recording:

- **Event Recording** (rate-per-minute, rate of occurrence) – counts the number of attempts students have to try a skill and the number of positive teacher-student interactions.

- **Duration Recording** – measures amount of time teacher spends on instructions, time spent on managing student activities, and time spent managing the participation of students.

- **Group Time Sampling/Playcheck Recording** – counts the number of students participating in the activity.

- **Self-Recording** – students sign in their arrival time to class and how many completed tasks they accomplish.

Student assessments that can facilitate changes in instructional strategies include:

- **Formal assessments** such as win/loss records, written tests, skills tests, performance records, and reviewing videotaped performances.

- **Informal assessments** such as rating scales, observational performance descriptions, completion of skills checklist, and observational time utilization.

Skill 2.4 **Demonstrate an understanding of types of evaluation such as norm-referenced, criterion-referenced, content-referenced, and authentic assessment.**

SEE Domain 6, Skill 1.1

Skill 2.5 **Demonstrate knowledge of formative and summative evaluation strategies.**

TYPES OF EVALUATION

Summative evaluation strategies involve assigning the student a letter or number grade, which can reflect both the student's performance and progress. Examples include:

- Performance evaluations – the instructor assigns a letter or number grade based on the student's performance on a task or set of tasks (e.g. push-ups and sit-ups, time to run one mile, etc.).

    o Appropriate for unbiased, objective assessment of performance, ability, and current level of competency.

- Progress evaluations – the instructor assigns a letter or number grade based on the student's improvement in the ability to perform a task or set of tasks.

    o Appropriate for assessment of effectiveness of physical education program in promoting improvement.

- Effort evaluations – the instructor assigns a letter or number grade based on the student's effort in working towards training goals.

    o Appropriate for assigning class grades, as instructors should reward effort and participation rather than natural ability.

- Behavior evaluations – the instructor assigns a letter or number grade based on the student's behavior in and attitude towards training and the training environment.

    o Appropriate for assigning class grades and maintaining an orderly, disciplined classroom.

Formative evaluation strategies do not provide a letter or number grade to the student, but rather focus on a textual analysis of the student's performance and progress. Examples include a written analysis of the student's performance, progress, effort, attitude, and behavior.

COMPETENCY 3.0   BASIC STATISTICAL APPLICATIONS

Skill 3.1   **Demonstrate knowledge of basic statistical applications, including central tendency and variability, standard scores, norms, and correlations.**

BASIC STATISTICAL APPLICATIONS

Statistical applications for physical education assessment purposes allow us to evaluate where the score of a given assessment stands in comparison to other assessments and compare different assessments of the same student's abilities (in other fields – tracking intra-individual differences, or in the same field over time – tracking the student's progress).

Central tendency and variability determine where a range of scores cluster on the assessment scale and whether they are all highly localized around one point on the scale, or spread out over a range.

Standard scores and norms allow us to evaluate where assessment results stand in relation to the 'normal' expected achievement level.

Correlations allow us to evaluate the frequency at which two assessment trends appear in conjunction. Note that correlation does not imply causation.

COMPETENCY 4.0 INTERPRETATION AND COMMUNICATION OF ASSESSMENT DATA

Skill 4.1 Apply skills for interpreting assessment data and for communicating test results, performance profiles, and assessment data to various audiences (e.g. students, parents, school board members).

Instructors should communicate assessment data should differently to students, parents, and school board members.

- **Assessment data communicated to students** should be encouraging, and should be limited to a textual analysis of the child's progress and effort (it is not helpful or encouraging to remind a child that he is below grade level norms, especially if he has worked hard and made progress). The ultimate purpose of assessment data communicated to a child is to encourage further hard work.

- **Assessment data communicated to parents** should also be encouraging and should focus on the child's progress and effort. That said, it is also important that a parent receive an accurate picture of the child's status relative to grade level norms, especially if the child is in need of remedial assistance.

- **Assessment data communicated to school board members** is generally more summative in nature (a letter or number grade). Since school board members will generally see evaluations of entire classes at a time without knowing the individual children, it is not important for them to receive an encouraging picture of an individual child's progress. It is more important for them to see both current achievement levels and rates of progress to properly assess curriculum design, lesson planning, and program evaluation.

DOMAIN 7. INTEGRATION OF CONCEPTS

COMPETENCY 1.0 INTERPRETATION AND APPLICATION OF THE SUBDISCIPLINES OF KINESIOLOGY

Skill 1.1 Interpret and apply knowledge of the subdisciplines of kinesiology to facilitate student skill acquisition and performance.

MOVEMENT SCIENCE AND KINESIOLOGY

The systematic study of human movement applied to the field of physical injury. It is concerned with the understanding of how and why we move and the factors that limit and enhance our capacity to move. This particular field also relates to studies about exercising for health or the regaining of function of an injured body.

Human Movement is based on a solid liberal arts and science education designed to foster development of human values and effective interpersonal skills. A scientific foundation is necessary for the study of the ability to function both didactically and clinically.

The aim of the study of human movement is to further the understanding of the mechanisms and processes underlying skilled movements and the means by which they are influenced by physiological, biomechanical, psychological and social factors.

Finally, kinesiology encompasses human anatomy, physiology, neuroscience, biochemistry, biomechanics, exercise psychology, and sociology of sport. Kinesiologists also study the relationship between the quality of movement and overall human health. Kinesiology is an important part of physical therapy, occupational therapy, chiropractics, osteopathy, exercise physiology, kinesiotherapy, massage therapy, ergonomics, physical education, and athletic coaching. The purpose of these applications may be therapeutic, preventive, or high-performance. The application of kinesiology can also incorporate knowledge from other academic disciplines such as psychology, sociology, cultural studies, ecology, evolutionary biology, and anthropology. The study of kinesiology is often part of the physical education curriculum and illustrates the truly interdisciplinary nature of physical education.

- **Sport History** – Understanding the sport history timeline and recounting key events to students can inspire and excite. Instructors can use stories of outdated, bad sports training practices as cautionary tales, contrasted with the methodologies that the instructor imparts to the student.

- **Nutrition** – Proper nutrition education will help students become more mindful of their diet throughout the course of their day and serve as a mental connection between their daily routine and physical education.

- **Sociology** – A solid grasp of the patterns of human behavior within a societal context (in this case, the behavior of students within a team and/or classroom environment) allows the instructor to tailor educational routines to accommodate, harness, and positively impact social dynamics within a group of students.

- **Sport Psychology** – Understanding the reciprocal relationship between motivation and physical activity and performance will allow the instructor to tailor the physical education experience to the psychological needs of the student, for maximum beneficial results.

- **Biomechanics** – The study of the way in which the body's mechanics (muscles, bones, tendons and ligaments) work to produce movement – is fundamental to the creation of a program meant to impart technical physical skills (e.g. executing a gymnastics technique). Such activities require that the instructor break down a series of motions so the student can practice them individually before connecting them in a kinetic chain.

- **Exercise Physiology** – Comprehension of the way in which movement activities interact with human physiology is key to the creation of a training program that aims at reaching specific goals (e.g. understanding differences between the role and function of slow-twitch and fast-twitch muscle fibers is necessary in order to create a program geared at strengthening a muscle for a specific purpose).

- **Motor Behavior** – Motor Behavior is the study of how various forces (cognitive and biomechanical) interact to produce motor skills. Understanding these interactions is key to monitoring the fine and gross motor development of children against age-appropriate norms, and for the design and implementation of activities for improvement of motor skills.

- **Pedagogy** – A solid grasp of Pedagogy – methodologies for imparting knowledge to students, and classroom management – is fundamental to the creation of a positive learning environment.

COMPETENCY 2.0 SELECTING, ADAPTING, AND MODIFYING ACTIVITIES

Skill 2.1 Use developmental information to appropriately select, adapt, and modify sports and games based on goals, skill levels, individual needs, and disabilities.

SEE ALSO Domain 2, Skill 4.4

Physical education helps individuals attain a healthy level of fitness and renders significant experiences in movement. It provides an opportunity to refine and develop motor skills, stamina, strategies and the pure pleasure of physical activity and participation. Children, infants, and the disabled are all entitled to benefit from physical education. Physical activities can be adapted by recognizing the individual's abilities, learning skills, and needs. This requires knowledge about the science of movement, the process of skill development, social and psychological components, physical fitness, assessment of the practices of physical activities, and development and implementation of proper and appropriate activities.

Children are at a developmental stage where their physical, emotional, motor, and social skills are not fully constructed. Children in different age groups have distinct and urgent developmental needs. A developmental need varies from child to child. Instructors should respect each child's developmental needs and pace of learning and deal with all students patiently. Instructors should put each child in an environment that stimulates him and offers challenges that are appropriate to his age, developmental needs, and ability. Instructors should not force a child to take up an activity. Coercion discourages the child and he resists learning. However, incorporating motivation and stimulation into the activity can encourage the child without direct intervention of an adult. Self-motivation is the best tool for learning. Children need to challenge themselves through constant exploration and experimentation. The activity should suit the developmental age of the child so that he/she can perform it with minimal outside assistance. An adult should act as an assistant who provides help only when it is required.

The physical education program for children should be geared to suit their developmental needs (i.e., constructing their motor skills, concept of movement). Physical activity should be fun, pleasurable and aimed at developing and maintaining health. Motor skills are comprised of locomotor skills, non-locomotor skills and manipulative and coordination skills. Games like Bean Bag, parachute, hoola hoop, gymnastics and ball activities modified and adapted to suit the particular needs of children, are particularly helpful. Physical activity should have the scope to adapt itself to suit an individual child's needs and goals. Instructors can incorporate activities, such as wheelchair races or activities that require use of the hands, to accommodate handicapped students that cannot use their legs. For children in the grades 1 – 3, instructors should incorporate concepts of movement and motor skills, allowing the child to perfect them. Concepts of movements like spatial consciousness regarding location, level or height and direction, body awareness and recognition of how the body can be manipulated to perform an activity, effort required regarding time, flow and force, relationship to the various objects and to others, are developed through various activities.

Instructor must also emphasize the significance of personal hygiene. With greater development of motor skills and concepts about movement, instructors can introduce more energetic and vigorous physical activities like volleyball, gymnastics, football, and hockey. Along with these skills, the curriculum should help develop group participation skills. It is essential to instill the values of physical education and its connection to general well-being and health. Apart from this, physical education for middle grade children should help develop a good body image and enhance their social skills. Instructors can teach activities like advanced volleyball, dance, and gymnastics that will help to develop these areas.

SPECIFIC DEVELOPMENTAL ISSUES

There are several important developmental issues for an educator to consider that affect the different stages of human growth. Play is a fundamental process for learning in young children. It is a method by which they come to grips with their reality and experiment with the world (e.g. playing with toys), experiment with their concept of roles in general, and experiment with their particular roles (e.g. playing "make believe"). Children will also participate in solitary play, parallel play (multiple children playing near each other, but not including each other in their games), and cooperative play (multiple children playing the same game, together). These types of play are ways for children to define their personal comfort levels with the different types of interactions with their peers.

Participation in physical activity in the socialization process is very important, as most human interaction has a physical component to it (though the amount of physical interaction has decreased since the advent of remote communication technology). Physical activity during the socialization process creates an opportunity for children to define personal comfort levels with different types of physical interaction, as well as establish guidelines for what is (and is not) acceptable physical behavior as related to their relationship with other individuals and the scenario in which they find themselves.

Another issue to consider is the preoccupation with physical appearance that surfaces in adolescence (especially earlier adolescence, ages 12-14). This comes from several factors, primarily their burgeoning sexual identities with which they have not yet come to grips that make them care a great deal about the impression they make on members of the opposite sex. Similarly, children at this age are in the process of creating their own identities, separate from the major players in their environments (i.e. their parents). This coupled with their intense concern with their social stature and perceptions in the eyes of their peers, all contribute to the preoccupation with physical appearance (which they will outgrow).

TECHNIQUES TO MAXIMIZE PARTICIPATION

There are three options for maximizing participation: activity modification, multi-activity designs, and homogeneous or heterogeneous grouping.

Activity modification is the first option to achieve maximum participation by simply modifying the type of equipment used or the activity rules. However, keep activity as close to the original as possible (i.e. substitute a yarn ball for a birdie for badminton).

Multi-activity designs permit greater diversification of equipment and more efficient use of available facilities (keeps all students involved).

Homogeneous and heterogeneous grouping for the purpose of individualized instruction, enhancing self-concepts, equalizing competition, and promoting cooperation among classmates.

Furthermore, plan activities that encourage the greatest amount of participation by utilizing all available facilities and equipment, involving students in planning class work/activities, and being flexible. Instructors can also use tangible rewards and praise.

COMPETENCY 3.0 DEVELOPMENTAL PROGRESSIONS

Skill 3.1 Demonstrate knowledge of appropriate developmental progressions within and between individual movement skills.

A normal three-year-old should be able to walk up and down the stairs, jump from the lowest step, and land on both the feet without falling. They should also be capable of standing on one foot and balancing and kicking a large ball (though not with a lot of force). A three-year-old can jump on the same spot, ride on a small tricycle, and throw a ball (although not very straight and with limited distance). The large motor skills are more or less developed, but fine motor skills and hand-eye coordination need refining. For example, a three-year-old may not be able to dodge a ball or play games like badminton, which require greater hand-eye coordination, speed, and balance, but a three-year-old can catch a big ball thrown to him/her from a short distance.

A four-year-old is capable of walking on a straight line, hopping using one foot, and pedaling a tricycle with confidence. A four-year-old can climb ladders and trees with relative ease. A four-year-old child can run around obstacles, maneuver, and stop when necessary. A four-year-old can throw a ball a greater distance and is capable of running around in circles.

A five-year-old is capable of walking backwards, using the heel and then the toe, and is able to easily climb up and down steps by alternating feet without any outside help. Five-year-olds can touch their toes without bending at the knee and balance on a beam. They may be able to do somersaults provided it is taught in a proper and safe manner. A five-year-old can ride a tricycle with speed and dexterity, make almost ten jumps or hops without losing balance and falling, and stand on one foot for about ten seconds.

Early elementary school children have already acquired many large motor and fine motor skills. Their movement is more accurate and with purpose, though some clumsiness may persist. An elementary student is always on the run and restless. A child older than five finds pleasure in more energetic and vigorous activities. He/she can jump, hop, and throw with relative accuracy and concentrate on an activity which sustains his/her interest. However, concentration on a single activity usually does not last long. Early elementary students enjoy challenges and can benefit greatly from them.

When proper and appropriate physical education is available, by the time a child finishes the fourth grade he is able to demonstrate well-developed locomotor movements. He is also capable of manipulative and nonlocomotor movement skills like kicking and catching. He is capable of living up to challenges like balancing a number of objects or controlling a variety of things simultaneously. Children at this developmental age begin to acquire specialized movement skills like dribbling. When a child has finished eighth grade, he is able to exhibit expertise in a variety of fine and modified movements (e.g. dance steps). Children begin to develop the necessary skills for competitive and strategic games. Despite a lack of competency in a game, they learn to enjoy the pleasure of physical activity. By the time the children finish the twelfth grade they can demonstrate competency in a number of complex and modified movements with relative ease (e.g. gymnastics, dual sports, dance). Students at this age display their interest in gaining a greater degree of competency at their favorite game or activity.

COMPETENCY 4.0   LEARNING CONCEPTS AND PRINCIPLES

Skill 4.1   Use concepts and principles of learning to analyze observed individual differences.

Events and conditions such as accidents, trauma, and congenital or neurological defects can affect development (physical or mental) and hinder motor skill functions. Each individual has distinct needs, goals, learning abilities, skills, and limitations. When a physical education teacher recognizes these individual differences and modifies, alters, and adapts the process of teaching physical activity based on these differences, it becomes more effective.

Active participation is an effective method in physical education. In other words, learning can become more efficient through active participation of the student. A physical education instructor can observe the personal experiences of the student while performing or undergoing a particular training. The student should let the instructor know what he is comfortable with and what he is afraid of. Discussions about which physical activity a student enjoys and why, and how he can learn it best, help the student learn faster. Open discussions can bring personal problems, difficulties, doubts, anxiety, and fears into the open. This not only gives the instructor an opportunity to dispel the fears and doubts, but to adopt a better approach of physical education to better suit the individual's specific needs. Moreover, the openness and active participation helps to establish the much needed rapport between the student and the instructor.

Every individual has a distinct capability for learning, even within the same developmental stage. Instructors must respect these individual differences. A certain individual may be better at fine motor skills, while another at large motor skills. Recognizing these differences enables an instructor to utilize the skills and capabilities of an individual in the best possible manner. Learning cannot take place in a stifling atmosphere or an untidy surrounding. An abusive and excessively strict instructor kills the urge to learn and de-motivates the student. Praising success and being tolerant of failure helps the student to feel motivated.

Ultimately, however, motivation should come from within. Self-motivation is of great importance. Thus, if a four-year-old is disinterested in performing an activity, an instructor should not coerce him to do so. Instead, the performance or failure of other children of the same age and the appealing and attractive equipment can serve to motivate the child in the future. A child learns to compete with himself and derive satisfaction when he realizes successive challenges or goals. Thus, realization of the goal itself is the incentive. Instructors should incorporate control of error within the activity so that a student requires minimal or very little assistance. Learning through self-experience and exploration is more effective. Thus, for a six-year-old child performing a climbing exercise, there should be a padded surface in case the child falls. The equipment should be designed so that the child can climb back on without any assistance. Physical education programs and equipment should be challenging but still within the limitations of the developmental age.

COMPETENCY 5.0   CONNECTIONS BETWEEN PHYSICAL EDUCATION AND OTHER DISCIPLINES

Skill 5.1   Demonstrate knowledge of connections between physical education and other subject areas such as life and physical sciences, social science, health, mathematics, language arts, and visual and performing arts.

The lines between different fields of study are growing ever more vague and blurry. Today we understand that not only is it possible to blend fields of study together, it is in the best interest of the child to do so. Increased connections between fields of knowledge in a child's mind reinforce all of the associated fields. Physical education connects to other subject areas in the following ways:

- **Life and Physical Sciences** – Giving students an understanding of the life and physical sciences that stand behind physical education can greatly reinforce the learning experience for children. For example, the physics of force and leverage can give children insight into the mechanics of gymnastic activities. The biology of carbohydrates turning into fuel for the muscles and protein used to rebuild muscle tissue, can grant insight into the study of nutrition.

- **Social Sciences** – Examination of the styles of interaction within and between groups in competitive team-based games and sports (e.g. soccer, dodge ball), interactions between children in competitive individual activities (e.g. running a race), and interactions between children engaging in personal-achievement, individual activities (e.g. gymnastics training, where no one is competing), help children understand concepts of social organization and interaction, and helps them to draw parallels with physical education experiences and other contexts.

- **Health Sciences** – Children who are taught the relationship between physical activity and health – not just in a general "exercise is good for you" sort of way, but in a more detailed manner (e.g. aerobic fitness training stimulates the cardiovascular system, strengthening the heart and increasing the yield of oxygen per heartbeat) – are much more likely to look to fitness training as a potential response to health problems.

- **Mathematics and Language Arts** – These two fields are more peripherally connected to physical education. The connections here are more in the use of mathematics and language arts as mediums to better quantify and communicate achievements.

- **Visual and Performing Arts** – There is a great deal of overlap between movement activities and visual and performing arts – whether it is the strenuous work of painting a large canvas, or the more obviously artistic activities of gymnastics or martial arts. Helping students to see the connections between these two disciplines can stimulate crossovers from one to the other, helping children to broaden their horizons.

TEACHER CERTIFICATION STUDY GUIDE

Annotated List of Resources

This list identifies some resources that may help candidates prepare to take the Physical Education examination. While not a substitute for coursework or other types of teacher preparation, these resources may enhance a candidate's knowledge of the content covered on the examination. The references listed do not represent a comprehensive listing of all potential resources. Candidates need not read all of the materials listed below, and passage of the examination will not require familiarity with these specific resources. When available, we have provided a brief summary for the reference cited. We have organized the resources alphabetically and by content domain in subtest order.

GROWTH, MOTOR DEVELOPMENT, AND MOTOR LEARNING

Colvin, A. Vonnie; Nancy J.; and Walker, Pamela. (2000). *Teaching the Nutes and Bolts of Physical Education: Building Basic Movement Skills.* Champaign, IL: Human Kinetics.

> Provides foundational content knowledge in locomotor and manipulative skills. Topics include rolling, throwing, catching, passing, dribbling, striking, kicking, and punting.

Fronske, H. (2001). *Teaching Cues for Sports Skills* (2nd edition). San Francisco, CA: Pearson/Cummings.

> Designed to provide verbal and alternate teaching cues and point out common errors in a variety of sports.

Graham, George. (1992). *Teaching Children Physical Education: Becoming a Master Teacher.* Champaign, IL: Human Kinetics.

> Includes the skills and techniques that successful teachers use to make their classes more interesting and developmentally appropriate. A reference for K-5 teachers and physical education department chairs and administrators.

Lawson, H.A. (1984). *Invitation to Physical Education.* Champaign IL: Human Kinetics.

> Shows students and practitioners how to apply basic business management principles to a variety of health promotion programs.

Pangrazi, Robert. (2004). *Dynamic Physical Education for Elementary School Children* (14th edition). San Francisco, CA: Pearson/Cummings.

> Provides step-by-step techniques for teaching physical education while navigating through today's challenging educational terrain.

Powers, S.K., and Howley, E.T. (2003). *Exercise Physiology* (5th edition). New York, NY: McGraw Hill.

> Explains theory of exercise science and physical education with application and performance models to increase understanding of classroom learning.

Schmidt, R.A., and Lee, T.D. (1999). *Motor Control Learning: A Behavioral Emphasis* (3rd Edition). Champaign: IL: Human Kinetics.

> Addresses many factors that affect the quality of movement behaviors and the ease with which students can learn them.

PHYSICAL EDUCATION

Sherrill, C. (1998). *Adapted Physical Activity, Recreation and Sport: Cross-disciplinary and Lifespan* (5th edition). Dubuque, IA: WCB McGraw Hill.
> Emphasizes attitude change, inclusion, and psychosocial perspectives for understanding individual differences.

Siedentop, D. (1994). *Sport Education.* Champaign, IL: Human Kinetics.
> Shows how sport can help students learn fair play, leadership skills, and self-responsibility, in addition to becoming competent players. Also shows physical educators how to implement effective sport education programs to achieve these goals.

Summers, J.J. (1992). *Approaches to the Study of Motor Control and Learning.* Amsterdam: Elsevier Science.
> Provides analysis of research with particular emphasis on the methods and paradigms employed and the future direction of their work.

Thomas, Katherine, et al. (2003). *Physical Education Methods for Elementary Teachers.* Champaign, IL: Human Kinetics.
> Takes a research approach and offers a user-friendly technique to applicable teaching modalities for physical education for grades K-12.

Winnick, J.P. (2000). *Adapted Physical Education and Sport* (3rd edition). Champaign, IL: Human Kinetics.
> Provides a thorough introduction for students preparing to work with individuals with disabilities in a variety of settings.

THE SCIENCE OF HUMAN MOVEMENT

Birrell, S., and Cole, C.L. (1994). *Women, Sport, and Culture.* Champaign, IL: Human Kinetics.
> A collection of essays that examine the relationship between sport and gender.

Grantham, W.C.; Patton, R.W.; Winick, M.L.; and York, T.D. (1998). *Health Fitness Management.* Champaign, IL: Human Kinetics.
> Brings conventional business management principles and operational guidelines to the unconventional business of health and fitness.

Hall, S. (2003). *Basic Biomechanics.* Boston, MA: McGraw-Hill.

Hamill, J., and Knutzen, K. (1995). *Biomechanical Basis of Human Movement.* Hagerstown, MD: Lippincott, Williams & Wilkins.
> Integrates aspects of functional anatomy, physics, calculus, and physiology into a comprehensive discussion of human movement.

Hopper, Chris; Fisher, Bruce; and Muniz, Kathy. (1997). *Health-Related Fitness: Grades 1-2, 3-4, 5-6.* Champaign, IL: Human Kinetics.
> These three books provide a wealth of health and fitness information and are an excellent resource for classroom teachers with limited backgrounds in physical education.

Lawson, H.A. (1984). *Invitation to Physical Education.* Champaign, IL: Human Kinetics.
> Shows students and practitioners how to apply basic business management principles to a variety of health promotion programs.

Sample Test

1. The Greek's best-known early contribution to the physical education profession was: (Easy) (Skill1.1)

   A. The Pentathlon

   B. The Olympics

   C. The Pankration

   D. Acrobatics

2. The physical education philosophy based on experience is: (Average Rigor) (Skill 1.1)

   A. Naturalism

   B. Pragmatism

   C. Idealism

   D. Existentialism

3. The modern physical education philosophy that combines beliefs from different philosophies is: (Rigorous) (Skill 1.1)

   A. Eclectic

   B. Humanistic

   C. Individualism

   D. Realism

4. Which of the following is not a skill assessment test to evaluate student performance? (Average Rigor) (Skill 1.1)

   A. Harrocks Volley

   B. Rodgers Strength Test

   C. Iowa Brace Test

   D. AAHPERD Youth Fitness Test

5. All of the following are methods to evaluate the affective domain except: (Average Rigor) (Skill 1.1)

   A. Adams Prosocial Inventory

   B. Crowell Personal Distance Scale

   C. Blanchard Behavior Rating Scale

   D. McCloy's Prosocial Behavior Scale

6. Educators can evaluate the cognitive domain by all of the following methods except: (Rigorous) (Skill 1.1)

   A. Norm-Referenced Tests

   B. Criterion Referenced Tests

   C. Standardized Tests

   D. Willis Sports Inventory Tests

7. Using the same foot to take off from a surface and land is which locomotor skill? (Easy) (Skill 1.1)

   A. Jumping

   B. Vaulting

   C. Leaping

   D. Hopping

8. Which nonlocomotor skill entails movement around a joint where two body parts meet? (Easy) (Skill 1.1)

   A. Twisting

   B. Swaying

   C. Bending

   D. Stretching

9. A sharp change of direction from one's original line of movement is which nonlocomotor skill? (Easy) (Skill 1.1)

   A. Twisting

   B. Dodging

   C. Swaying

   D. Swinging

10. Which movement concept involves students making decisions about an object's positional changes in space? (Rigorous) (Skill 1.1)

    A. Spatial Awareness

    B. Effort Awareness

    C. Body Awareness

    D. Motion Awareness

11. Applying the mechanical principles of balance, time, and force describes which movement concept? (Average Rigor) (Skill 1.1)

    A. Spatial Awareness

    B. Effort Awareness

    C. Body Awareness

    D. Motion Awareness

12. Having students move on their hands and knees, move on lines, and/or hold shapes while moving develops which quality of movement? (Average Rigor) (Skill 1.1)

    A. Balance

    B. Time

    C. Force

    D. Inertia

13. **What is the proper order of sequential development for the acquisition of locomotor skills? (Rigorous) (Skill 1.1)**

    A. Creep, crawl, walk, jump, run, slide, gallop, hop, leap, skip; step-hop.

    B. Crawl, walk, creep, slide, walk, run, hop, leap, gallop, skip; step-hop.

    C. Creep, crawl, walk, slide, run, hop, leap, skip, gallop, jump; step-hop.

    D. Crawl, creep, walk, run, jump, hop, gallop, slide, leap, skip; step-hop.

14. **Having students pretend they are playing basketball or trying to catch a bus develops which locomotor skill? (Easy) (Skill 1.1)**

    A. Galloping

    B. Running

    C. Leaping

    D. Skipping

15. **Having students play Fox and Hound develops: (Easy) (Skill 1.1)**

    A. Galloping

    B. Hopping

    C. Stepping-hopping

    D. Skipping

16. **Having students take off and land with both feet together develops which locomotor skill? (Easy) (Skill 1.1)**

    A. Hopping

    B. Jumping

    C. Leaping

    D. Skipping

17. **What is the proper sequential order of development for the acquisition of nonlocomotor skills? (Average Rigor) (Skill 1.1)**

    A. Stretch, sit, bend, turn, swing, twist, shake, rock & sway, dodge; fall.

    B. Bend, stretch, turn, twist, swing, sit, rock & sway, shake, dodge; fall.

    C. Stretch, bend, sit, shake, turn, rock & sway, swing, twist, dodge; fall.

    D. Bend, stretch, sit, turn, twist, swing, sway, rock & sway, dodge; fall.

18. Activities such as pretending to pick fruit off a tree or reaching for a star develop which non-locomotor skill? (Easy) (Skill 1.1)

    A. Bending

    B. Stretching

    C. Turning

    D. Twisting

19. Picking up coins, tying shoes, and petting animals develop this nonlocomotor skill. (Easy) (Skill 1.1)

    A. Bending

    B. Stretching

    C. Turning

    D. Twisting

20. Having students collapse in their own space or lower themselves as though they are a raindrop or snowflake develops this nonlocomotor skill. (Easy) (Skill 1.1)

    A. Dodging

    B. Shaking

    C. Swinging

    D. Falling

21. Which is the proper sequential order of development for the acquisition of manipulative skills? (Rigorous) (Skill 1.1)

    A. Striking, throwing, bouncing, catching, trapping, kicking, ball rolling; volleying.

    B. Striking, throwing, kicking, ball rolling, volleying, bouncing, catching; trapping.

    C. Striking, throwing, catching, trapping, kicking, ball rolling, bouncing; volleying.

    D. Striking, throwing, kicking, ball rolling, bouncing; volleying.

22. Having students hit a large balloon with both hands develops this manipulative skill. (Average Rigor) (Skill 1.1)

    A. Bouncing

    B. Striking

    C. Volleying

    D. Trapping

23. Progressively decreasing the size of a target that balls are projected at develops which manipulative skill. (Average Rigor) (Skill 1.1)

    A. Throwing

    B. Trapping

    C. Volleying

    D. Kicking

24. Hitting a stationary object while in a fixed position, then incorporating movement, develops this manipulative skill. (Average Rigor) (Skill 1.1)

    A. Bouncing

    B. Trapping

    C. Throwing

    D. Striking

25. Which of the following body types is the most capable of motor performance involving endurance? (Average Rigor) (Skill 1.2)

    A. Endomorph

    B. Ectomorph

    C. Mesomorph

    D. Metamorph

26. A major event in the history of physical education occurred among the Romans. Which of the following did the Romans identify?(Average Rigor) (Skill2.1)

    A. Severe physical training

    B. Harmonious development of the body, mind, and spirit

    C. The worth of physical education

    D. Physical training only for warriors

27. President Eisenhower was alerted to the poor fitness levels of American youths. How was the poor physical conditioning of youths discovered in the Eisenhower Administration? (Average Rigor) (Skill 2.1)

    A. By WWII Selective Service Examination

    B. By organizations promoting physical fitness

    C. By the Federal Security Agency

    D. By the Kraus-Webber Tests

28. In 1956, the AAHPER Fitness Conferences established: (Rigorous) (Skill 2.1)

   A. The President's Council on Youth Fitness

   B. The President's Citizens' Advisory Committee

   C. The President's Council on Physical Fitness

   D. A and B

29. Students that paddle balls against a wall or jump over objects with various heights are demonstrating which quality of movement? (Rigorous) (Skill 2.1)

   A. Balance

   B. Time

   C. Force

   D. Inertia

30. All of the following affect force except: (Easy) (Skill 2.1)

   A. Magnitude

   B. Energy

   C. Motion

   D. Mass

31. For a movement to occur, applied force must overcome inertia of an object and any other resisting forces. What concept of force does this describe? (Rigorous) (Skill 2.1)

   A. Potential energy

   B. Magnitude

   C. Kinetic energy

   D. Absorption

32. The energy of an object to do work while recoiling is which type of potential energy? (Average Rigor) (Skill 2.1)

   A. Absorption

   B. Kinetic

   C. Elastic

   D. Torque

33. Gradually decelerating a moving mass by utilization of smaller forces over a long period of time is: (Average Rigor) (Skill 2.1)

   A. Stability

   B. Equilibrium

   C. Angular force

   D. Force absorption

34. Which of the following principles is not a factor to assess to correct errors in performance for process assessment? (Average Rigor) (Skill 2.1)

    A. Inertia

    B. Action/Reaction

    C. Force

    D. Acceleration

35. An instructor used a similar movement from a skill learned in a different activity to teach a skill for a new activity. The technique used to facilitate cognitive learning was: (Average Rigor) (Skill 2.1)

    A. Conceptual thinking

    B. Transfer of learning

    C. Longer instruction

    D. Appropriate language

36. A teacher rewards students for completing tasks. Which method is the teacher using to facilitate psychomotor learning? (Average Rigor) (Skill 2.1)

    A. Task/Reciprocal

    B. Command/Direct

    C. Contingency/Contract

    D. Physical/Reflex

37. All of the following are Systematic Observational Evaluations except: (Rigorous) (Skill 2.3)

    A. Reflective Recording

    B. Event Recording

    C. Duration Recording

    D. Self Recording

38. A physical education teacher emphasizes healthy attitudes and habits. She conducts her classes so that students acquire and interpret knowledge and learn to think/analyze, which is necessary for physical activities. The goals and values utilized and the philosophy applied by this instructor is: (Average Rigor) (Skill 3.1)

    A. Physical Development Goals and Realism Philosophy

    B. Affective Development Goals and Existentialism

    C. Motor Development Goals and Realism Philosophy

    D. Cognitive Development Goals and Idealism Philosophy

39. Social skills and values developed by activity include all of the following except: (Easy) (Skill 3.1)

    A. Winning at all costs

    B. Making judgments in groups

    C. Communicating and cooperating

    D. Respecting rules and property

40. Activities that enhance team socialization include all of the following except: (Easy) (Skill 3.1)

    A. Basketball

    B. Soccer

    C. Golf

    D. Volleyball

41. Through physical activities, John has developed self-discipline, fairness, respect for others, and new friends. John has experienced which of the following? (Rigorous) (Skill 3.1)

    A. Positive cooperation psycho-social influences

    B. Positive group psycho-social influences

    C. Positive individual psycho-social influences

    D. Positive accomplishment psycho-social influences

42. Which of the following psycho-social influences is not negative? (Rigorous) (Skill 3.1)

    A. Avoidance of problems

    B. Adherence to exercise

    C. Ego-centeredness

    D. Role conflict

43. The affective domain of physical education contributes to all of the following except: (Rigorous) (Skill 3.1)

    A. Knowledge of exercise, health, and disease

    B. Self-actualization

    C. An appreciation of beauty

    D. Good sportsmanship

44. A physical education instructor anticipates and prevents potential injuries, watches for hidden injuries, and takes an injury evaluation of the entire class. Which of the following strategies to prevent injuries is the teacher demonstrating? (Average Rigor) (Skill 3.1)

    A. Maintaining hiring standards

    B. Proper use of equipment

    C. Proper procedures for emergencies

    D. Participant screening

45. An instructor notices that class participation is much lower than expected. By making changes in equipment and rules, the instructor applied which of the following concepts to enhance participation? (Rigorous) (Skill 3.1)

    A. Homogeneous grouping

    B. Heterogeneous grouping

    C. Multi-activity designs

    D. Activity modification

46. Using tactile clues is a functional adaptation that can assist which type of students? (Rigorous) (Skill 3.1)

    A. Deaf students

    B. Blind students

    C. Asthmatic students

    D. Physically challenged students

47. There are two sequential phases to the development of spatial awareness. What is the order of these phases? (Rigorous) (Skill 3.1)

    A. Locating more than one object in relation to each object; the location of objects in relation to one's own body in space.

    B. The location of objects in relation to one's own body in space; locating more than one object in relation to one's own body.

    C. Locating more than one object independent of one's body; the location of objects in relation to one's own body.

    D. The location of objects in relation to one's own body in space; locating more than one object in relation to each object and independent of one's own body.

48. Equilibrium is maintained as long as: (Average Rigor) (Skill 3.1)

    A. Body segments are moved independently.

    B. The center of gravity is over the base of support

    C. Force is applied to the base of support.

    D. The center of gravity is lowered.

49. Which of the following does not enhance equilibrium? (Average Rigor) (Skill 3.1)

   A. Shifting the center of gravity away from the direction of movement.

   B. Increasing the base of support.

   C. Lowering the base of support.

   D. Increasing the base of support and lowering the center of support.

50. The most effective way to promote the physical education curriculum is to: (Rigorous) (Skill 3.2)

   A. Relate physical education to higher thought processes

   B. Relate physical education to humanitarianism

   C. Relate physical education to the total educational process

   D. Relate physical education to skills necessary to preserve the natural environment

51. Which of the following is not a consideration for the selection of a facility? (Rigorous) (Skill 3.2)

   A. Community involvement

   B. Custodial staff

   C. Availability to women, minorities, and the handicapped

   D. Bond issues

52. Which of the following is not a class-management technique? (Easy) (Skill 3.2)

   A. Explaining procedures for roll call, excuses, and tardiness

   B. Explaining routines for changing and showering

   C. Explaining conditioning

   D. Promoting individual self-discipline

53. Long-term planning is essential for effective class management. Identify the management techniques not essential to long-term planning. (Easy) (Skill 3.2)

   A. Parental observation

   B. Progress evaluation

   C. Precise activity planning

   D. Arrangements for line markings

54. Although Mary is a paraplegic, she wants to participate in some capacity in the physical education class. What federal legislative act entitles her to do so? (Rigorous) (Skill 3.2)

   A. PE 94-142

   B. Title IX

   C. PL 94-142

   D. Title XI

55. A legal wrong resulting in a direct or an indirect injury is: (Average Rigor) (Skill 3.2)

   A. Negligence

   B. A Tort

   C. In loco parentis

   D. Legal liability

56. All of the following actions help avoid lawsuits except: (Average Rigor) (Skill 3.2)

   A. Ensuring equipment and facilities are safe

   B. Getting exculpatory agreements

   C. Knowing each students' health status

   D. Grouping students with unequal competitive levels

57. Which of the following actions does not promote safety? (Rigorous) (Skill 3.2)

   A. Allowing students to wear the current style of shoes

   B. Presenting organized activities

   C. Inspecting equipment and facilities

   D. Instructing skill and activities properly

58. The tendency of a body/object to remain in its present state of motion unless some force acts to change it is which mechanical principle of motion? (Average Rigor) (Skill 3.2)

   A. Acceleration

   B. Inertia

   C. Action/Reaction

   D. Linear motion

59. The movement response of a system depends not only on the net external force, but also on the resistance to movement change. Which mechanical principle of motion does this definition describe? (Rigorous) (Skill 3.2)

    A. Acceleration

    B. Inertia

    C. Action/Reaction

    D. Air Resistance

60. Which of the following mechanical principles of motion states that every motion has a similar, contrasting response? (Easy) (Skill 3.2)

    A. Acceleration

    B. Inertia

    C. Action/Reaction

    D. Centripetal force

61. A subjective, observational approach to identifying errors in the form, style, or mechanics of a skill is accomplished by: (Rigorous) (Skill 4.1)

    A. Product assessment

    B. Process assessment

    C. Standardized norm-referenced tests

    D. Criterion-referenced tests

62. What type of assessment objectively measures skill performance? (Rigorous) (Skill 4.1)

    A. Process assessment

    B. Product assessment

    C. Texas PE Test

    D. Iowa Brace Test

63. Process assessment does not identify which of the following errors in skill performance. (Average Rigor) (Skill 4.1)

    A. Style

    B. Form

    C. End result

    D. Mechanics

64. Determining poor performance of a skill using process assessment can best be accomplished by: (Average Rigor) (Skill 4.1)

    A. Observing how fast a skill is performed.

    B. Observing how many skills are performed.

    C. Observing how far or how high a skill is performed.

    D. Observing several attributes comprising the entire performance of a skill.

65. Which of the following methods measures fundamental skills using product assessment? (Rigorous) (Skill 4.1)

    A. Criterion-referenced tests

    B. Standardized norm-referenced tests

    C. Both A and B

    D. Neither A nor B

66. Product assessment measures all of the following except: (Rigorous) (Skill 4.1)

    A. How the student performs the mechanics of a skill.

    B. How many times the student performs a skill.

    C. How fast the student performs a skill.

    D. How far or high the student performs a skill.

67. Instructors can evaluate skill level of achievement in archery by: (Average Rigor) (Skill 4.1)

    A. Giving students a written exam on terminology.

    B. Having students demonstrate the correct tension of arrow feathers.

    C. Totaling a student's score obtained on the target's face.

    D. Time how long a student takes to shoot all arrows.

68. Instructors can determine skill level achievement in golf by: (Average Rigor) (Skill 4.1)

   A. The number of "birdies" that a student makes.

   B. The number of "bogies" a student makes.

   C. The score obtained after several rounds

   D. The total score achieved throughout the school year.

69. Instructors can determine skill level achievement in swimming by: (Average Rigor) (Skill 4.1)

   A. How long a student can float

   B. How many strokes it takes a student to swim a specified distance.

   C. How long a student can stay under the water without moving.

   D. How many times a student can dive in five minutes.

70. Instructors can assess skill level achievement in bowling by: (Easy) (Skill 4.1)

   A. Calculating a student's average score.

   B. Calculating how many gutter-balls the student threw.

   C. Calculating how many strikes the student threw.

   D. Calculating how many spares the student threw.

71. Although they are still hitting the target, the score of some students practicing archery has decreased as the distance between them and the target has increased. Which of the following adjustments will improve their scores? (Rigorous) (Skill 4.1)

   A. Increasing the velocity of their arrows.

   B. Increasing the students' base of support.

   C. Increasing the weight of the arrows.

   D. Increasing the parabolic path of the arrows.

72. Some students practicing basketball are having difficulty with "free throws," even though the shots make it to and over the hoop. What adjustment will improve their "free throws?" (Average Rigor) (Skill 4.1)

   A. Increasing the height of release (i.e. jump shot).

   B. Increasing the vertical path of the ball.

   C. Increasing the velocity of the release.

   D. Increasing the base of support.

73. An archery student's arrow bounced off the red part of the target face. What is the correct ruling? (Average Rigor))Skill 4.1)

   A. No score.

   B. Re-shoot arrow.

   C. 7 points awarded.

   D. Shot receives same score as highest arrow shot that did not bounce off the target.

74. A student playing badminton believed that the shuttlecock was going to land out-of-bounds. The shuttlecock landed on the line. What is the correct ruling? (Easy) (Skill 4.1)

   A. The shuttlecock is out-of-bounds.

   B. The shuttlecock is in-bounds.

   C. The point is replayed.

   D. That player is charged with a feint.

75. A mechanical pinsetter accidentally knocked down the only bowling pin left standing for a spare attempt after clearing all the other pins knocked down by the first ball thrown. What is the correct ruling?(Rigorous) (Skill 4.1)

   A. Foul

   B. Spare

   C. Frame is replayed

   D. No count for that pin

76. The ball served in racquetball hits the front line and lands in front of the short line. What is the ruling? (Easy) (Skill 4.1)

    A. Fault

    B. Reserve

    C. Out-of-bounds

    D. Fair ball

77. Two opposing soccer players are trying to gain control of the ball when one player "knees" the other. What is the ruling? (Easy) (Skill 4.1)

    A. Direct free kick

    B. Indirect free kick

    C. Fair play

    D. Ejection from the game

78. Two students are playing badminton. When receiving the shuttlecock, one student consistently stands too deep in the receiving court. What strategy should the server use to serve the shuttlecock? (Average Rigor) (Skill 4.1)

    A. Smash serve

    B. Clear serve

    C. Overhead serve

    D. Short serve

79. A basketball team has an outstanding rebounder. In order to keep this player near the opponent's basket, which strategy should the coach implement? (Easy) (Skill 4.1)

    A. Pick-and-Roll

    B. Give-and-Go

    C. Zone defense

    D. Free-lancing

80. When a defensive tennis player needs more time to return to his position, what strategy should he apply? (Rigorous) (Skill 4.1)

    A. Drop shot

    B. Dink shot

    C. Lob shot

    D. Down-the-line shot

81. An overhead badminton stroke used to hit a fore-hand-like overhead stroke that is on the backhand side of the body is a(n): (Rigorous) (Skill 4.1)

    A. Around-the-head-shot

    B. Down-the-line shot

    C. Lifting the shuttle

    D. Under hand shuttle

82. A maneuver when an offensive player passes to a teammate and then immediately cuts in toward the basket for a return pass is: (Average Rigor) (Skill 4.1)

   A. Charging

   B. Pick

   C. Give-and-go

   D. Switching

83. A bowling pin that remains standing after an apparently perfect hit is a: (Rigorous) (Skill 4.1)

   A. Tap

   B. Turkey

   C. Blow

   D. Leave

84. A soccer pass from the outside of the field near the end line to a position in front of the goal is a: (Average Rigor) (Skill 4.1)

   A. Chip

   B. Settle

   C. Through

   D. Cross

85. A volleyball that opponents simultaneously contact and momentarily hold above the net is a(n): (Easy) (Skill 4.1)

   A. Double fault

   B. Play over

   C. Overlap

   D. Held ball

86. Volleyball player LB on team A digs a spiked ball. The ball deflects off LB's shoulder. What is the ruling? (Average Rigor) (Skill 4.1)

   A. Fault

   B. Legal hit

   C. Double foul

   D. Play over

87. Playing "Simon Says" and having students touch different body parts applies which movement concept? (Average Rigor) (Skill 4.2)

   A. Spatial Awareness

   B. Effort Awareness

   C. Body Awareness

   D. Motion Awareness

88. Having students move in a specific pattern while measuring how long they take to do so develops which quality of movement? (Average Rigor) (Skill 4.2)

    A. Balance

    B. Time

    C. Force

    D. Inertia

89. Aerobic dance develops or improves each of the following skills or health components except… (Rigorous) (Skill 4.2)

    A. Cardio-respiratory function

    B. Body composition

    C. Coordination

    D. Flexibility

90. Rowing develops which health or skill related component of fitness? (Rigorous) (Skill 4.2)

    A. Muscle endurance

    B. Flexibility

    C. Balance

    D. Reaction time

91. Calisthenics develops all of the following health and skill related components of fitness except: (Average Rigor) (Skill 4.2)

    A. Muscle strength

    B. Body composition

    C. Power

    D. Agility

92. Which health or skill related component of fitness is developed by rope jumping? (Average Rigor) (Skill 4.2)

    A. Muscle Force

    B. Coordination

    C. Flexibility

    D. Muscle strength

93. Swimming does not improve which health or skill related component of fitness? (Rigorous) (Skill 4.2)

    A. Cardio-respiratory function

    B. Flexibility

    C. Muscle strength

    D. Foot Speed

94. Data from a cardio-respiratory assessment can identify and predict all of the following except: (Rigorous) (Skill 4.2)

   A. Functional aerobic capacity

   B. Natural over-fatness

   C. Running ability

   D. Motivation

95. Data from assessing _____ identifies an individual's potential of developing musculoskeletal problems and an individual's potential of performing activities of daily living. (Rigorous) (Skill 4.2)

   A. Flexibility

   B. Muscle endurance

   C. Muscle strength

   D. Motor performance

96. A 17-year-old male student performed 20 sit-ups, ran a mile in 8 minutes, and has a body fat composition of 17%. Which is the best interpretation of his fitness level? (Rigorous) (Skill 4.2)

   A. Average muscular endurance, good cardiovascular endurance; appropriate body fat composition.

   B. Low muscular endurance, average cardiovascular endurance; high body fat composition.

   C. Low muscular endurance, average cardiovascular endurance; appropriate body fat composition.

   D. Low muscular endurance, low cardiovascular endurance; appropriate body fat composition.

97. Based on the information given in the previous question, what changes would you recommend to improve this person's level of fitness? (Average Rigor) (Skill 4.2)

    A. Muscle endurance training and cardiovascular endurance training.

    B. Muscle endurance training, cardiovascular endurance training, and reduction of caloric intake.

    C. Muscle strength training and cardio-vascular endurance training.

    D. No changes necessary.

98. An obese student's fitness assessments were poor for every component of fitness. Which would you recommend first? (Easy) (Skill 4.2)

    A. A jogging program.

    B. A weight lifting program.

    C. A walking program.

    D. A stretching program.

99. Coordinated movements that project a person over an obstacle are: (Easy) (Skill 4.4)

    A. Jumping

    B. Vaulting

    C. Leaping

    D. Hopping

100. Which manipulative skill uses the hands to stop the momentum of an object? (Rigorous) (Skill 4.4)

    A. Trapping

    B. Catching

    C. Striking

    D. Rolling

101. Which professional organization protects amateur sports from corruption? (Easy) (Skill 5.1)

    A. AIWA

    B. AAHPERD

    C. NCAA

    D. AAU

102. Which professional organization works with legislatures? (Average Rigor) (Skill 5.1)

   A. AIWA

   B. AAHPERD

   C. ACSM

   D. AAU

103. Research in physical education is published in all of the following periodicals except the: (Average Rigor) (Skill 5.1)

   A. School PE Update

   B. Research Quarterly

   C. Journal of Physical Education

   D. YMCA Magazine

104. A teacher who modifies and develops tasks for a class is demonstrating knowledge of which appropriate behavior in physical education activities. (Rigorous) (Skill 5.1)

   A. Appropriate management behavior

   B. Appropriate student behavior

   C. Appropriate administration behavior

   D. Appropriate content behavior

105. The ability for a muscle(s) to repeatedly contract over a period of time is: (Average Rigor) (Skill 5.1)

   A. Cardiovascular endurance

   B. Muscle endurance

   C. Muscle strength

   D. Muscle force

106. The ability to change rapidly the direction of the body is: (Average Rigor) (Skill 5.1)

   A. Coordination

   B. Reaction time

   C. Speed

   D. Agility

107. Students are performing the vertical jump. What component of fitness does this activity assess? (Rigorous) (Skill 5.1)

   A. Muscle strength

   B. Balance

   C. Power

   D. Muscle endurance

108. Using the Karvonen Formula, compute the 60% - 80% THR for a 16-year old student with a RHR of 60. (Rigorous) (Skill 5.1)

   A. 122-163 beats per minute

   B. 130-168 beats per minute

   C. 142-170 beats per minute

   D. 146-175 beats per minute

109. Using Cooper's Formula, compute the THR for a 15 year old student. (Rigorous) (Skill 5.1)

   A. 120- 153 beats per minute

   B. 123-164 beats per minute

   C. 135-169 beats per minute

   D. 147-176 beats per minute

110. Which is not a common negative stressor? (Rigorous) (Skill5.1)

   A. Loss of significant other

   B. Personal illness or injury.

   C. Moving to a new state.

   D. Landing a new job.

111. Which of the following is a negative coping strategy for dealing with stress?(Average Rigor)(Skill5.1)

   A. Recreational diversions

   B. Active thinking

   C. Alcohol use

   D. Imagery

112. The most important nutrient the body requires, without which life can only be sustained for a few days, is: (Easy)(Skill5.1)

   A. Vitamins

   B. Minerals

   C. Water

   D. Carbohydrates

113. With regard to protein content, foods from animal sources are usually⊗ (Average Rigor)(Skill5.1)

   A. Complete

   B. Essential

   C. Nonessential

   D. Incidental

114. Fats with room for two or more hydrogen atoms per molecule-fatty acid chain are: (Rigorous)(Skill 5.1)

   A. Monounsaturated

   B. Polyunsaturated

   C. Hydrosaturated

   D. Saturated

115. An adequate diet to meet nutritional needs consists of: (Rigorous)(Skill 5.1)

   A. No more than 30% caloric intake from fats, no more than 50 % caloric intake from proteins, and at least 20% caloric intake from carbohydrates.

   B. No more than 30% caloric intake from fats, no more than 40% caloric intake from proteins, and at least 30% caloric intake from carbohydrates.

   C. No more than 30% caloric intake from fats, no more than 15% caloric intake from proteins, and at least 55% caloric intake from carbohydrates.

   D. No more than 30 % caloric intake from fats, no more than 30% caloric intake from proteins, and at least 40% caloric intake from carbohydrates.

116. Maintaining body weight is best accomplished by: (Average Rigor) (Skill 5.1)

   A. Dieting

   B. Aerobic exercise

   C. Lifting weights

   D. Equalizing caloric intake relative to output

117. Most high-protein diets: (Average Rigor) (Skill 5.1)

   A. Are high in cholesterol

   B. Are high in saturated fats

   C. Require vitamin and mineral supplements

   D. All of the above

118. Which one of the following statements about low-calorie diets is false? (Rigorous) (Skill 5.1)

   A. Most people who "diet only" regain the weight they lose.

   B. They are the way most people try to lose weight.

   C. They make weight control easier.

   D. They lead to excess worry about weight, food, and eating.

119. Physiological benefits of exercise include all of the following except: (Rigorous) (Skill 5.1)

    A. Reducing mental tension

    B. Improving muscle strength

    C. Cardiac hypertrophy

    D. Quicker recovery rate

120. Psychological benefits of exercise include all of the following except: (Rigorous) (Skill 5.1)

    A. Improved sleeping patterns

    B. Improved energy regulation

    C. Improved appearance

    D. Improved quality of life

121. Which of the following conditions is not associated with a lack of physical activity? (Average Rigor) (Skill 5.1)

    A. Atherosclerosis

    B. Longer life expectancy

    C. Osteoporosis

    D. Certain cancers

122. Which of the following pieces of exercise equipment best applies the physiological principles? (Average Rigor) (Skill 5.1)

    A. Rolling machine

    B. Electrical muscle stimulator

    C. Stationary Bicycle

    D. Motor-driven rowing machine

123. To enhance skill and strategy performance for striking or throwing objects, for catching or collecting objects, and for carrying and propelling objects, students must first learn techniques for: (Rigorous) (Skill 5.3)

    A. Offense

    B. Defense

    C. Controlling objects

    D. Continuous play of objects

124. Which of the following is not a type of tournament? (Average Rigor) (Skill 5.3)

    A. Spiderweb

    B. Pyramid

    C. Spiral

    D. Round Robin

125. Which of the following is not a type of meet? (Average Rigor) (Skill 5.3)

    A. Extramural

    B. Intramural

    C. Interscholastic

    D. Ladder

126. Activities to specifically develop cardiovascular fitness must be: (Rigorous) (Skill 6.1)

    A. Performed without developing an oxygen debt

    B. Performed twice daily.

    C. Performed every day.

    D. Performed for a minimum of 10 minutes.

127. Which is not a sign of stress? (Rigorous) (Skill 6.1)

    A. Irritability

    B. Assertiveness

    C. Insomnia

    D. Stomach problems

128. Students are performing trunk extensions. What component of fitness does this activity assess? (Average Rigor) (Skill 9.1)

    A. Balance

    B. Flexibility

    C. Body Composition

    D. Coordination

129. Working at a level that is above normal is which exercise training principle? (Rigorous) (Skill 9.1)

    A. Intensity

    B. Progression

    C. Specificity

    D. Overload

130. Students on a running program to improve cardio-respiratory fitness apply which exercise principle. (Rigorous) (Skill 9.1)

    A. Aerobic

    B. Progression

    C. Specificity

    D. Overload

131. Adding more reps to a weightlifting set applies which exercise principle. (Average Rigor) (Skill 9.1)

    A. Anaerobic

    B. Progression

    C. Overload

    D. Specificity

132. Which of the following does not modify overload? (Rigorous) (Skill 9.1)

    A. Frequency

    B. Perceived exertion

    C. Time

    D. Intensity

133. Prior to activity, students perform a 5-10 minute warm-up. Which is not recommended as part of the warm-up? (Easy) (Skill 9.1)

    A. Using the muscles that will be utilized in the following activity.

    B. Using a gradual aerobic warm-up.

    C. Using a gradual anaerobic warm-up.

134. Which is not a benefit of warming up? (Rigorous) (Skill 9.1)

    A. Releasing hydrogen from myoglobin.

    B. Reducing the risk of musculoskeletal injuries.

    C. Raising the body's core temperature in preparation for activity.

    D. Stretching the major muscle groups to be used in the activity.

135. Which is not a benefit of cooling down? (Rigorous) (Skill 9.1)

    A. Preventing dizziness.

    B. Redistributing circulation.

    C. Removing lactic acid.

    D. Removing myoglobin.

136. Overloading for muscle strength includes all of the following except: (Rigorous) (Skill 9.1)

    A. Raising heart rate to an intense level.

    B. Lifting weights every other day.

    C. Lifting with high resistance and low reps.

    D. Lifting 60% to 90% of assessed muscle strength.

137. Which of the following applies the concept of progression? (Rigorous) (Skill 9.1)

    A. Beginning a stretching program every day.

    B. Beginning a stretching program with 3 sets of reps.

    C. Beginning a stretching program with ballistic stretching.

    D. Beginning a stretching program holding stretches for 15 seconds and work up to holding stretches for 60 seconds.

138. Which of following overload principles does not apply to improving body composition? (Average Rigor) (Skill 9.1)

    A. Aerobic exercise three times per week.

    B. Aerobic exercise at a low intensity.

    C. Aerobic exercise for about an hour.

    D. Aerobic exercise in intervals of high intensity.

139. Which of the following principles of progression applies to improving muscle endurance? (Rigorous) (Skill 9.1)

    A. Lifting weights every day.

    B. Lifting weights at 20% to 30% of assessed muscle strength.

    C. Lifting weights with low resistance and low reps.

    D. Lifting weights starting at 60% of assessed muscle strength.

Answer Key

1.	B	36.	C	71.	D	106.	D
2.	B	37.	A	72.	B	107.	C
3.	A	38.	D	73.	C	108.	D
4.	A	39.	A	74.	B	109.	B
5.	D	40.	C	75.	D	110.	D
6.	D	41.	B	76.	A	111.	C
7.	D	42.	B	77.	A	112.	C
8.	C	43.	A	78.	D	113.	A
9.	B	44.	D	79.	C	114.	B
10.	A	45.	D	80.	C	115.	C
11.	B	46.	B	81.	A	116.	D
12.	B	47.	D	82.	C	117.	D
13.	D	48.	B	83.	A	118.	C
14.	B	49.	A	84.	D	119.	A
15.	A	50.	C	85.	D	120.	B
16.	B	51.	A	86.	B	121.	B
17.	C	52.	C	87.	C	122.	C
18.	B	53.	A	88.	B	123.	C
19.	A	54.	C	89.	D	124.	C
20.	D	55.	B	90.	A	125.	D
21.	B	56.	D	91.	C	126.	A
22.	C	57.	A	92.	B	127.	B
23.	A	58.	B	93.	D	128.	B
24.	D	59.	A	94.	B	129.	D
25.	B	60.	C	95.	A	130.	C
26.	C	61.	B	96.	C	131.	B
27.	D	62.	B	97.	A	132.	B
28.	D	63.	C	98.	C	133.	C
29.	C	64.	D	99.	B	134.	A
30.	D	65.	C	100.	B	135.	D
31.	B	66.	A	101.	D	136.	A
32.	C	67.	C	102.	B	137.	D
33.	D	68.	C	103.	A	138.	A
34.	C	69.	B	104.	D	139.	B
35.	B	70.	A	105.	B		

Rationales with Sample Questions

1. **The Greek's best known early contribution to the profession Physical Education was: (Easy) (Skill 1.1)**
    A. The Pentathlon
    B. The Olympics
    C. The Pankration
    D. Acrobatics

(B.) The Olympics are a premiere athletic meeting that originated in ancient Greece and still exists in modern times. The Greeks held the games in ancient times on the plain of Olympia in Greece every four years. Greek citizens put aside political and religious differences as athletes from all of the Greek cities and districts competed in the Olympics. The games included patriotic and religious rituals as well as athletic contests. The winners received high honors.

2. **The physical education philosophy based on experience is: (Average Rigor) (Skill 1.1)**
    A. Naturalism
    B. Pragmatism
    C. Idealism
    D. Existentialism

(B.) Pragmatism, as a school of philosophy, is a collection of different ways of thinking. Given the diversity of thinkers and the variety of schools of thought that have adopted this term over the years, the term pragmatism has become almost meaningless in the absence of further qualification. Most of the thinkers who describe themselves as pragmatists indicate some connection with practical consequences or real effects as vital components of both meaning and truth.

3. **The modern physical education philosophy that combines beliefs from different philosophies is: (Rigorous) (Skill 1.1)**
    A. Eclectic
    B. Humanistic
    C. Individualism
    D. Realism

(A.) Eclectics are so-called philosophers who attach themselves to no system in particular. Instead, they select what, in their judgment, is true out of the other philosophes. In antiquity, the Eclectic philosophy is that which sought to unite into a coherent whole, the doctrines of Pythagoras, Plato, and Aristotle. There is eclecticism in art as well as philosophy. The term was applied to an Italian school which aimed at uniting the excellence of individual intellectual masters.

TEACHER CERTIFICATION STUDY GUIDE

4. Which of the following is not a skill assessment test to evaluate student performance? (Average Rigor) (Skill 1.1)
   A. Harrocks Volley
   B. Rodgers Strength Test
   C. Iowa Brace Test
   D. AAHPERD Youth Fitness Test

(A.) Harrocks Volley is a volleyball code for a popular player named James.

5. All of the following are methods to evaluate the affective domain except: (Average Rigor) (Skill1.1)
   A. Adams Prosocial Inventory
   B. Crowell Personal Distance Scale
   C. Blanchard Behavior Rating Scale
   D. McCloy's Prosocial Behavior Scale

(D.) McCloy's Prosocial Behavior scale provided one of the earliest discussions on the influence of participation in sports and on the development of socially desirable character traits. Not surprisingly, large voids still exist in the knowledge about athletes' moral reasoning. One area that has thus far received little attention by social psychologists is the relationship between sport involvement, moral development, and aggression.

6. Educators can evaluate the cognitive domain by all of the following methods except: (Rigorous) (Skill1.1)
   A. Norm-Referenced Tests
   B. Criterion Referenced Tests
   C. Standardized Tests
   D. Willis Sports Inventory Tests

(D.) The Willis Sports Inventory Test is the tally of all wins and losses of the popular basketball player, Willis.

7. Using the same foot to take off from a surface and land is which locomotor skill? (Easy) (Skill 1.1)
   A. Jumping
   B. Vaulting
   C. Leaping
   D. Hopping

(D.) Hopping is a move with light, bounding skips or leaps. Basically, it is the ability to jump on one foot.

PHYSICAL EDUCATION

8. Which nonlocomotor skill entails movement around a joint where two body parts meet? (Easy) (Skill 1.1)
   A. Twisting
   B. Swaying
   C. Bending
   D. Stretching

(C.) Bending is a deviation from a straight-line position. It is also means to assume a curved, crooked, or angular form or direction, to incline the body, to make a concession, yield, to apply oneself closely, or to concentrate (e.g., *she bent to her task*).

9. A sharp change of direction from one's original line of movement is which nonlocomotor skill? (Easy) (Skill 1.1)
   A. Twisting
   B. Dodging
   C. Swaying
   D. Swinging

(B.) Dodging is the ability to avoid something by moving or shifting quickly aside.

10. Which movement concept involves students making decisions about an object's positional changes in space? (Rigorous) (Skill1.1)
    A. Spatial Awareness
    B. Effort Awareness
    C. Body Awareness
    D. Motion Awareness

(A.) Spatial awareness is an organized awareness of objects in the space around us. It is also an awareness of our body's position in space. Without this awareness, we would not be able to pick food up from our plates and put it in our mouths. We would have trouble reading, because we could not see the letters in their correct relation to each other and to the page. Athletes would not have the precise awareness of the position of other players on the field and the movement of the ball, which is necessary to play sports effectively.

11. **Applying the mechanical principles of balance, time, and force describes which movement concept? (Average Rigor) (Skill (1.1)**
    A. Spatial Awareness
    B. Effort Awareness
    C. Body Awareness
    D. Motion Awareness

(B.) Effort Awareness is the knowledge of balance, time, and force and how they relate to athletic movements and activities.

12. **Having students move in a specific pattern while measuring how long they take to do so develops which quality of movement? (Average Rigor) (Skill4.2)**
    A. Balance
    B. Time
    C. Force
    D. Inertia

(B.) Time is a sequential arrangement of all events or the interval between two events in such a sequence. We can discuss the concept of time on several different levels: physical, psychological, philosophical, scientific, and biological. Time is the non-spatial continuum in which events occur, in apparently irreversible succession, from the past through the present to the future.

TEACHER CERTIFICATION STUDY GUIDE

13. What is the proper order of sequential development for the acquisition of locomotor skills? (Rigorous) (Skill1.1)
   A. Creep, crawl, walk, jump, run, slide, gallop, hop, leap, skip; step-hop.
   B. Crawl, walk, creep, slide, walk, run, hop, leap, gallop, skip; step-hop.
   C. Creep, crawl, walk, slide, run, hop, leap, skip, gallop, jump; step-hop.
   D. Crawl, creep, walk, run, jump, hop, gallop, slide, leap, skip; step-hop.

(D.) LOCOMOTOR SKILL: A skill that utilizes the feet and moves you from one place to another.

CRAWL: A form of locomotion where the person moves in a prone position with the body resting on or close to the ground or on the hands and knees.

CREEP: A slightly more advanced form of locomotion in which the person moves on the hands and knees.

WALK: A form of locomotion in which body weight is transferred alternately from the ball (toe) of one foot to the heel of the other. At times one foot is on the ground and during a brief phase, both feet are on the ground. There is no time when both feet are off the ground.

RUN: A form of locomotion much like the walk except that the tempo and body lean may differ. At times one foot is on the ground and during a brief phase both feet are off the ground. There is no time when both feet are on the ground simultaneously.

14. Having students pretend they are playing basketball or trying to catch a bus develops which locomotor skill? (Easy) (Skill1.1)
   A. Galloping
   B. Running
   C. Leaping
   D. Skipping

(B.) Playing basketball involves near constant running up and down the court. In addition, chasing is a good example to use with children to illustrate the concept of running.

15. Having students play Fox and Hound develops⊗ Easy) (Skill1.1)
   A. Galloping
   B. Hopping
   C. Stepping-hopping
   D. Skipping

(A.) Fox and Hound is an activity that emphasizes rapid running. The form of the exercise most closely resembles a gallop, especially in rhythm and rapidity. It can develop or progress at an accelerated rate.

16. **Having students take off and land with both feet together develops which locomotor skill? (Easy) (Skill 1.1)**
    A. Hopping
    B. Jumping
    C. Leaping
    D. Skipping

(B.) Jumping is a skill that most humans and many animals share. It is the process of getting one's body off of the ground for a short time using one's own power, usually by propelling oneself upward via contraction and then forceful extension of the legs. One can jump up to reach something high, jump over a fence or ditch, or jump down. One can also jump while dancing and as a sport in track and field.

17. **What is the proper sequential order of development for the acquisition of nonlocomotor skills? (Average Rigorous) (Skill 1.1)**
    A. Stretch, sit, bend, turn, swing, twist, shake, rock & sway, dodge; fall.
    B. Bend, stretch, turn, twist, swing, sit, rock & sway, shake, dodge; fall.
    C. Stretch, bend, sit, shake, turn, rock & sway, swing, twist, dodge; fall.
    D. Bend, stretch, sit, turn, twist, swing, sway, rock & sway, dodge; fall.

(C.) Each skill in the progression builds on the previous skills.

18. **Activities such as pretending to pick fruit off a tree or reaching for a star develop which non-locomotor skill? (Easy) (Skill 1.1)**
    A. Bending
    B. Stretching
    C. Turning
    D. Twisting

(B.) Stretching is the activity of gradually applying tensile force to lengthen, strengthen, and lubricate muscles, often performed in anticipation of physical exertion and to increase the range of motion within a joint. Stretching is an especially important accompaniment to activities that emphasize controlled muscular strength and flexibility. These include ballet, acrobatics or martial arts. Stretching also may help prevent injury to tendons, ligaments, and muscles by improving muscular elasticity and reducing the stretch reflex in greater ranges of motion that might cause injury to tissue. In addition, stretching can reduce delayed onset muscle soreness (DOMS).

19. **Picking up coins, tying shoes, and petting animals develop this nonlocomotor skill. (Easy) (Skill 1.1)**
    A. Bending
    B. Stretching
    C. Turning
    D. Twisting

(**A.**) Bending is the action of moving the body across a skeletal joint. In each of the sample activities, one must bend from the waist or knees to reach a low object.

20. **Having students collapse in their own space or lower themselves as though they are a raindrop or snowflake develops this nonlocomotor skill. (Easy) (Skill 1.1)**
    A. Dodging
    B. Shaking
    C. Swinging
    D. Falling

(**D.**) **Falling** is a major cause of personal injury in athletics. Athletic participants must learn how to fall in such a way as to limit the possibility of injury.

21. **Which is the proper sequential order of development for the acquisition of manipulative skills? (Rigorous) (Skill 1.1)**
    A. Striking, throwing, bouncing, catching, trapping, kicking, ball rolling; volleying.
    B. Striking, throwing, kicking, ball rolling, volleying, bouncing, catching; trapping.
    C. Striking, throwing, catching, trapping, kicking, ball rolling, bouncing; volleying.
    D. Striking, throwing, kicking, ball rolling, bouncing; volleying.

(**B.**) Striking, throwing, kicking, ball rolling, volleying, bouncing, catching, and trapping is the proper sequential order of development for the acquisition of manipulative skills. Each skill in this progression builds on the previous skill.

22. **Having students hit a large balloon with both hands develops this manipulative skill?** (Average Rigor) (Skill 1.1)
    A. Bouncing
    B. Striking
    C. Volleying
    D. Trapping

(C.) In a number of ball games, a volley is the ball that a player receives and delivers without touching the ground. The ability to volley a ball back and forth requires great body control and spatial awareness.

23. **Progressively decreasing the size of a target that balls are projected at develops which manipulative skill.** (Average Rigor) (Skill 1.1)
    A. Throwing
    B. Trapping
    C. Volleying
    D. Kicking

(A.) Children develop throwing skills (the ability to propel an object through the air with a rapid movement of the arm and wrist) by projecting balls at progressively smaller targets.

24. **Hitting a stationary object while in a fixed position, then incorporating movement, develops this manipulative skill.** (Average Rigor) (Skill 1.1)
    A. Bouncing
    B. Trapping
    C. Throwing
    D. Striking

(D.) Striking is the process of hitting something sharply, as with the hand, the fist, or a weapon.

25. **Which of the following body types is the most capable of motor performance involving endurance?** (Average Rigor) (Skill 1.2)
    A. Endomorph
    B. Ectomorph
    C. Mesomorph
    D. Metamorph

(B.) Characteristically, ectomorphs are lean and slender with little body fat and musculature. Ectomorphs are usually capable of performing at high levels in endurance events.

26. A major event in the history of physical education occurred among the Romans. Which of the following did the Romans identify? (Average Rigor) (Skill 2.1)
   A. Severe physical training
   B. Harmonious development of the body, mind, and spirit
   C. The worth of physical education was dignified
   D. Physical training only for warriors

(C.) The Romans first established the worth of physical education for its own sake. Answers A and D describe the Spartans, who emphasized severe physical training for warriors. Answer B describes the Athenians, who valued the harmonious development of mind, body, and spirit.

27. President Eisenhower was alerted to the poor fitness levels of American youths. How was the poor physical conditioning of youths discovered in the Eisenhower Administration? (Average Rigor) (Skill 2.1)
   A. By WWII Selective Service Examination
   B. By organizations promoting physical fitness
   C. By the Federal Security Agency
   D. By the Kraus-Webber Tests

(D.) This is one of the programs that President Dwight Eisenhower implemented during his presidency. Using a test devised by Drs. Hans Kraus and Sonja Weber of New York Presbyterian Hospital, Bonnie began testing children in Europe, Central America, and the United States. The Kraus-Weber test involved six simple movements and took 90 seconds to administer. It compared US children to European children in the realms of strength and flexibility. The fitness emphasis in schools started by Kraus-Weber declined in the 1970s and early 1980s. The President's Council on Physical Fitness and Sports was one result of the Kraus-Weber test results.

TEACHER CERTIFICATION STUDY GUIDE

28. In 1956, the AAHPER Fitness Conferences established: (Rigorous) (Skill 2.1)
    A. The President's Council on Youth Fitness
    B. The President's Citizens' Advisory Committee
    C. The President's Council on Physical Fitness
    D. A and B

(D. A, and B.) The **President's Council on Youth Fitness** was founded on July 16, 1956 to encourage American children to be healthy and active after a study indicated that American youths were less physically fit than European children. President Eisenhower created the President's Council on Youth Fitness with cabinet-level status. The Executive Order specified "one" objective. The first Council identified itself as a "catalytic agent" concentrating on creating public awareness. A President's Citizens-Advisory Committee on Fitness of American Youth was confirmed to give advice to the Council.

29. Students that paddle balls against a wall or jump over objects with various heights are demonstrating which quality of movement? (Rigorous) (Skill 2.1)
    A. Balance
    B. Time
    C. Force
    D. Inertia

(C.) Force is the capacity to do work or create physical change, energy, strength, or active power. It is a classical **force** that causes a free body with mass to accelerate. A net (or resultant) force that causes such acceleration may be the non-zero additive sum of many different forces acting on a body.

30. All of the following affect force except (Easy) (Skill 2.1)
    A. Magnitude
    B. Energy
    C. Motion
    D. Mass

(D.) Mass is a property of a physical object that quantifies the amount of matter and energy it contains. Unlike weight, the mass of something stays the same regardless of location. Every object has a unified body of matter with no specific shape.

PHYSICAL EDUCATION

31. For a movement to occur, applied force must overcome inertia of an object and any other resisting forces. What concept of force does this describe? (Rigorous) (Skill 2.1)
    A. Potential energy
    B. Magnitude
    C. Kinetic energy
    D. Absorption

(B.) Speaking of magnitude in a purely relative way states that nothing is large and nothing small. If everything in the universe increased in bulk one thousand diameters, nothing would be any larger than it was before. However, if one thing remained unchanged, all of the others would be larger than they had been. To a person familiar with the relativity of magnitude and distance, the spaces and masses of the astronomer would be no more impressive than those of the microscopist would. To the contrary, the visible universe may be a small part of an atom, with its component ions floating in the life-fluid (luminiferous ether) of some animal.

32. The energy of an object to do work while recoiling is which type of potential energy? (Average Rigor) (Skill 2.1)
    A. Absorption
    B. Kinetic
    C. Elastic
    D. Torque

(C.) In materials science, the word elastomer refers to a material that is very elastic (like rubber). We often use the word elastic colloquially to refer to an elastomeric material such as rubber or cloth/rubber combinations. It is capable of withstanding stress without injury. Elastic potential energy describes the energy inherent in flexible objects.

33. Gradually decelerating a moving mass by utilization of smaller forces over a long period of time is⊗(Average Rigor) (Skill 2.1)
    A. Stability
    B. Equilibrium
    C. Angular force
    D. Force absorption

(D.) Force absorption is the gradual deceleration of a moving mass by utilization of smaller forces over a long period of time.

TEACHER CERTIFICATION STUDY GUIDE

34. Which of the following principles is not a factor to assess to correct errors in performance for process assessment? (Average Rigor) (Skill 2.1)
    A. Inertia
    B. Action/Reaction
    C. Force
    D. Acceleration

(C.) Force is not a factor to focus on in process assessment.

35. An instructor used a similar movement from a skill learned in a different activity to teach a skill for a new activity. The technique used to facilitate cognitive learning was® (Rigorous) (Skill 2.1)
    A. Conceptual thinking
    B. Transfer of learning
    C. Longer instruction
    D. Appropriate language

(B.) Using a previously used movement to facilitate a new task is a transfer of learning. The individual relates the past activity to the new one, enabling him/her to learn it more easily. Conceptual thinking is related to the transfer of learning, but it does not give the exact idea. Rather, it emphasizes the history of all learning.

36. A teacher rewards students for completing tasks. Which method is the teacher using to facilitate psychomotor learning? (Average Rigor) (Skill 2.1)
    A. Task/Reciprocal
    B. Command/Direct
    C. Contingency/Contract
    D. Physical/Reflex

(C.) Since the teacher is rewarding the student, the contingency/contract method is in place. The command/direct method involves the interaction between student and teacher when the student fails to fulfill the requirements.

PHYSICAL EDUCATION

37. All of the following are Systematic Observational Evaluations except⊗ (Rigorous) (Skill 2.3)
    A. Reflective Recording
    B. Event Recording
    C. Duration Recording
    D. Self Recording

(A.) Reflective recording is not a type of systematic observational evaluation. Event, duration, and self recordings are all methods used in systematic observational evaluations.

38. A physical education teacher emphasizes healthy attitudes and habits. She conducts her classes so that students acquire and interpret knowledge and learn to think/analyze, which is necessary for physical activities. The goals and values utilized and the philosophy applied by this instructor is: (Average Rigor) (Skill 3.1)
    A. Physical Development Goals and Realism Philosophy
    B. Affective Development Goals and Existentialism
    C. Motor Development Goals and Realism Philosophy
    D. Cognitive Development Goals and Idealism Philosophy

(D.) Educators use cognitive development goals to describe the act of teaching children in a manner that will help them develop as personal and social beings. Concepts that fall under this term include social and emotional learning, moral reasoning/cognitive development, life-skills education, health education, violence prevention, critical thinking, ethical reasoning, and conflict resolution and mediation. This form of education involves teaching children and teenagers such values as honesty, stewardship, kindness, generosity, courage, freedom, justice, equality, and respect. Idealism is an approach to philosophical inquiry that asserts direct and immediate knowledge can only be had as ideas or mental pictures. We can only know the objects that are the basis of these ideas indirectly.

39. Social skills and values developed by activity include all of the following except: (Easy) (Skill 3.1)
    A. Winning at all costs
    B. Making judgments in groups
    C. Communicating and cooperating
    D. Respecting rules and property

(A.) Winning at all costs is not a desirable social skill. Instructors and coaches should emphasize fair play and effort over winning. Answers B, C, and D are all positive skills and values developed in physical activity settings.

TEACHER CERTIFICATION STUDY GUIDE

40. Activities that enhance team socialization include all of the following except: (Easy) (Skill 3.1)
    A. Basketball
    B. Soccer
    C. Golf
    D. Volleyball

(C.) Golf is mainly an individual sport. Though golf involves social interaction, it generally lacks the team element inherent in basketball, soccer, and volleyball.

41. Through physical activities, John has developed self-discipline, fairness, respect for others, and new friends. John has demonstrated which of the following? (Rigorous) (Skill 3.1)
    A. Positive cooperation psycho-social influences
    B. Positive group psycho-social influences
    C. Positive individual psycho-social influences
    D. Positive accomplishment psycho-social influences

(B.) Through physical activities, John developed his social interaction skills. Social interaction is the sequence of social actions between individuals (or groups) that modify their actions and reactions due to the actions of their interaction partner(s). In other words, they are events in which people attach meaning to a situation, interpret what others mean, and respond accordingly. Through socialization with other people, John feels the influence of the people around him.

42. Which of the following psycho-social influences is not negative? (Rigorous) (Skill 3.1)
    A. Avoidance of problems
    B. Adherence to exercise
    C. Ego-centeredness
    D. Role conflict

(B.) The ability of an individual to adhere to an exercise routine due to her/his excitement, accolades, etc. is not a negative psycho-social influence. Adherence to an exercise routine is healthy and positive.

TEACHER CERTIFICATION STUDY GUIDE

43. The affective domain of physical education contributes to all of the following except: (Rigorous) (Skill 3.1)
   A. Knowledge of exercise, health, and disease
   B. Self-actualization
   C. An appreciation of beauty
   D. Good sportsmanship

(A.) The affective domain encompasses emotions, thoughts, and feelings related to physical education. Knowledge of exercise, health, and disease is part of the cognitive domain.

44. A physical education instructor anticipates and prevents potential injuries, watches for hidden injuries, and takes an injury evaluation of the entire class. Which of the following strategies to prevent injuries is the teacher demonstrating? (Average Rigor) (Skill 3.1)
   A. Maintaining hiring standards
   B. Proper use of equipment
   C. Proper procedures for emergencies
   D. Participant screening

(D.) In order for the instructor to know each student's physical status, she takes an injury evaluation. Such surveys are one way to know the physical status of an individual. It chronicles past injuries, tattoos, activities, and diseases the individual may have or had. It helps the instructor to know the limitations of each individual. Participant screening covers all forms of surveying and anticipation of injuries.

45. An instructor notices that class participation is much lower than expected. By making changes in equipment and rules, the instructor applied which of the following concepts to enhance participation? (Rigorous) (Skill 3.1)
   A. Homogeneous grouping
   B. Heterogeneous grouping
   C. Multi-activity designs
   D. Activity modification

(D.) Activity modification involves changing rules and equipment to fit the needs of students of different ability levels and physical development levels. Activity modification can encourage participation by making games and activities more enjoyable and allowing for more student success.

TEACHER CERTIFICATION STUDY GUIDE

46. Using tactile clues is a functional adaptation that can assist which type of students? (Rigorous) (Skill 3.1)
   A. Deaf students
   B. Blind students
   C. Asthmatic students
   D. Physically challenged students

(B.) Blind people use tactile clues to identify colors. Instructors should use tactile clues to help students see or hear targets by adding color, making them larger, or moving them closer. It will help cooperation in a creative way.

47. There are two sequential phases to the development of spatial awareness. What is the order of these phases? (Rigorous) (Skill 3.1)
   A. Locating more than one object to each object; the location of objects in relation to one's own body in space.
   B. The location of objects in relation to ones' own body in space; locating more than one object in relation to one's own body.
   C. Locating more than one object independent of one's body; the location of objects in relation to one's own body.
   D. The location of objects in relation to one's own body in space; locating more than one object in relation to each object and independent of one's own body.

(D.) The order of the two sequential phases to develop spatial awareness are as follows: the location of objects in relation to one's own body in space, and locating more than one object in relation to each object and independent of one's own body.

48. Equilibrium is maintained as long as® (Average Rigor) (Skill 3.1)
   A. Body segments are moved independently.
   B. The center of gravity is over the base of support
   C. Force is applied to the base of support.
   D. The center of gravity is lowered.

(B.) Equilibrium is a condition in which all acting influences are canceled by others, resulting in a stable, balanced, or unchanging system. It allows humans and animals to walk without falling. An object maintains equilibrium as long as its center of gravity is over its base of support.

PHYSICAL EDUCATION 265

49. Which of the following does not enhance equilibrium? (Average Rigor) (Skill 3.1)

   A. Shifting the center of gravity away from the direction of movement.

   B. Increasing the base of support.

   C. Lowering the base of support.

   D. Increasing the base of support and lowering the center of support.

(A.) Equilibrium is a state of balance. When a body or a system is in equilibrium, there is no net tendency toward change. In mechanics, equilibrium has to do with the forces acting on a body. When no force acts to make a body move in a line, the body is in translational equilibrium. When no force acts to make the body turn, the body is in rotational equilibrium. A body in equilibrium while at rest is in static equilibrium. Increasing the base of support, lowering the base of support, and increasing the base of support and lowering the center of support all enhance equilibrium by balancing forces.

50. The most effective way to promote the physical education curriculum is to: (Rigorous) (Skill 3.2)
   A. Relate physical education to higher thought processes
   B. Relate physical education to humanitarianism
   C. Relate physical education to the total educational process
   D. Relate physical education to skills necessary to preserve the natural environment

(C.) The government treats the physical education curriculum as one of the major subjects. Because of all of the games that we now participate in, many countries have focused their hearts and set their minds on competing with rival countries. Physical education is now one of the major, important subjects and instructors should integrate physical education into the total educational process.

51. Which of the following is not a consideration for the selection of a facility? (Rigorous) (Skill 3.2)
   A. Community involvement
   B. Custodial staff
   C. Availability to women, minorities, and the handicapped
   D. Bond issues

(A.) While community involvement positively impacts the communities where individuals live and work, it is not a major consideration in facility selection. Factors that are more important are staffing, accessibility, and financial considerations.

TEACHER CERTIFICATION STUDY GUIDE

52. Which of the following is not a class-management technique? (Easy) (Skill 3.2)
    A. Explaining procedures for roll call, excuses, and tardiness
    B. Explaining routines for changing and showering
    C. Explaining conditioning
    D. Promoting individual self-discipline

(C.) Explaining conditioning is not a class management technique. It is an instructional lesson.

53. Long-term planning is essential for effective class management. Identify the management techniques not essential to long-term planning. (Easy) (Skill 3.2)
    A. Parental observation
    B. Progress evaluation
    C. Precise activity planning
    D. Arrangements for line markings

(A.) While it is important that a child have support from his/her parents, parental observation is not an essential consideration in long-term planning. Progress evaluation, precise activity planning, and arranging line markings are all essential management techniques for long-term planning.

54. Although Mary is a paraplegic, she wants to participate in some capacity in the physical education class. What federal legislative act entitles her to do so? (Rigorous) (Skill 3.2)
    A. PE 94-142
    B. Title IX
    C. PL 94-142
    D. Title XI

(C.) It is the purpose of Act PL 94-142 to assure that all handicapped children have available to them, within the time periods specified in section 612(2), (B.), a free, appropriate public education that emphasizes special education and related services designed to meet their unique needs, to assure that the rights of handicapped children and their parents/guardians are protected, to assist states and localities to provide for the education of all handicapped children, and to assess and assure the effectiveness of efforts to educate handicapped children.

55. **A legal wrong resulting in a direct or an indirect injury is: (Average Rigor) (Skill 3.2)**
    A. Negligence
    B. A Tort
    C. In loco parentis
    D. Legal liability

(B.) A tort is damage, injury, or a wrongful act done willfully, negligently, or in circumstances involving strict liability, but not involving breach of contract, for which the injured party can bring a civil suit.

56. **All of the following actions help avoid lawsuits except: (Average Rigor) (Skill 3.2)**
    A. Ensuring equipment and facilities are safe
    B. Getting exculpatory agreements
    C. Knowing each students' health status
    D. Grouping students with unequal competitive levels

(D.) Grouping students with unequal competitive levels is not an action that can help avoid lawsuits. Such a practice could lead to injury because of the inequality in skill, size, and strength.

57. **Which of the following actions does not promote safety? (Rigorous) (Skill 3.2)**
    A. Allowing students to wear the current style of shoes
    B. Presenting organized activities
    C. Inspecting equipment and facilities
    D. Instructing skill and activities properly

(A.) Shoes are very important in physical education and the emphasis on current shoe styles does not promote safety because they focus more on the look of the clothing, rather than functionality.

58. The tendency of a body/object to remain in its present state of motion unless some force acts to change it is which mechanical principle of motion? (Average Rigor) (Skill 3.2)
    A. Acceleration
    B. Inertia
    C. Action/Reaction
    D. Linear motion

(B.) Inertia (ĭnûr'shə) is a term used in physics that describes the resistance of a body to any alteration in its state of motion. Inertia is a property common to all matter. Galileo first observed this property and Newton later restated it. Newton's first law of motion is sometimes called the law of inertia. Newton's second law of motion states that the external force required to affect the motion of a body is proportional to that acceleration. The constant of proportionality is the mass, which is the numerical value of the inertia. The greater the inertia of a body, the less acceleration is needed for a given, applied force.

59. The movement response of a system depends not only on the net external force, but also on the resistance to movement change. Which mechanical principle of motion does this definition describe? (Rigorous) (Skill 3.2)
    A. Acceleration
    B. Inertia
    C. Action/Reaction
    D. Air Resistance

(A.) Acceleration is the change in the velocity of a body with respect to time. Since velocity is a vector quantity involving both magnitude and direction, acceleration is also a vector. In order to produce acceleration, a force must on a body. The magnitude of the force (F) must be directly proportional to both the mass of the body (m) and the desired acceleration (a), according to Newton's second law of motion ($F=ma$). The exact nature of the acceleration depends on the relative directions of the original velocity and force. A force acting in the same direction as the velocity changes only the speed of the body. An appropriate force, acting always at right angles to the velocity, changes the direction of the velocity but not the speed.

TEACHER CERTIFICATION STUDY GUIDE

60. **Which of the following mechanical principles of motion states that every motion has a similar, contrasting response? (Easy) (Skill 3.2)**
    A. Acceleration
    B. Inertia
    C. Action/Reaction
    D. Centripetal force

(C.) The principle of action/reaction is an assertion about the nature of motion from which we can determine the trajectory of an object subject to forces. The path of an object yields a stationary value for a quantity called the **action**. Thus, instead of thinking about an object accelerating in response to applied forces, one might think of them as picking out the path with a stationary action.

61. **A subjective, observational approach to identify errors in the form, style, or mechanics of a skill is accomplished by: (Rigorous) (Skill 4.1)**
    A. Product assessment
    B. Process assessment
    C. Standardized norm-referenced tests
    D. Criterion-referenced tests

(B.) Process assessment is one way to identify errors in the skills of an individual. It is one way to know the limitations and skills that every individual possesses.

62. **What type of assessment objectively measures skill performance? (Rigorous) (Skill 4.1)**
    A. Process assessment
    B. Product assessment
    C. Texas PE Test
    D. Iowa Brace Test

(B.) Product assessment measures the skills of an individual. This process is a methodical evaluation of the characteristics of your product or service in the eyes of potential users and customers. The two principle types of assessments are principle-based assessments and usability testing.

TEACHER CERTIFICATION STUDY GUIDE

63. **Process assessment does not identify which of the following errors in skill performance? (Average Rigor) (Skill 4.1)**
    A. Style
    B. Form
    C. End result
    D. Mechanics

(C.) Process assessment does not evaluate end results. Process assessment emphasizes analysis of style, form, and mechanics.

64. **Determining poor performance of a skill using process assessment can best be accomplished by⊗ (Average Rigor) (Skill 4.1)**
    A. Observing how fast a skill is performed.
    B. Observing how many skills are performed.
    C. Observing how far or how high a skill is performed.
    D. Observing several attributes comprising the entire performance of a skill.

(D.) To determine the source of the error in the poor performance of an individual, we use observations of several attributes that compromise the entire performance of a skill. Instructors should observe limitations and mistakes and determine how to best address these problems to improve future performance.

65. **Which of the following methods measures fundamental skills using product assessment? (Rigorous) (Skill 4.1)**
    A. Criterion-referenced tests
    B. Standardized norm-referenced tests
    C. Both A and B
    D. Neither A nor B

(C.) Criterion-referenced tests and standardized norm-referenced tests are both methods that can prove and measure skills in product assessment. They can help to prevent or lessen errors.

TEACHER CERTIFICATION STUDY GUIDE

66. Product assessment measures all of the following except⊗ (Rigorous) (Skill 4.1)
   A. How the student performs the mechanics of a skill.
   B. How many times the student performs a skill.
   C. How fast the student performs a skill.
   D. How far or high the student performs a skill.

(A.) Product assessment evaluates student performance and gives insight into how students can correct errors. Product assessment measures results. Thus, how the student performs the mechanics of a skill is not relevant to product assessment.

67. Instructors can evaluate skill level of achievement in archery by: (Average Rigor) (Skill 4.1)
   A. Giving students a written exam on terminology.
   B. Having students demonstrate the correct tension of arrow feathers.
   C. Totaling a student's score obtained on the target's face.
   D. Time how long a student takes to shoot all arrows.

(C.) Archery is the practice of using a bow to shoot arrows. Totaling a student's score is the only method, of the possible choices, that evaluates skill level. Choices A and B test knowledge and choice D is an arbitrary measure.

68. Instructors can determine skill level achievement in golf by: (Average Rigor) (Skill 4.1)
   A. The number of "birdies" that were made.
   B. The number of "bogies" that were made.
   C. The score obtained after several rounds.
   D. The total score achieved throughout the school year.

(C.) Instructors can determine skill level in golf by evaluating a golfer's score after several rounds. The number of bogies or birdies is not necessarily indicative of skill level because they are isolated events (i.e. the score on one hole). The player who consistently scores the lowest likely has the most impressive golf skills. Therefore, a player's score is the best way to determine his/her skill level. Finally, several rounds is a sufficient sample to determine skill level. An entire year's worth of scores is not necessary.

TEACHER CERTIFICATION STUDY GUIDE

69. **Instructors can determine skill level achievement in swimming by : (Average Rigor) (Skill 4.1)**
    A. How long a student can float.
    B. How many strokes it takes to swim a specified distance.
    C. How long a student can stay under the water without moving.
    D. How many times a student can dive in five minutes.

(B.) Instructors can determine skill level in swimming by counting the strokes a swimmer takes when covering a certain distance. The arm movement, the strength, and the tactic to move quickly gives the swimmer an ability to swim faster. The ability to float, stay under water, and dive quickly is not relevant to swimming ability.

70. **Instructors can assess skill level achievement in bowling by: (Easy) (Skill 4.1)**
    A. Calculating a student's average.
    B. Calculating how many gutter-balls were thrown.
    C. Calculating how many strikes were thrown.
    D. Calculating how many spares were thrown.

(A.) Instructors can determine the skill level of a bowler by calculating the student's average game score. There is a possibility that some coincidences take place (e.g., bowling a strike). To check the consistency, we determine the average instead of looking at only the score from a single game.

71. **Although they are still hitting the target, the score of some students practicing archery has decreased as the distance between them and the target has increased. Which of the following adjustments will improve their scores? (Rigorous) (Skill 4.1)**
    A. Increasing the velocity of their arrows.
    B. Increasing the students' base of support.
    C. Increasing the weight of the arrows.
    D. Increasing the parabolic path of the arrows.

(D.) Increasing the parabolic path of the arrows will increase accuracy and precision at greater distances.

72. Some students practicing basketball are having difficulty with "free throws," even though the shots make it to and over the hoop. What adjustment will improve their "free throws?" (Average Rigor) (Skill 4.1)
    A. Increasing the height of release (i.e. jump shot).
    B. Increasing the vertical path of the ball.
    C. Increasing the velocity of the release.
    D. Increasing the base of support.

(B.) In this case, increasing the vertical path of the ball will help the students make more free throws. Increased vertical path provides greater margin for error, allowing the ball to drop more easily through the hoop. Increasing the velocity cannot work due to common sense. Finally, increasing the height of release and base of support are not viable options in this case because the students are having no problem getting the ball to the basket.

73. An archery student's arrow bounced off the red part of the target face. What is the correct ruling? (Average Rigor) (Skill 4.1)
    A. No score.
    B. Re-shoot arrow.
    C. 7 points awarded.
    D. Shot receives same score as highest arrow shot that did not bounce off the target.

(C.) When an arrow bounces off the red area of a target, the archer receives 7 points, the value of the shot had the arrow stuck in the target.

74. A student playing badminton believed that the shuttlecock was going to land out-of-bounds. The shuttlecock landed on the line. What is the correct ruling? (Easy) (Skill 4.1)
    A. The shuttlecock is out-of-bounds.
    B. The shuttlecock is in-bounds.
    C. The point is replayed.
    D. That player is charged with a feint.

(B.) If a shuttlecock lands on the line, it is inbounds by the rules of badminton.

TEACHER CERTIFICATION STUDY GUIDE

75. **A mechanical pinsetter accidentally knocked down the only bowling pin left standing for a spare attempt, after clearing all the other pins knocked down by the first ball thrown. What is the correct ruling? (Rigorous) (Skill 4.1)**
    A. Foul
    B. Spare
    C. Frame is replayed
    D. No count for that pin

(D.) When the mechanical pin setter touches a pin and knocks it down, there is no count for the pin because the pin fell because of mechanical fault and the player had nothing to do with it. The other pins count and there is no foul for the player.

76. **The ball served in racquetball hits the front line and lands in front of the short line. What is the ruling? (Easy) (Skill 4.1)**
    A. Fault
    B. Reserve
    C. Out-of-bounds
    D. Fair ball

(A.) If a served ball falls in front of the short line, it is a fault according to a rule that states that a ball must fall within the short line frame at the time of serving. It is not out-of-bounds, as it is still within the limits of the pitch. However, it is also not a fair ball due to the service rule.

77. **Two opposing soccer players are trying to gain control of the ball when one player "knees" the other. What is the ruling? (Easy) (Skill 4.1)**
    A. Direct free kick
    B. Indirect free kick
    C. Fair play
    D. Ejection from a game

(A.) Assuming that the soccer player didn't intentionally hit the other player's knee, the result would be a direct free kick. If the foul was intentional, the referee can eject the offender from the game. Minor offenses and offenses not involving contact result in indirect free kicks.

78. Two students are playing badminton. When receiving the shuttlecock, one student consistently stands too deep in the receiving court. What strategy should the server use to serve the shuttlecock? (Average Rigor) (Skill 4.1)
   A. Smash serve
   B. Clear serve
   C. Overhead serve
   D. Short serve

(D.) The short serve would give land short in the court so the opponent would not be able to reach the shuttlecock. Therefore, the short serve would win the point. A clear or overhead serve enables the opponent to hit the shuttlecock and continue the game. A smash serve runs a higher risk of falling out-of-bounds. Neither of these scenarios are goals of the server.

79. A basketball team has an outstanding rebounder. In order to keep this player near the opponent's basket, which strategy should the coach implement? (Easy) (Skill 4.1)
   A. Pick-and-Roll
   B. Give-and-Go
   C. Zone defense
   D. Free-lancing

(C.) A zone defense, where each player guards an area of the court rather than an individual player, allows an outstanding rebounder to remain near the basket. The give-and-go, pick-and-roll, and free-lancing are offensive strategies that do not affect rebounding.

80. When a defensive tennis player needs more time to return to his position, what strategy should he apply? (Rigorous) (Skill 4.1)
   A. Drop shot
   B. Dink shot
   C. Lob shot
   D. Down-the-line shot

(C.) When a tennis player is off the court and needs time to return to his position, the player should play a lob shot. Down-the-line shots and drop shots are offensive shots and are too risky in this situation. The dink shot would allow the opponent to take control of the point.

81. **An overhead badminton stroke used to hit a forehand-like overhead stroke that is on the backhand side of the body is called: (Rigorous) (Skill 4.1)**
    A. Around-the-head-shot
    B. Down-the-line shot
    C. Lifting the shuttle
    D. Under hand shuttle

(A.) A shot played from the backhand side and over the head is known as an around-the-head shot. It is played when the shuttlecock is high and cannot be reached any other way.

82. **A maneuver when an offensive player passes to a teammate and then immediately cuts in toward the basket for a return pass is: (Average Rigor) (Skill 4.1)**
    A. Charging
    B. Pick
    C. Give-and-go
    D. Switching

(C.) In the game of basketball, a give-and-go is an offensive play where a player passes to a teammate and immediately cuts toward the basket for a return pass. Charging is an offensive foul, a pick is a maneuver to free up a teammate for a pass or shot, and switching is a defensive maneuver.

83. **A bowling pin that remains standing after an apparently perfect hit is called a: (Rigorous) (Skill 4.1)**
    A. Tap
    B. Turkey
    C. Blow
    D. Leave

(A.) A bowling pin that remains standing, even after a perfect shot, is known as a tap. Other options, like turkeys and blows, are not relevant to the standing pin.

84. **A soccer pass from the outside of the field near the end line to a position in front of the goal is called: (Average Rigor) (Skill 4.1)**
    A. Chip
    B. Settle
    C. Through
    D. Cross

(D.) Any long pass from the sides of the field toward the middle is a cross, since the hitter hits it across the field. A chip is a high touch pass or shot. A through pass travels the length of the field through many players. Finally, settling is the act of controlling the ball after receiving a pass.

85. **A volleyball that is simultaneously contacted above the net by opponents and momentarily held upon contact is a(n): (Easy) (Skill 4.1)**
    A. Double fault
    B. Play over
    C. Overlap
    D. Held ball

(D.) In volleyball, if two players simultaneously contact the ball above the net, the ball is a held ball.

86. **Volleyball player LB on team A digs a spiked ball. The ball deflects off of LB's shoulder. What is the ruling? (Average Rigor) (Skill 4.1)**
    A. Fault
    B. Legal hit
    C. Double foul
    D. Play over

(B.) Since the spiked ball does not touch the ground and instead deflects off LB's shoulder, it is a legal hit. In order for a point to end, the ball must touch the ground. In this instance, it does not.

87. **Playing "Simon Says" and having students touch different body parts applies which movement concept? (Average Rigor) (Skill 4.2)**
    A. Spatial Awareness
    B. Effort Awareness
    C. Body Awareness
    D. Motion Awareness

(C.) Body Awareness is a method that integrates European traditions of movement and biomedical knowledge with the East Asian traditions of movement (e.g. Tai chi and Zen meditation).

TEACHER CERTIFICATION STUDY GUIDE

88. Having students move in a specific pattern while measuring how long they take to do so develops which quality of movement? (Average Rigor) (Skill 4.2)
    A. Balance
    B. Time
    C. Force
    D. Inertia

(B.) Time is a sequential arrangement of all events or the interval between two events in such a sequence. We can discuss the concept of time on several different levels: physical, psychological, philosophical, scientific, and biological. Time is the non-spatial continuum in which events occur, in apparently irreversible succession, from the past through the present to the future.

89. Aerobic dance develops or improves each of the following skills or health components except: (Rigorous) (Skill 4.2)
    A. Cardio-respiratory function
    B. Body composition
    C. Coordination
    D. Flexibility

(D.) Aerobic dance does not develop flexibility, as flexibility results from stretching and not aerobic exercise. Ballet dancing, however, does develop flexibility. Aerobic dance develops cardio-respiratory function due to the unusual body movements performed. It also improves body composition and coordination due to the movement of various body parts.

90. Rowing develops which health or skill related component of fitness? (Rigorous) (Skill 4.2)
    A. Muscle endurance
    B. Flexibility
    C. Balance
    D. Reaction time

(A.) Rowing helps develop muscle endurance because of the continuous arm movement against the force of the water. However, flexibility, balance, and reaction time are not important components of rowing. Rowing also develops the lower abdominal muscles while the individual is in the sitting position when rowing.

91. Calisthenics develops all of the following health and skill related components of fitness except: (Average Rigor) (Skill 4.2)
    A. Muscle strength
    B. Body composition
    C. Power
    D. Agility

(C.) Calisthenics is a sport that actually helps to keep a body fit in by combining gymnastic and aerobic activities. Calisthenics develop muscle strength and agility and improves body composition. However, calisthenics do not develop power because they do not involve resistance training or explosiveness.

92. Which health or skill related component of fitness is developed by rope jumping? (Average Rigor) (Skill 4.2)
    A. Muscle Force
    B. Coordination
    C. Flexibility
    D. Muscle strength

(B.) Rope jumping is a good mental exercise and it improves coordination. Many athletes (e.g. boxers, tennis players) jump rope to improve coordination and quickness. Muscle strength is secondary to that.

93. Swimming does not improve which health or skill related component of fitness? (Rigorous) (Skill 4.2)
    A. Cardio-respiratory function
    B. Flexibility
    C. Muscle strength
    D. Foot Speed

(D.) Swimming involves every part of the body. It works on the cardio-respiratory system and it develops flexibility because of the intense body movement in the water. It also improves muscle strength as swimmers must move their bodies against the force of water. Increased foot speed is not an outcome of swimming.

TEACHER CERTIFICATION STUDY GUIDE

94. Data from a cardio-respiratory assessment can identify and predict all of the following except: (Rigorous) (Skill 4.2)
    A. Functional aerobic capacity
    B. Natural over-fatness
    C. Running ability
    D. Motivation

(B.) The data from cardio-respiratory assessment can identify and predict running ability, motivation, and functional aerobic capacity. However, it cannot predict natural over-fatness, as natural over-fatness is a part of the human body. It is not artificially developed like running ability and motivation.

95. Data from assessing _____ identifies an individual's potential of developing musculoskeletal problems and an individual's potential of performing activities of daily living. (Rigorous) (Skill 4.2)
    A. Flexibility
    B. Muscle endurance
    C. Muscle strength
    D. Motor performance

(A.) Flexibility.

96. A 17-year-old male student performed 20 sit-ups, ran a mile in 8 minutes, and has a body fat composition of 17%. Which is the best interpretation of his fitness level? (Rigorous) (Skill 4.2)
    A. Average muscular endurance, good cardiovascular endurance; appropriate body fat composition.
    B. Low muscular endurance, average cardiovascular endurance; high body fat composition.
    C. Low muscular endurance, average cardiovascular endurance; appropriate body fat composition.
    D. Low muscular endurance, low cardiovascular endurance; appropriate body fat composition.

(C.) A 17-year-old male who performs 20 sit-ups, runs a mile in 8 minutes and has 17% fat composition has low muscular endurance, average cardiovascular endurance, and appropriate fat composition. 20 sit-ups is a relatively low number. An 8-minute mile is an average time for a 17-year-old male. Finally, a body fat composition of 17% is appropriate.

97. **Based on the information given in the previous question, what changes would you recommend to improve this person's level of fitness? (Average Rigor) (Skill 4.2)**
    A. Muscle endurance training and cardiovascular endurance training.
    B. Muscle endurance training, cardiovascular endurance training, and reduction of caloric intake.
    C. Muscle strength training and cardio-vascular endurance training.
    D. No changes necessary.

(A.) The person requires both muscle endurance and cardiovascular training while keeping the other bodily intakes normal. An appropriate program would include moderate weightlifting and regular aerobic activity.

98. **An obese student's fitness assessments were poor for every component of fitness. Which would you recommend first? (Easy) (Skill 4.2)**
    A. A jogging program.
    B. A weight lifting program.
    C. A walking program.
    D. A stretching program.

(C.) An obese person should begin by walking and then progress to jogging. Weightlifting and stretching are not as important initially. They are also dangerous because the student may not have the ability to complete such strenuous tasks safely.

99. **Coordinated movements that project a person over an obstacle are: (Easy) (Skill 4.4))**
    A. Jumping
    B. Vaulting
    C. Leaping
    D. Hopping

(B.) Vaulting is the art of acrobatics on horseback. Vaulting is an internationally recognized, competitive sport that is growing in popularity. At the most basic level vaulting enhances riding skills. At any skill-level, this ancient dance between horse and rider deepens the sense of balance, timing, and poise for the rider, as well as a sensitivity to and respect for the horse-rider relationship. Participants can vault in competition individually or on a team of 8 people with up to 3 people on the horse at once.

100. **Which manipulative skill uses the hands to stop the momentum of an object? (Rigorous) (Skill 4.4)**
    A. Trapping
    B. Catching
    C. Striking
    D. Rolling

(B.) The ability to use the hands to catch an object is a manipulative skill. Catching stops the momentum of an object. A successful catch harnesses the force of the oncoming object to stop the object's momentum.

101. **Which professional organization protects amateur sports from corruption? (Easy) (Skill5.1)**
    A. AIWA
    B. AAHPERD
    C. NCAA
    D. AAU

(D.) The Amateur Athletic Union (AAU) is one of the largest non-profit, volunteer sports organizations in the United States. A multi-sport organization, the AAU dedicates itself exclusively to the promotion and development of amateur sports and physical fitness programs. Answer C may be a tempting choice, but the NCAA deals only with college athletics.

102. **Which professional organization works with legislatures? (Average Rigor) (Skill 5.1)**
    A. AIWA
    B. AAHPERD
    C. ACSM
    D. AAU

(B.) AAHPERD, or American Alliance for Health, Physical Education, Recreation and Dance, is an alliance of 6 national associations. AAHPERD is the largest organization of professionals supporting and assisting those involved in physical education, leisure, fitness, dance, health promotion, and education, as well as all other specialties related to achieving a healthy lifestyle. AAHPERD is an alliance designed to provide members with a comprehensive and coordinated array of resources, support, and programs to help practitioners improve their skills and in turn, further the health and well-being of the American public.

TEACHER CERTIFICATION STUDY GUIDE

103. Research in physical education is published in all of the following periodicals except the: (Average Rigor) (Skill 5.1)
    A. School PE Update
    B. Research Quarterly
    C. Journal of Physical Education
    D. YMCA Magazine

(A.) Each school has a PE Update that publishes their own periodicals about physical activities. It aims at helping the students to catch-up on what is happening around them. The school produces this update to encourage their students to become more interested in all of the physical activities that they offer. School PE Updates, however, do not include research findings.

104. A teacher who modifies and develops tasks for a class is demonstrating knowledge of which appropriate behavior in physical education activities. (Rigorous) (Skill 5.1)
    A. Appropriate management behavior
    B. Appropriate student behavior
    C. Appropriate administration behavior
    D. Appropriate content behavior

(D.) In this case, the teacher is demonstrating knowledge of a behavior in reference to physical activity. It is known as appropriate content behavior. The other options are not related to physical activities.

105. The ability for a muscle(s) to repeatedly contract over a period of time is⊗ (Average Rigor) (Skill 5.1)
    A. Cardiovascular endurance
    B. Muscle endurance
    C. Muscle strength
    D. Muscle force

(B.) Muscle endurance gives the muscle the ability to contract over a period of time. Muscle strength is a prerequisite for the endurance of muscle. Cardiovascular endurance involves aerobic exercise.

TEACHER CERTIFICATION STUDY GUIDE

106. **The ability to change rapidly the direction of the body is: (Average Rigor) (Skill 5.1)**
    A. Coordination
    B. Reaction time
    C. Speed
    D. Agility

(D.) Agility is the ability of the body to change position quickly. Reaction time, coordination, and speed are not the right words to describe the ability to move quickly, as we always say that the goalkeeper is agile.

107. **Students are performing the vertical jump. What component of fitness does this activity assess? (Rigorous) (Skill 5.1)**
    A. Muscle strength
    B. Balance
    C. Power
    D. Muscle endurance

(C.) Vertical jumping assesses the power of the entire body. It shows the potential of the legs to hold the upper body and the strength in the joints of the legs. Balance and muscle strength are secondary requirements. Power automatically ensures these secondary requirements.

108. **Using the Karvonen Formula, compute the 60% - 80% THR for a 16-year old student with a RHR of 60. (Rigorous) (Skill 5.1)**
    A. 122-163 beats per minute
    B. 130-168 beats per minute
    C. 142-170 beats per minute
    D. 146-175 beats per minute

(D.)

220 – 16 (age) = 204, 204 – 60 (RHR) = 144, 144 x .60 (low end of heart range) = 86, 86 + 60 (RHR) = **146 (bottom of THR)**

220 – 16 (age) = 204, 204 – 60 (RHR) = 144, 144 x 0.80 (high end of heart range) = 115, 115 + (RHR) = **175 (top of THR)**

146-175 beats per minute is the 60%-80% THR.

109. Using Cooper's Formula, compute the THR for a 15-year old student. (Rigorous) (Skill 5.1)
   A. 120-153 beats per minute
   B. 123-164 beats per minute
   C. 135-169 beats per minute
   D. 147-176 beats per minute

(B.) 123-164 beats per minute.

110. Which is not a common negative stressor? (Rigorous) (Skill 5.1)
   A. Loss of significant other
   B. Personal illness or injury.
   C. Moving to a new state.
   D. Landing a new job.

(D.) Landing a new job is generally not a cause of worry or stress. In fact, it is a positive event. Personal illness, loss of a significant other, or moving to a strange state can cause negative stress.

111. Which of the following is a negative coping strategy for dealing with stress? (Average Rigor) (Skill 5.1)
   A. Recreational diversions
   B. Active thinking
   C. Alcohol use
   D. Imagery

(C.) The use of alcohol is a negative coping strategy for dealing with stress. Alcohol causes the brain to lose the stressful data thus soothing the individual, but it can be highly detrimental in the long run. Positive ways to deal with stress include active thinking, imagery, and recreational diversions.

112. The most important nutrient the body requires, without which life can only be sustained for a few days, is: (Easy) (Skill 5.1)
   A. Vitamins
   B. Minerals
   C. Water
   D. Carbohydrates

(C.) Although the body requires vitamins, minerals, and carbohydrates to achieve proper growth and shape, water is essential. Without it, the body gets dehydrated and death is a possibility. Water should be pure, as seawater can cause kidney failure and death.

113. With regard to protein content, foods from animal sources are usually: (Average Rigor) (Skill 5.1)
   A. Complete
   B. Essential
   C. Nonessential
   D. Incidental

(A.) Animal protein is complete, meaning it provides all of the amino acids that the human body requires. Although animal meat is not essential to a person's diet, it is an excellent source of protein.

114. Fats with room for two or more hydrogen atoms per molecule-fatty acid chain are: (Rigorous) (Skill 5.1)
   A. Monounsaturated
   B. Polyunsaturated
   C. Hydrosaturated
   D. Saturated

(B.) Polyunsaturated fatty acids contain multiple carbon-carbon double bonds. Thus, there is room for two or more hydrogens. Polyunsaturated fats are healthier than saturated fats.

115. An adequate diet to meet nutritional needs consists of: (Rigorous) (Skill 5.1)
   A. No more than 30% caloric intake from fats, no more than 50 % caloric intake from proteins, and at least 20% caloric intake from carbohydrates.
   B. No more than 30% caloric intake from fats, no more than 40% caloric intake from proteins, and at least 30% caloric intake from carbohydrates.
   C. No more than 30% caloric intake from fats, no more than 15% caloric intake from proteins, and at least 55% caloric intake from carbohydrates.
   D. No more than 30 % caloric intake from fats, no more than 30% caloric intake from proteins, and at least 40% caloric intake from carbohydrates.

(C.) General guidelines for nutritionally sound diets are 30% caloric intake from fats, no more than 15% caloric intake from proteins, and at least 55% caloric intake from carbohydrates.

TEACHER CERTIFICATION STUDY GUIDE

116. Maintaining body weight is best accomplished by: (Average Rigor) (Skill 5.1)
   A. Dieting
   B. Aerobic exercise
   C. Lifting weights
   D. Equalizing caloric intake relative to output

(D.) The best way to maintain a body weight is by balancing caloric intake and output. Extensive dieting (caloric restriction) is not a good option as this would result in weakness. Exercise is part of the output process that helps balance caloric input and output.

117. Most high-protein diets: (Average Rigor) (Skill 5.1)
   A. Are high in cholesterol
   B. Are high in saturated fats
   C. Require vitamin and mineral supplements
   D. All of the above

(D.) High-protein diets are high in cholesterol, saturated fats, and they require vitamin and mineral supplements.

118. Which one of the following statements about low-calorie diets is false? (Rigorous) (Skill 5.1)
   A. Most people who "diet only" regain the weight they lose.
   B. They are the way most people try to lose weight.
   C. They make weight control easier.
   D. They lead to excess worry about weight, food, and eating.

(C.) People who participate in low-calorie diets do not control their weight easily. They must work more and utilize their bodies in many other ways (e.g., walking) to keep themselves fit.

119. Physiological benefits of exercise include all of the following except: (Average Rigor) (Skill 5.1)
   A. Reducing mental tension
   B. Improving muscle strength
   C. Cardiac hypertrophy
   D. Quicker recovery rate

(A.) Physical exercises can help improve muscle strength by making the body move and they can help provide quicker recovery between exercise sessions and from injuries. However, physical activity does not directly relieve mental tension. It might reduce tension temporarily, but chances are the tension will persist.

TEACHER CERTIFICATION STUDY GUIDE

120. Psychological benefits of exercise include all of the following except: (Rigorous) (Skill 5.1)
   A. Improved sleeping patterns
   B. Improved energy regulation
   C. Improved appearance
   D. Improved quality of life

(B.) The psychological benefits of exercise include improved sleeping patterns, improved appearances, and an improved quality of life. Improved energy regulation is a physical benefit, not a psychological one.

121. Which of the following conditions is not associated with a lack of physical activity? (Average Rigor) (Skill I5.1)

   A. Atherosclerosis
   B. Longer life expectancy
   C. Osteoporosis
   D. Certain cancers

(B.) A lack of physical activity can contribute to atherosclerosis, osteoporosis, and certain cancers. Conversely, regular physical activity can contribute to longer life expectancy.

122. Which of the following pieces of exercise equipment best applies the physiological principles? (Average Rigor) (Skill 5.1)
   A. Rolling machine
   B. Electrical muscle stimulator
   C. Stationary Bicycle
   D. Motor-driven rowing machine

(C.) A stationary bicycle is the best option to support the body physically as it includes all of the operations related to an individual's body (e.g., movement of legs, position of arms, back exercise, stomach movement). Electrical muscle stimulators are very dangerous as they can cause muscles to loosen too much. Other machines may provide an unnecessarily extensive workout that is dangerous for muscle.

123. To enhance skill and strategy performance for striking or throwing objects, for catching or collecting objects, and for carrying and propelling objects, students must first learn techniques for: (Rigorous) (Skill5.3)
   A. Offense
   B. Defense
   C. Controlling objects
   D. Continuous play of objects

(C.) For enhancing the catching, throwing, carrying, or propelling of objects, a student must learn how to control the objects. The control gives the player a sense of the object. Thus, offense, defense, and continuous play come naturally, as they are part of the controlling process.

124. Which of the following is not a type of tournament? (Average Rigor) (Skill 5.3)
   A. Spiderweb
   B. Pyramid
   C. Spiral
   D. Round Robin

(C.) A spiral is not a type of tournament.

125. Which of the following is not a type of meet? (Average Rigor) (Skill 5.3)
   A. Extramural
   B. Intramural
   C. Interscholastic
   D. Ladder

(D.) A ladder is not a type of meet.

126. Activities to specifically develop cardiovascular fitness must be (Rigorous) (Skill 6.1)
   A. Performed without developing an oxygen debt
   B. Performed twice daily.
   C. Performed every day.
   D. Performed for a minimum of 10 minutes.

(A.) The development of cardiovascular fitness is not dependent on specific time limits or routine schedules. Participants should perform aerobic activities without developing an oxygen debt.

TEACHER CERTIFICATION STUDY GUIDE

127. Which is not a sign of stress? (Average Rigor) (Skill 6.1)
A. Irritability
B. Assertiveness
C. Insomnia
D. Stomach problems

(B.) Assertiveness is not a sign of stress. Irritability, insomnia, and stomach problems are all related to stress.

128. Students are performing trunk extensions. What component of fitness does this activity assess? (Average Rigor) (Skill 9.1)
A. Balance
B. Flexibility
C. Body Composition
D. Coordination

(B.) The core component of trunk extensions is flexibility. Trunk extensions also indicate the body's capacity for full expansion and emphasize areas such as the stomach, arms, and shoulder joints.

129. Working at a level that is above normal is which exercise training principle? (Rigorous) (Skill 9.1)
A. Intensity
B. Progression
C. Specificity
D. Overload

(D.) Overloading is exercising above normal capacities. Intensity and progression are supporting principles in the process of overload. Overloading can cause serious issues within the body, either immediately or after some time.

130. Students on a running program to improve cardio-respiratory fitness apply which exercise principle. (Rigorous) (Skill 9.1)
A. Aerobic
B. Progression
C. Specificity
D. Overload

(C.) Running to improve cardio-respiratory fitness is an example of specificity. Specificity is the selection of activities that isolate a specific body part or system. Aerobics is also a good option, but it deals with the entire body, including areas not specific to cardio-respiratory fitness.

131. Adding more reps to a weightlifting set applies which exercise principle. (Average Rigor) (Skill 9.1)
A. Anaerobic
B. Progression
C. Overload
D. Specificity

(B.) Adding more repetitions (reps) to sets when weightlifting is an example of progression. Adding reps can result in overload, but the guiding principle is progression.

132. Which of the following does not modify overload? (Rigorous) (Skill 9.1)
A. Frequency
B. Perceived exertion
C. Time
D. Intensity

(B.) Time extension, frequency of movement, and intensity are all indicators of overload. However, exertion is not a good indicator of overload, because measuring exertion is subjective and difficult to monitor.

133. Prior to activity, students perform a 5-10 minute warm-up. Which is not recommended as part of the warm-up? (Easy) (Skill 9.1)
A. Using the muscles that will be utilized in the following activity.
B. Using a gradual aerobic warm-up.
C. Using a gradual anaerobic warm-up.
D. Stretching the major muscle groups to be used in the activity.

(C.) Warm-up is always necessary, but it should not be an anaerobic warm-up. The muscle exercises, the stretching, and even the aerobics are all helpful and athletes should complete these exercises within the normal breathing conditions. In fact, athletes should focus more closely on proper breathing. Athletes should engage in anaerobic stretching after activity, when muscles are loose and less prone to injury.

TEACHER CERTIFICATION STUDY GUIDE

134. Which is not a benefit of warming up? (Rigorous) (Skill 9.1)
   A. Releasing hydrogen from myoglobin.
   B. Reducing the risk of musculoskeletal injuries.
   C. Raising the body's core temperature in preparation for activity.
   D. Stretching the major muscle groups to be used in the activity.

(A.) Warm-up can reduce the risk of musculoskeletal injuries, raise the body's temperature in preparation for activity, and stretch the major muscle groups. However, a warm-up does not release hydrogen from myoglobin. Myoglobin binds oxygen, not hydrogen.

135. Which is not a benefit of cooling down? (Rigorous) (Skill 9.1)
   A. Preventing dizziness.
   B. Redistributing circulation.
   C. Removing lactic acid.
   D. Removing myoglobin.

(D.) Cooling down helps the body to regain blood circulation and to remove lactic acid. It also prevents dizziness, which may occur after extensive exercises. The only thing that cooling down does not support is removing myoglobin. However, it can help myoglobin get a strong hold in the muscles.

136. Overloading for muscle strength includes all of the following except® (Rigorous) (Skill 9.1)
   A. Lifting heart rate to an intense level.
   B. Lifting weights every other day.
   C. Lifting with high resistance and low reps.
   D. Lifting 60% to 90% of assessed muscle strength.

(A.) Overloading muscle strength is possible by lifting the weights every other day or by lifting weights with high resistance and low repetition. Overloading does not cause or require an intense increase in heart rate. However, overloading has many other possibilities.

137. **Which of the following applies the concept of progression? (Rigorous) (Skill 9.1)**
    A. Beginning a stretching program every day.
    B. Beginning a stretching program with 3 sets of reps.
    C. Beginning a stretching program with ballistic stretching.
    D. Beginning a stretching program holding stretches for 15 seconds and work up to holding stretches for 60 seconds.

(D.) Progression is the process of starting an exercise program slowly and cautiously before proceeding to more rigorous training. Answer D is the only answer that exemplifies progression.

138. **Which of following overload principles does not apply to improving body composition? (Average Rigor) (Skill 9.1)**
    A. Aerobic exercise three times per week.
    B. Aerobic exercise at a low intensity.
    C. Aerobic exercise for about an hour.
    D. Aerobic exercise in intervals of high intensity.

(A.) To improve body composition, a person should engage in aerobic exercise daily, not three times per week. However, an individual can do aerobics for at least half an hour daily, he/she can exercise at a low intensity, or he/she can train with intervals of high intensity.

139. **Which of the following principles of progression applies to improving muscle endurance? (Rigorous) (Skill 9.1)**
    A. Lifting weights every day.
    B. Lifting weights at 20% to 30% of assessed muscle strength.
    C. Lifting weights with low resistance and low reps.
    D. Lifting weights starting at 60% of assessed muscle strength.

(B.) To improve muscle endurance, a person should lift weights at 20 to 30% of the assessed muscle strength. Lifting weights daily is counterproductive because it does not allow for adequate rest. In addition, lifting at 60% of the assessed muscle strength can damage the muscle.

Rigor Table

Question #s

Easy %20	Average Rigor %40	Rigorous %40
1,7,8,9,14,15,16,18,19,20, 30,39,40,52,53,60,70,74, 76,77,79,85,98,99,101,112 133	2, 4,5,11,12,17,22,23,24, 25,26,27,32,33,34,36,38 44,48,49,55,56,58,63,64 67,68,69,72,73,78,82,84 86,87,88,91,92,97,102,103 105,106,111,113,116,117 119,121,122,124,125,127, 128,131,138,	3,6,10,13,21,28,29,31, 35,37,41,42,43,45,46, 47,50,51,54,57,59,61, 62,65,66,71,75,80,81, 83,89,90,93,94,95,96, 100,104,107,108,109, 110,114,115,118,120, 123,126,129,130,132, 134,135,136,137,139

TEACHER CERTIFICATION STUDY GUIDE

Sample Written Assignment

The sample written assignment consists of a brief scenario followed by a sequence of questions or topics to discuss. You should draft an essay of 150-300 words addressing all of the topics or questions. It is important that you organize your response and demonstrate a thorough understanding of the subject matter. Content is more important than writing style, though poor grammar, punctuation, spelling, and sentence structure can detract from your response.

Use the information below to complete the exercise that follows.

Evan is a 10-year-old fifth grade student who recently completed a physical fitness evaluation in his physical education class. Evan was able to perform 6 push-ups and no pull-ups. He completed the mile run in 6:58. The evaluation also showed that Evan had below average flexibility.

Evan is a physically active child, participating in tennis and soccer outside of school. Evan is a very talented athlete looking to improve his performance in his sporting activities. Evan is also a very reserved, shy child who does not make friends easily or interact much with other children. In addition, Evan's parents feel Evan is an unusually gifted tennis player and should stop playing soccer to focus on tennis.

Based on your knowledge of physical fitness construct a written response that addresses the following:

- interpret the results of Evan's fitness evaluation; determine the components of fitness that Evan needs to address

- identify two age-appropriate fitness activities that will help Evan achieve his goals

- advise Evan's parents on their desire to have Evan focus on tennis taking into account the social and psychological aspects of participation in sports and fitness activities

Strong Response to the Sample Written Assignment

The results of Evan's physical fitness assessment show that he has a high level of cardiovascular endurance (good mile run time), a low level of muscular endurance (poor results on push-up and pull-up test), and a low level of flexibility. Thus, a fitness program for Evan should focus on developing muscular endurance and flexibility. In addition, because Evan participates in soccer and tennis, he likely receives more than enough aerobic activity in these aerobically intensive sports.

Flexibility and muscular endurance are important, and often overlooked, aspects of tennis and soccer. Thus, developing these areas will improve Evan's athletic performance. Because Evan is only 10-years-old, I would recommend he engage in body support exercises, rather than resistance training exercises, to increase his muscular endurance. Such exercises include push-ups, pull-ups, sit-ups, lunges, and squats. I would not recommend weight training for a 10-year-old because lifting weights is dangerous and possibly detrimental for developing bodies. Evan should also engage in a regular stretching program after his tennis and soccer practices and matches. Stretching improves flexibility and stretching after physical activity is safest and most effective.

Finally, I would advise Evan's parents that he should continue to play both soccer and tennis. Sport specialization is not necessary at Evan's age to maximize performance and asking Evan to give up soccer could have other detrimental effects. Because Evan is shy and reserved, the social aspects of a team sport like soccer are important to his development. Participation in team sports promotes the development of social skills, leadership, teamwork, and interpersonal relationships. Evan will benefit from such interaction with other children and will improve his self-esteem, especially because he is a talented player. While tennis is an excellent sport, it is mainly an individual sport, and the opportunity for socialization and the development of friendships is limited.

www.ingramcontent.com/pod-product-compliance
Lightning Source LLC
Chambersburg PA
CBHW080535300426
44111CB00017B/2733